Talking All Night

The New York Poets:

Interviews, Photographs, Letters

Mark Hillringhouse

Talking All Night

The New York Poets:
Interviews, Photographs, Letters

Mark Hillringhouse

SERVING HOUSE BOOKS

Talking All Night
The New York Poets
Interviews, Photographs, Letters

Copyright © 2025 by Mark Hillringhouse

All Rights Reserved

Published by Serving House Books
Raleigh, NC

www.servinghousebooks.com

ISBN: 978-1-947175-66-2

Library of Congress Control Number: 2025933115

No part of this book may be used or reproduced in any manner whatsoever without the prior written permission of the copyright holder except for brief quotations in critical articles or reviews.

Member of The Independent Book Publishers Association

First Serving House Books Edition 2025

Cover Design: Peter Selgin

Serving House Books Logo: Barry Lereng Wilmont

Talking All Night

The New York Poets:
Interviews, Photographs, Letters

Mark Hillringhouse

SERVING HOUSE BOOKS

Talking All Night
The New York Poets
Interviews, Photographs, Letters

Copyright © 2025 by Mark Hillringhouse

All Rights Reserved

Published by Serving House Books
Raleigh, NC

www.servinghousebooks.com

ISBN: 978-1-947175-66-2

Library of Congress Control Number: 2025933115

No part of this book may be used or reproduced in any manner whatsoever without the prior written permission of the copyright holder except for brief quotations in critical articles or reviews.

Member of The Independent Book Publishers Association

First Serving House Books Edition 2025

Cover Design: Peter Selgin

Serving House Books Logo: Barry Lereng Wilmont

Dedication

WALTER CUMMINS

For Walter Cummins:
Teacher, Mentor, Friend—

Whose guidance and inspiration made this book possible

Acknowledgments

Magazines where the interviews were first published.

Ashbery, John, *New York Arts Journal* #24, Fall 1981.

Baraka, Amiri, *Mag City* #13, Summer 1982.

Berrigan, Ted, *The World*, #39, Winter 1983.

Denby, Edwin, *Mag City* #14, Fall 1983.

Guest, Barbara, *The American Poetry Review*, Vol. 21/No. 4, July/August 1992.

Koch, Kenneth, *New York Arts Journal* #25-26, Spring 1982.

Merwin, W. S., *Sequoia*, Stanford University, Winter 1984.

Schuyler, James, *The American Poetry Review*, Vol. 14/No. 2 March/April, 1985.

Stern, Gerald, *The American Poetry Review*, Vol. 13/No. 2 March/April, 1984.

Violi, Paul, *Hanging Loose,* Vol. 100, 2012.

Waldman, Anne, *American Poetry*, Vol. 2/No. 3, Spring 1985.

Contents

Acknowledgments 6
About the Author 9
Introduction 11
The Interview Process 24
The Interviews
John Ashbery 26
Amiri Baraka 47
Ted Berrigan 64
Edwin Denby 84
Barbara Guest 109
Bob Holman and Tom Pickard 152
Kenneth Koch 166
Bernadette Mayer and Phil Good 191
W.S. Merwin 208
Howard Moss 221
Simon Pettet 250
James Schuyler 262
Gerald Stern 292
Tony Towle 320
Paul Violi 331
Anne Waldman 365
Appendix: Alice in Brooklyn 386
Letters and Photographs 391
Selected Bibliography 395

Thanks

I want to thank Renée Ashley for giving me the idea to put all of my interviews together in a book. And I want to thank Walter Cummins for helping me arrange and edit and for formatting all this material into a publishable form. I also want to thank my wife, Linda, for her careful and close reading of my drafts. I also want to thank my brother, Jeff, who gave me my first camera. I want to acknowledge David Bonanno, longtime editor of *The American Poetry Review* who died in 2017, for publishing several of my first interviews. I want to thank David Lehman for publishing several excerpts from my interviews in his book on the New York School, *The Last Avant-Garde*. I also want to thank Robert Hershon, who kindly published my interview with Paul Violi in his magazine, *Hanging Loose*. I want to thank Martin Stannard who was a mutual friend of Paul Violi's and who reprinted several of my published interviews in his British poetry journal titled *Joe Soap's Canoe*. In addition, I want to thank Anne-Marie Macari, poet, and partner of Gerald Stern's, for all the lovely evenings we shared together in their home. And a big thanks to Louise Stahl, who proofread the entire manuscript. And finally, I want to acknowledge all the poets who gave generously of their time to sit down with me to do these interviews.

Mark Hillringhouse with Alice Notley and Tom Savage (above) 101 Saint Mark's Place, 1982

About the Author

Mark Hillringhouse began his interviews with New York poets starting with Ted Berrigan in 1980 and continued working on his series of interviews for over a decade. He was a contributing editor for the *New York Arts Journal*, and a founding editor of the *American Book Review*, as well as a member of the National Book Critics' Circle, and the Geraldine R. Dodge Foundation's Poetry Program.

He writes frequently about photography and he is an award-winning photographer who has taught photography for many years, as well as having taught poetry and creative writing.

His published writing has appeared in many anthologies, books, journals, and magazines including *The American Poetry Review*, *The Chicago Tribune*, *The Literary Review*, *The New York Times*, *The Paterson Literary Review*, *New Jersey Monthly*, *View Camera*, *The Photo Review*, *Photo-Eye*, and elsewhere. Serving House Books published *Between Frames*, a book of his black and white photographs alongside his poems, and *Paterson Light and Shadow*, a collection of Maria Mazziotti Gillan's Paterson poems with Hillringhouse's black and white Paterson photographs.

He is the winner of the Allen Ginsberg Poetry Award, and the Chester H. Jones Poetry Competition and three Pushcart Prizes, and he is also the recipient of several poetry fellowships from the New Jersey State Council on the Arts. His recent photography exhibitions include shows at the Paterson Museum, the Soho Gallery of Digital Art, the Main Street Gallery's "Juried Competition," and the Salmagundi Art Club's Juried Graphics and Photography Competition, and one-man shows at the Hamilton Club Art Gallery at Passaic County College, and at the Ben Shahn Gallery at William Paterson University.

He holds degrees from Hope College, BA in French and English, Montclair State University, MA in English and Comparative Literature, and Fairleigh Dickinson University, MFA in Creative Writing.

He retired from his full-time teaching position as a member of the English and Fine Arts Department at Passaic County College in 2020.

Introduction

When I think about how I got to interview all these poets, I have to go back to where I started, which was back in college. The first poet I ever knew was my English professor, Dirk Jellema, who taught Modern Poetry and Creative Writing at Hope College. I took all his classes. He reminded me of Hemingway with his gray beard and gruff manner, and he would often be seen at the local bar sitting in a corner drinking by himself looking lost in thought. I was lost, too, and my head wasn't in anything like a career or an academic frame of mind, and I drifted from biology and pre-med to French and English.

When I saw a program on the local public broadcasting station in the early '70s about local Michigan poets, Jim Harrison's name came up, and I became interested in his poetry. I had started writing my freshman year, and I even published a poem that won my college's literary award, and I was heavily into reading.

Emotionally, I was unstable and depressed. A bad break-up with a girlfriend who had left me for someone else had a debilitating effect on me and I missed several weeks of classes. And it was hard getting over her, but it was with poetry that I was trying to understand my feelings and pull myself together. I aligned my depression with Eliot's "Prufrock" and other poems like his that spoke to what was going on in my head.

As a French major I took a year abroad in France and two professors at the French university who were poets introduced me to their favorite poets, and I fell in love with Baudelaire, Rimbaud, Mallarmé, and Desnos. Those poets, too, spoke to my ennui and restless longing and depression.

When I returned to college in Michigan, I dropped out soon after meeting a woman whom I fell in love with in a store downtown. I found a job in a local furniture factory (Herman Miller), and she and I dated briefly, but not long enough to really get to know each other. I made the mistake of asking her to marry me and we eloped and after a month I realized I had made a big mistake; I was too young and immature, and I tried to get out of the marriage by leaving.

So began the dark road that I had embarked upon.

Then in June, 1977, I said goodbye to my wife—she would file for divorce and we'd be divorced by September. We said goodbye with tears in our eyes, and all I had was my backpack, tent, and sleeping bag and I was headed north hitch-hiking.

After two nights sleeping on the road, I made it to Traverse City, and found a bookstore and inside the owner told me where Harrison lived—Lake Leelanau. After hitching the thirty miles up to Lake Leelanau, I stopped at a bar called the Bluebird and found a pay phone on the wall and the phone book and found Harrison's phone number. I called the number, and Harrison answered. I said I was a young poet who wanted to meet him. He told me he was busy working (writing) and that I should call him tomorrow afternoon.

There was a wooded lot by the bar and that is where I pitched my tent. The next day, I called Harrison again and he answered and came to meet me at the Bluebird. He came with his wife, Linda, and after a few drinks, and some food (Harrison made me try the whitefish), he and his wife offered to take me back to their place, an old farmhouse with a barn in the back (Harrison's writing studio) and he let me pitch my tent on his front lawn. It was after midnight, Linda had gone to bed, and Harrison was up making tamales (he was still hungry after a night of drinking) at his stove and he had me sit at his kitchen table. He wanted me to try his tamales with sour cream and hot sauce (which were very good), and sat across from me so I could ask him some questions about poetry. His stare unnerved me a bit with his one blind eye that wandered off by itself.

He told me that if you try to live out your fantasies that you will never write. And he mentioned that he owed the IRS back taxes and was working part-time laying cinder block to help pay off his debt. He had the cover of his last published novel framed on the kitchen wall behind him, a novel titled *Farmer* and told me he made no money on that novel. His last book of poetry was a chapbook titled *Letters to Yesenin*. I had a copy of his first novel, *Wolf*, that I bought in the bookstore in Traverse City, and had him sign it. He told me I should read his friend, the writer Tom McGuane. They were grad students together at Michigan State where they met. He mentioned his friend Dan Gerber who was a Michigan poet and scion of the Gerber Baby Food company. Gerber had published some of Harrison's poetry in his small press publication.

In the morning, Harrison's ten-year-old daughter, Anna, was outside my tent laughing. In my drunken state, I had pitched my tent inside out. Jim and Linda fed me breakfast and let me take a bath, and he drove me (in his weaving one-eyed way of driving) in his old yellow Chevy pick-up to the Mackinac Bridge where we said goodbye. He told me that he wished he could go with me up into Canada on a road trip. His fortunes would soon improve with his next publication, *Legends of The Fall*, that would make him famous.

After a week on the road hitch-hiking through Canada, I made it back home and I had to face my parents and their concern about my misguided life after having eloped. Eventually, I got divorce papers in the mail which I mailed back to her lawyers. All I wanted to do was read poetry and write. But after a couple of months living at home, I wanted to go back to Michigan and see if I could repair the damage I had done. And so, I ended up living back temporarily with my now ex-wife, and I found a job in a factory called Big Dutchman that made poultry feeders. The man who owned it had donated a cultural center in his name to the college I had attended.

Coming back to my ex-wife's rented house after work one day, I noticed that the door was open. I stepped inside and it was cleared out. She was gone. She had moved out and taken off. The only thing she left was a Polaroid of her on the mantle of the picture window in the living room. I deserved it. I had hurt her badly when I had deserted her. There was no way that she would reconcile with me, although I wanted a second chance. I never saw her again.

I got laid off from my factory job soon after, and I was collecting unemployment and I had moved in with a couple of college friends. The unemployment office placed me in a government work program called CETA and offered me a job at the public library. It was working at the library that I was able to take the classes I needed in the evening to finish my degree. While working at the library one of the jobs I was given was ordering poetry books which I loved. Some of the books I ordered like Charles Bukowski's *Love Is a Dog from Hell*, the director refused to put out on the shelves. I didn't last long in that job.

I went back home to New Jersey after I graduated, and I found a job working in Brentano's. This was where I would discover many of the New York School poets. It was Jim Harrison who told me to read Frank O'Hara. And Jim Harrison liked Ted Berrigan's poetry. Back in New York City, I walked into a book warehouse on 4th Avenue between East 9th Street and Astor Place and I picked up a remaindered copy of *So Going Around Cities, Berrigan's New & Selected Poems 1958-1979*.

I was reading the books of poetry that I took home from Brentano's and I was trying to write poetry. My interest in how someone could devote their life to writing poetry is what I wanted to explore as well as what went into the art and craft of poetry. I wanted to learn. Reading poetry, going to poetry readings, and contacting the poets I wanted to interview was my way of entering into this world.

Frank O'Hara

My aim in doing all these interviews was to gather as much information as I could from a diverse group of poets who formed a specific approach to poetry that ranged from the urbane and academic, to the urban and political. All were part of a place and a time in the New York literary world in the days before the internet and the smart phone.

During the time that I was working on the interviews, I got to sit in on several poetry classes. I realize now that I had created my own MFA. I sat in on Berrigan's poetry class at Stevens Institute of Technology in Hoboken, and John Ashbery's poetry writing class at Brooklyn College, and Kenneth Koch's Modern Poetry class at Columbia, and Paul Violi's class in British Romantic Poetry at Bloomfield College, and Gerald Stern's poetry writing workshop at the 92nd Street Y.

In addition, I was taking poetry workshops at the Poetry Project at Saint Mark's. The first one was John Godfrey's. On the first night, all the poets who lived in the area showed their support by attending including Ted Berrigan, Anne Waldman, and Ron Padgett. I realized that this was a tradition at the Poetry Project. Godfrey started the evening by reading a few of his favorite poems by Nazim Hikmet, and Guillaume Apollinaire and Robert Desnos, and Pablo Neruda. And he dug down deep into the poems in order to give us, his workshop students, what he got out of reading these important poets. I remember after the workshop going to the Saint Mark's Bookstore to purchase some of the books he read from. He finished by giving us prompts, and instructions to bring in our own poems photocopied for next class. He ended the workshop by reading a couple of his poems from *Dabble*, published by Ron Padgett's Full Court Press. Godfrey's poems impressed me with their word play, their intelligence and lightheartedness and gravity.

Ron Padgett ran the French Translation workshop that I attended and on the first night he had with him all the dictionaries that he used, including a dictionary of technical and mechanical and scientific terms. I was impressed by his focus on accuracy in terms of translating French into English. And the last workshop I attended was Simon Schuchat's Chinese Poetry Workshop. Simon had worked in the diplomatic corps in China attached to the U.S. Embassy in Beijing, and he walked in wearing his blue Mao winter coat. He influenced me to start reading the classic poets of China, Tu Fu and Li Po.

JOHN GODFREY

I kept expanding my interest in the New York poetry world, which at that time included many major poets from outside the Poetry Project at Saint Mark's, poets such as Howard Moss, then the longtime poetry editor of *The New Yorker* which led me to other poets who were contemporaries of Ashbery and Koch, poets such as Philip Levine and James Wright who I got to hear read in the city, as well as James Merrill, and the Russian poet Joseph Brodsky. This led me to interview some of the other major players in that New York literary world, including Daniel Halpern, a poet who was influential in publishing other poets with his press, Ecco.

I was hired as a contributing editor of the *New York Arts Journal*, a bi-monthly tabloid that was started by Richard Burgin along with some Columbia students (Burgin went on to start another literary journal titled *Boulevard* in the 1990s). I published my interview with John Ashbery there. My interviews with Ted Berrigan, Amiri Baraka, and Edwin Denby were published in *Mag City,* a small press journal that came out of the Poetry Project edited by Greg Masters,

Michael Scholnick, and Gary Lenhart.

One day I was walking down Saint Mark's Place to visit Ted Berrigan, and I see Ted talking to a man on the corner of Second Avenue. Ted introduces me to Ronald Sukenick, and tells him that he should hire me. Sukenick, an experimental novelist, was starting a book review, and he needed editors. From that introduction on the street, I was hired and became one of the founding editors of *The American Book Review*.

There was little money in any of these publications and we mostly we got paid through state grants and some city money for the arts, and some help from the Coordinating Council of Literary Magazines, and from some advertising. We met every month in each other's apartments and passed around the new review books coming in from major publishers and small presses. Then we'd take the review copies down to the Strand Book Store on 12th Street and Broadway to sell them.

It amazes me now in this digital age that things like that would happen on the street where poets would bump into each other. Bernadette Mayer said to me that what happened back at Saint Mark's in the 1970s and '80s, that that community would never happen again. It was possible back then to work in a bookstore and rent an apartment in the East Village.

How this poetry community began started when James Schuyler, who originally wanted to become an architect, came to Manhattan in 1950 after college and worked for a time as W. H. Auden's personal secretary. He also worked for the Voice of America Radio, the Museum of Modern Art, and *Art News* for which he wrote reviews. He met Frank O'Hara and John Ashbery in 1951 through John Bernard Meyers, a gallery owner, who saw one of Schuyler's poems he liked that Howard Moss had published in *The New Yorker*, and invited the young poet to a Larry Rivers vernissage—the New York School was launched.

As the New York Abstract Expressionist painters took off, the poets who came to their openings and who wrote reviews of their work, attracted a literary audience as they became more famous and began winning awards for their poetry. The major New York publishers took notice.

Frank O'Hara, as a curator at the Museum of Modern Art, was at the epicenter of bringing these two worlds together in the 1960s which attracted a younger generation of poets to come to New York, the "Second" generation that was drawn to O'Hara and who started the Poetry Project at Saint Mark's Church-in-the-Bowery—a second generation New York School was formed.

Following O'Hara's death in 1966, Anne Waldman was hired as an assistant to the Poetry Project at Saint Mark's. The "Poetry Project's" first official reading was in September, 1966. Prior to the nascent poetry readings at Saint Mark's, there was the Café le Metro readings which stopped in 1965. In 1965, the poet Paul Blackburn hosted a poetry reading series in the Saint Mark's parish hall. It should be noted that W. H. Auden lived nearby on Saint Mark's Place in the '60s and attended Saint Mark's Church for Sunday service. He was a devout Anglican and Saint Mark's was an Episcopal Church. In 1965, the poet Joel Oppenheimer was made director of the nascent poetry program under President Lyndon Johnson's "Office of Economic Opportunity," which funded this Poetry Project as a way to enhance the lives of youth living in the Lower East Side.

Alongside the budding Poetry Project readings, magazines were started to publish participants' poetry. *The World*, a mimeographed and hand-stapled magazine for poetry began. The poet Ed Sanders published *Fuck You, a magazine of the arts*. Le Roi Jones (Amiri Baraka) started *Floating Bear*. Ted Berrigan started 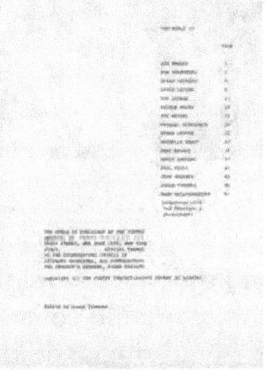*C Magazine,* and artists' drawings by Philip Guston, Joe Brainard, Alex Katz, Larry Rivers, and George Schneeman graced many of the covers.

Ted Berrigan was the epicenter of the "Second Generation." He and Alice Notley, his wife and also a poet, with their two kids, Anselm and Edmund, in their third-floor apartment on Saint Mark's Place was where I would run into any number of Saint Mark's poets coming and going. Bob Holman summed it up best when he said, "But Ted was the guy—he just—he and Alice lived the total poetry life and visiting them at 101 Saint Mark's Place was like walking into a poem."

And walk into a poem I did. I would visit Ted and sit at his bedside (he had a bad back and would be lying on his mattress on the floor) and he always had a Chesterfield cigarette in his mouth,

RON PADGETT, TED BERRIGAN, AND MARK HILLRINGHOUSE
AT THE SAINT MARK'S CHURCH POETRY PROJECT

and the ashes would fall on his chest. If Ted liked you, he would be happy to hold court. There was a phone by Ted's bedside and when it would ring and Ted always answered never pausing his conversation. I remember once it was his mother and I was touched by how sweet Ted was talking to her. Ted's kids were always playing in the next room or in their bunk beds, and Alice would be working on writing or reading in the living room at the front of the apartment that faced the street.

Ted and Alice's apartment was itself an artwork of murals and drawings by artist friends with broadsides of friends' poems and posters and postcards and poetry book covers and Polaroid photographs tacked to the walls, and looking back, I wish that there was a way to place Ted and Alice's apartment in a museum as a permanent display of what bohemian life looked like in the East Village during those years.

I remember when I got the news that Ted Berrigan had died. I thought of him as a poetry father, and he was that to me, and to other young poets as well. He was only forty-eight. I remember driving out with the funeral procession to Calverton National Cemetery for the burial. Ted was one of the few poets who was a veteran having served in Korea. I remember at the gravesite seeing Ed Sanders putting his hand on the flag-draped coffin and saying, "Goodbye dear friend." The honor guard folded the flag into a triangle and handed it to Alice. As the casket lowered, a military honor guard played "Taps" on trumpet.

I wrote an elegy for Ted that I read at his memorial held in the parish hall at Saint Mark's Church on his birthday, November 15, 1983, that had over seventy poets paying tribute. I look at the long list of poets' names now on that list of readers for Ted's memorial and it surprises me how many there were and how many were there because of the bond these poets all had with Ted Berrigan.

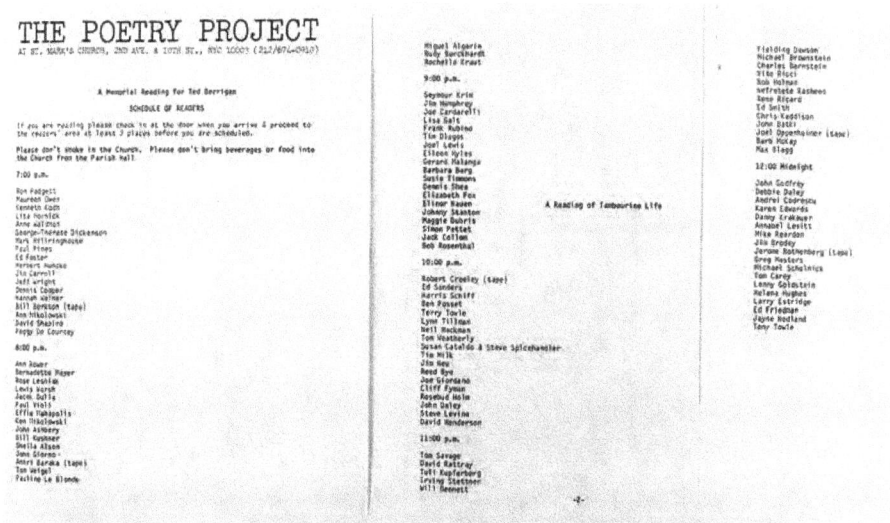

TED BERRIGAN MEMORIAL READING NOVEMBER 15, 1983

Jim Harrison
RR 1
Lake Leelanau, MI 49653

August 3, 1983

Dear Mark,

    Thank you for Ted's Selected Poems. It arrived the same day as the news of his death. Is there some sort of place I might send a donation?

    I had always felt he was the most interesting of that whole group of poets but never got to say so. Strangely enough, my favorite living poet in college was Frank O'Hara. Meanwhile, if you get out this way stop or ring and say hello.

Yrs.,

Jim Harrison

JH/jah

JIM HARRISON ON THE DEATH OF TED BERRIGAN

```
                                165 Haumana Road
                                Haiku, HI 96708
                                July 22, 1983
Dear Mark,

        Thank you for writing.  The news was a shock, even though
I'd known that Ted was in bad health, and he'd looked that way when I
last saw him, a year and a half ago.  But somehow one expects friends
to be immortal.
        I can't say that I knew him well, but every time we saw each
other I felt again his great affection and dignity, a magnanimity of
spirit that I welcomed and respected and loved.  I valued his evident
esteem for my own writing and I've been very fond of poems of his, for
years.  I am writing to Alice, whom I met once many years ago, and
say more or less that - what else can one say? And again I'm touched
and grateful to you for writing to tell me.
        We're here until Labor Day, and then, we're rather appalled
to keep remembering, we've committed ourselves to coming back to the
city until Christmas.  Apart from this grief I hope you have been having
a good summer.

                                Sincerely,

                                Bill
```

W.S. MERWIN ON THE DEATH OF TED BERRIGAN

GEM SPA OPEN 24 HOURS ON ST. MARK'S PLACE
WHERE TED BERRIGAN WAS OFTEN FOUND

The Interview Process

For each of these interviews, I began by reading all the books that each poet had published. In addition, I would look up articles on each poet at libraries where I could find the many art magazines and poetry journals where they had published individual poems or art reviews. Some of this published material, starting back in the 1950s, was only available at research libraries, so I spent many hours at the main branch of the New York Public Library at 42nd Street and 5th Ave. I also used the Bobst Library at NYU, and spent many hours there looking at microfilm strips of old magazines and newspaper articles and other sources, as well as going to the Butler Library at Columbia University to do the same.

Once I had read all the books by the poet I was going to interview, and after I had done the background research, I wrote out by hand all the questions that I wanted to ask and then I typed those and kept them with me when I went to do the interview.

Setting up a date and time with the poet was done at first by writing a letter asking where and when would be a good place and time to talk, and after I got a letter in reply, or a phone call, I would confirm the date and time of my visit. Two hours taping the interview was about the most time I ever spent in one sitting. In some cases, I needed to return to continue the interview.

I had a cassette tape player/recorder that I brought with me with many blank one-hour cassettes, and I would later transcribe the cassette recordings word for word. I transcribed all this on yellow legal pads. After that, I would sit and type up what I had handwritten on the legal pads and I would send a photocopy of the typed interview to the poet for corrections.

After I got the photocopied typed manuscript of the interview back from the poet, I would fix misspellings, fix names and dates, make changes, or deletions. Then I would retype the interview for a clean copy before sending it off for publication.

In addition, I asked each poet to sit or stand for a photographic portrait. I used my 35mm SLR and Kodak Tri-X 400 black and white film for the photographs.

Interview with John Ashbery

A few years after I published my interview with Ashbery, he published his twelfth book of poems, *April Galleons*, which I believe now to be his strongest work. Many of the poets I interviewed consider *Houseboat Days* or *Self-Portrait in a Convex Mirror* to be his best, but I remember having to sit down to write him a letter about how much I loved the new work, and the title poem which appeared on the last page.

I had been studying Emerson at the time and reading his essays and I made an immediate connection to Ashbery's title poem "April Galleons" to Emerson's essay "Experience" and Emerson's first line "Where do we find ourselves?"—a very Ashbery-like line of inquiry. And it struck me that Ashbery was our "Emerson" in poetic form.

Ashbery has been written about so much that it is almost impossible to come up with any new major insights into his work. But I still find new surprises going back and reading him again. He has that quality. And of all the New York School poets that I interviewed, his poetry, and Barbara Guest's, seemed to me to be the hardest to penetrate, but reading his work has given me the pleasure of going to places that I never would have traveled to.

MH: *R. P. Blackmur says that it is more difficult to assent to a poet's music than to his will or subject matter. I find that the opposite is true for your poetry, that it is more difficult to assent to its subject matter.*

JA: I don't know how difficult it is to assent to any aspect of my work since I am not the reader of it.

MH: *I can go into your poetry and come out of it with a new impression each time. Like music, it affects you differently every time you hear it.*

JA: (leaning back on his sofa) Wallace Stevens said, "The poem

JOHN ASHBERY WITH MARK HILLRINGHOUSE

should resist the intelligence almost completely."

MH: *Stevens is your favorite poet?*

JA: One of them. But I certainly prefer, for my own reading, poetry that offers a certain resilience, that doesn't resist the mind completely, but almost completely.

MH: *Why should poetry resist the mind?*

JA: Just because it then occupies you and gives you something to do. And as I say, offers a certain resilience which keeps you coming back until you come to terms with it rather than something you swallow immediately and forget.
 Poetry that I enjoy would fall under that category. Right now, I can't think of any serious poetry that doesn't do that. Robert Service doesn't. Well, Frost I guess would be a serious poet whose poetry doesn't offer enormous difficulties. On the other hand, I don't enjoy it as much as I do Stevens or John Wheelwright, who are much more intellectual than I am.

MH: Getting back to subject matter, it seems that you usually start with a subject, but then almost never go on to develop it or take it in an expectable direction.

JA: I think the development does occur though the poetry doesn't develop in expectable ways.

MH: Kenneth Koch in his new anthology of Modern Poetry, Sleeping on The Wing, says, "Ashbery's poems are full of just thinking, not thinking of the kind that necessarily leads to any conclusion, but the kind that goes on in dreams."

JA: I like the dream process because it just happens by itself and we're part of it happening. When things are too real we can't contemplate them.

MH: There's a line from your long poem "The Skaters" in your book, Rivers and Mountains, that goes, "Back to dreaming, my most important activity."

JA: It's most important, but it's certainly not everything. We all manage to do whatever jobs we have; we're not dreaming all the time.

MH: There's a theory that the dream process continues throughout our waking day.

JA: It's certainly there, but we're not totally irrational.

MH: You once said that your poetry was a conscious rather than unconscious exploration.

JA: I said that!

MH: Mainly because you said consciousness takes up more of our time.

JA: Oh no, I didn't say that. What I said was, that it occupies some of our time. That occasionally we all behave like conscious, rational human beings. Therefore, even surrealism's false because it suppresses that aspect of us.

MH: *Does your poetry then try to reflect the style of the mind?*

JA: Yes, the style of my mind. I wouldn't go so far as to say that everybody's functions the way mine functions or malfunctions (laughing).

MH: *Do things in themselves stand out and become important? I'm thinking of Williams's "No ideas but in things."*

JA: I like Williams Carlos Williams tremendously but I don't reflect on "things" very much in the way he would; they do intrude themselves into my poetry, of course.

MH: *Do you like Olson?*

JA: I don't like Charles Olson. I like Robert Creeley and Robert Duncan, whom I don't know whether to consider as Olson's stepchildren or not. But I've never cared for Olson's poetry, it always seemed like a kind of simplistic Williams. But you better not put that in the interview or I'll be attacked from both coasts (both laughing).

MH: *Is the look of the poem on the page important?*

JA: I think that the look and the meaning are very much connected with each other. The look is very important to me. I've always felt that Elizabeth Bishop is the person who does that supremely well. The actual sort of physical aspect of her poems, even if you didn't know English, would somehow please you.

MH: *Do you read your poems out loud?*

JA: No, I try to forget them as fast as I can—I do forget them; I don't try.

MH: *Even when writing, in composing a poem, do you read it out?*

JA: No, it's all silent.

MH: *How do you write then?*

JOHN ASHBERY IN HIS 22ND STREET CHELSEA APARTMENT

JA: Well, I don't stare at objects or meditate on them. I don't know how I write and would rather not know.

MH: *The act of writing then is mysterious in itself?*

JA: It is almost by definition, I think. And it seems to work better for me to wade into whatever today may be and start writing.

MH: *James Merrill says his life would not make any sense without poetry; why do you write?*

JA: I don't think I write poetry to make sense out of my life. I'm not sure I'm capable of doing that by any means or process. In fact, that's a question people always ask, "Why do you write?" I've never been able to come up with a satisfactory answer and this is often construed as arrogance on my part—but I don't know. They'll say, "Ah, come on; you must know. Don't give us that!"

MH: Back to how you write, is it longhand, on the typewriter, listening to music?

JA: On the typewriter, and I listen to classical music most of the time on WNCN, New York's twenty-four-hour classical music station. The music works very well as an ambience and occasionally, when there are announcements or commercials, they get sucked into the poem, as do all kinds of things in my immediate environment: papers that happen to be on my desk at the time, or letters, stray books, magazines.

MH: Don't you get distracted?

JA: I don't mind distraction. I probably got this idea from John Cage who feels that contemporary music should be open to the sounds outside it.

MH: *I was going to say Frank O'Hara, because he was able to write with people in the room, the telephone ringing, the TV going.*

JA: In his case, I think he was able to wall out whatever was around him and write what he was going to write anyway. In my case, I feel open and vulnerable to the things that are happening around me. I always answer the phone when I'm writing and I frequently find that it has helped me either to forget an unprofitable line of thinking, or that whoever I'm talking to will say something that gives me an idea.

MH: *Your poetry is really open-ended in a way, open to all those intrusions; it is really just a part of your day, your unconscious; you can incorporate everything going on around you.*

JA: Yes, it should be that way because these things are very important. They're the environment that we live in, and there's no point in trying to pretend that it's different or should be different.

MH: *Did you know O'Hara?*

JA: Yes, but I lived in France for ten years so I didn't see much of him then, and I missed out on the '50s in America. Actually, I was here for the first half of the '50s but missed the poetry scene in New

York, which really began in the mid-'50s, by which time I was gone. And you see Frank was very friendly with all these artists. I never really knew them although everybody thinks I did. I was just hanging out with him.

MH: *O'Hara made a statement that in the '50s in art, it was the artists like Jackson Pollock who were steering the boat and not the poets, although they were still in the boat. Who do you think is steering now?*

JA: (lighting one of his French cigarettes) I think it's drifting rudderless.

MH: *So, you feel today's poetry is more disheveled, looser?*

JA: Disheveled yes, but I think it's better. I'm all in favor of dishevelment—I mean, look at me!

MH: *(looking around the room at the Persian rugs on the floor and original artwork on the walls) Well, I wouldn't call this disheveled. You've done well for yourself (both laughing). The poet James Schuyler said that once you tried to emulate the artist Leger. Could you comment on that?*

JA: Well, Leger was never one of my favorite artists but I sort of got a take on him from something Jane Freilicher once said. We were looking at an exhibit of Leger's work and she exclaimed, "He's a very mysterious artist." I looked again, and sure enough, he was. I like him because she told me he was mysterious.

He is rather mysterious—he has people with disc faces and factory chimneys with circular smoke coming out of them! That's nicely perverse (laughs).

MH: *Do you like art, being an art critic as well as a poet?*

JA: Onto the next question (both laughing). I'm more auditory than visual. I like hearing music anytime, really. Schoenberg I never liked until Frank O'Hara explained to me how important he was. Most of my ideas come from other people. I appreciate things because others tell me that they're good.

MH: *I get an impression from a lot of your poetry, as in your book* Houseboat Days, *of wonder and resignation.*

JA: Those would seem to be almost incompatible (laughing).

MH: *There's a "Prufrock" feeling I get from reading the poem "Loving Mad Tom," for instance. Lines like— "Best to leave it there" ... "The music ended anyway" ... "On some busy, deserted metropolitan avenue" ... "and night falls anyway." Sounds like it could be inspired by Eliot's "half-deserted streets, and voices dying with a dying fall" ... ?*

JA: Hmmm, I have been very influenced by a line by Laura Riding from a rare book of hers called *Progress of Stories*.

MH: *You've been influenced by her?*

JA: Yes, I have, but if you say that, I'll get an angry letter from her saying, "You couldn't possibly have been influenced by me!" (both laughing). (quoting Laura Riding) "What one does for others makes one old and ugly, but what one does for oneself comes as easy as breathing," she distinctly said. "And never do anything for yourself, it's always someone else who benefits in the end anyway." This is from a character in her story "Reality as Port Huntlady."

MH: *Well, now I see where you picked that up. But I also get an Eliot-Prufrock feeling from your lines: "You didn't see the miserable dawns piled up, one after the other, stretching away ... to the opposite shore, where it was all coming true."*

Sounds reminiscent of Eliot's, "I've come to know them all already, known them all, mornings, evenings, afternoons ..." There's that resignation of future time already imagined, of admitting defeat even before the battle has started.

JA: But I would say that my poetry tends to be much more naively optimistic than jaded Prufrock.

I never cared for Eliot when I was young, actually, it's only been in recent times that I've come to enjoy his work.

MH: *But wouldn't the overriding tone of your poetry (over ten books) be one of the passing of time?*

JA: Unfortunately, I would say that the passage of time is certainly a theme that keeps recurring in my work, and more so as I've gotten older and more time has elapsed. Although, I used to think my poetry didn't have subject matter in the conventional way, it now seems to me that growing older and witnessing time is probably the subject, and is probably the subject of everything.

MH: *Is poetry then a way of recapturing time, or a way of restructuring it in some Proustian manner? Ted Berrigan told me he thought there were three times in a poem: the time the poet writes it, the time about which the poet is writing, and the time when the reader will read it.*

JA: Yes, and I think there'll even be a fourth, since the reader will be thinking about things in his own past suggested by the poem.
   When I put myself in a state of mind to write, when that happens, I remember things from years ago that are suddenly suggested by the process of writing. It opens me up to all the times I have experienced or times I haven't experienced.

MH: *So, time recaptured, in a way?*

JA: Yeah, but you can never recapture it, just remember it.

MH: *Laura Riding in an essay on Proust says that he introduces something very false into the novel because he's infringing on the poet.*

JA: I can see why she would say that. Her own opinion of poetry isn't very high.

MH: *But all art falsifies to some extent.*

JA: I suppose it does.

MH: *There's no real connection with reality; it's an invention, a fiction.*

JA: Yes, but I think that's precisely why we enjoy it, and the enjoyment we get from these fictions is certainly real. Therefore, they are involved with reality somehow. Of course basically it is true, that poetry does falsify, that it isn't real.

MH: *Raymond Roussel said that the work must contain nothing real, no observation on the world, the mind, nothing but completely imaginary combinations.*

JA: Well, of course that's a very extreme position and I don't think anybody but Roussel could have made that statement. In fact, he was discussing his own work, not prescribing formulas.

MH: *Why did you take to him?*

JA: Something about the totally mechanical nature of his writing attracted me. I don't entirely know why. His work is a kind of supreme fiction and that attracted me.

MH: *Did he give you a model for your own poetry?*

JA: Yes, his long poem "La Vue" which is an elaborate description of a scene set in the base of a pen holder, in which all kinds of objects in a landscape are described in a detail that could not possibly be seen by the naked eye even if they had been there intrigued me. And that sort of heightened voyeurism had an influence on my poem "The Instruction Manual" from my first book *Some Trees* (1956), which is a poem describing in detail a scene in Guadalajara, a city in Mexico that I've never been to. And I think the poignancy of not having been there and of being in the situation of actually describing it was something that attracted me.

Influences are always so strange. I feel that perhaps I've been influenced more by novels.

MH: *Like Henry Green?*

JA: Very much. He was very chic at the time I was trying to find a subject for a thesis at Columbia in 1950. Then he immediately went out of fashion and now has been coming back into fashion a little bit.

MH: *What is it in his style that you like?*

JA: I like his earlier works, although not the novel *Blindness* which was reprinted recently. But there was one titled *Living* which was about working-class people in Birmingham, England, and just the way they talked and the crude way they expressed themselves was very good. I love people expressing themselves in crude ways, or the dumb way people have of talking when they're really trying to say what's on their minds.

Ivy Compton-Burnett is another of my favorite writers and so is Ronald Firbank.

MH: *The language seems to be a brother to you.*

JA: Oh yeah, I love it, but I love it because of the things it says, it's like—I don't like money, I just like the things it can buy (both laughing).

MH: *When you were away from this country for ten years, did it bother you that you could not use your language?*

JA: Yes, it did, but it took me almost two years before I was able to speak French.

MH: *Is it a good thing for a poet to get outside his native language and experience a foreign culture?*

JA: Yes, I enjoyed it very much once I got over the culture shock. I didn't even want to come back, though I enjoy America.

MH: *You once said that you had a period of about two years when you couldn't write.*

JA: That started during the time of the Korean War. I don't know if that was what caused it, but it certainly didn't help matters.

MH: *Do you feel that this present political climate will get as bad?*

JA: It's worse, I think! There are so many new technologies that bad guys can use.

MH: *How do you get through a period of dryness in yourself when nothing is coming?*

JA: Well, it's not pleasant. You live through it. I haven't had much of that happen in recent times. It mostly happened when I was in my early twenties and later when I went to France as a Fulbright scholar. It took me a long time to get adjusted to another culture before I could write anything. During a dry period in Paris when I felt out of touch with the American language I missed hearing around me, I'd go through an issue of *Esquire* or some other magazine and just copy down phrases and put them in poems. Those weren't very satisfactory either. I get a great deal of material for poetry from what I overhear people saying in the streets.

MH: *As an aide to writing, Ted Berrigan says that he'll take one of your poems, double space the lines, then write his lines in-between, then erase your lines and see if he's come up with a poem.*

JA: Yeah, and sometimes he doesn't bother to erase my lines (both laughing).

MH: *But you seem to work purely in the language as if you're writing with a fearless use of syntax and vocabulary.*

JA: A lady once came up to me after a reading and said, "I just love your vocabulary" (both laughing).
  When you talk about pure language though, what does that mean? Because language can't be pure, it refers to things. It doesn't exist by itself because it always incorporates something other than itself. It's a hybrid no matter how pure it is.

MH: *Clark Coolidge says that you took one of your poems and demonstrated how you could rewrite it by stating the lines differently.*

JA: I did that with one of my own poems in *As We Know*; there's a poem called "The Shower," which is a rewrite of a poem by the same title which was in my second book *The Tennis Court Oath*.

MH: *Is there any amount of prophecy in your work?*

JA: Like what?

MH: *There seems to be some sort of future riding out of the poems;*

that something is always about to happen.

JA: I'm not seriously prophesying anything. I might adopt the tone of a prophet as I adopt other voices.

MH: *The last stanza of your poem "The Pursuit of Happiness" in your most recent book* Shadow Train *is a good example:*

> ... *knowing*
>
> *That it would always ever afterward be this way*
> *Caused the eyes to faint, the ears to ignore warnings.*
> *We knew how to get by on what comes along, but the idea*
> *Warning, waiting there like a forest, not emptied, beckons.*

You seem to be prophesying the inevitability of time and the inevitability of people being as stupid as always.

JA: I don't think I'm going out on a limb there (laughing).

MH: *The tone is pervasive throughout your work even in the first stanza of the poem "Night Life" out of the same book:*

> *I thought it was you but I couldn't tell.*
> *It's so hard, working with people, you want them all*
> *To like you and be happy, but they get in the way*
> *Of their own predilections, it's like a stone*
>
> *Blocking the mouth of a cave.*

You place people in a dilemma; describe an anxiety that exists in just being a person.

JA: Well, that poem you've just quoted and others like it, deal with just how hard it is to be natural. You're always wondering if you are being natural when you're attempting to be. On the other hand, it's probably very easy since the way you are is natural for you. You worry about it but you don't have to.

MH: *Like telling somebody not to be nervous?*

JA: Yes (laughing).

MH: *Doesn't this bring out a certain amount of cynicism, this kind of seeing, of knowing how people react?*

JA: That's one of the things one tries to avoid when trying to be natural. It may be there but no one wants to be thought of as a cynic. I certainly don't. But maybe I am cynical.

MH: *There's this tangle of "how I got here" that your poetry appears to be a series of meditations on the same dilemma. Beckett, in a rare interview said, "Let's write about the mess." In your book* Three Poems, *in the poem "The New Spirit," I found the line, "We must drink the confusion." Very similar.*

JA: That's curious. There's a line in "The Ivory Tower" from *Shadow Train* that startled me because it sounded rather like William Carlos Williams— "There is always some impurity. Help it along! Make room for it!" I don't think that this is something that Williams would necessarily have said, but the way of saying it could have been his. It sounded like a cheerful induction of the "mess."

MH: *Things are so different now. The mess is everywhere. Paris has skyscrapers!*

JA: I know, and everybody always gets very upset about that. But I guess part of my mental make-up is that it doesn't upset me at all. I like to see things get fucked up in a certain way. There's always some innate room for it; help it out. And I think that the very artificial city of Paris is even more pleasing now that it has those grotesque skyscrapers in it!

MH: *Does decadence have an appeal for you, seeing things get as bad as possible?*

JA: Only if it can bring us back to our senses.

MH: *Alfred Kazin says, "Ashbery's poetry is vaguely unreachable, haunting rather than moving."*

JA: That's an interesting statement; I mean, "vaguely unreachable" sounds like "a little bit pregnant" doesn't it?

MH: *Do you feel that critics live off you? That you've become prey to a bunch of brilliant predators?*

JA: No, but I wouldn't want the opposite situation either. Very often the ambiguity and obscurity that critics write about in my poetry seems to have rubbed off on them and they end up contradicting themselves.

MH: *How does it feel to be singled out by a critic and scholar such as Harold Bloom?*

JA: Nice.

MH: *What about Bloom's anxiety of influence?*

JA: I know that it exists. One falls under the spell of some writer and probably feels a certain amount of anxiety about him also. But I never felt anxious about Wallace Stevens. One thing Bloom has ignored, although I've told him, is that I feel that Auden has been more of an influence than Stevens.

Auden was the first poet to really speak to me. I had the same difficulty with Modern Poetry everybody else has—it didn't make any sense when I first started reading it. At first, I was really put off by the fact that Auden used ordinary everyday speech as the language of poetry. And little by little, I began to see the beauty of that.

MH: *Did you like Dylan Thomas?*

JA: I liked him very much when I was first discovering Modern Poetry because he was so obscure. It turned out he wasn't all that obscure. From a certain distance now, his poetry seems self-consciously rhetorical and imposing. "The force that through the green fuse drives the flower" seemed like one of the most beautiful lines I've ever read, but now it sounds kind of hollow.

MH: *Do you still consider yourself to be a New York poet?*

JA: No, I don't, but everybody else does. There's a tremendous regionalism, but that's one of the funny things about American Poetry, that it is so intensely regional. You go to the Northwest and the people think that the only viable poetry is that written by Roethke, Wagoner, and Hugo. You go to Tennessee and Robert Penn Warren is the only poet of importance. In San Francisco it's Ferlinghetti or Duncan.

MH: *Do you like their poetry?*

JA: Well, yes, some of them, and many of the poets that I like are unlike me. I read to be entertained and not to find something that I might have written.

MH: *How about confessional poetry?*

JA: I sometimes write confessionally. But that doesn't qualify me to be a confessional poet because you can't be a part-time confessional poet or a part-time anything. Your label must adhere to you and you mustn't try to wiggle out from under it.

My poem "Soonest Mended" from *The Double Dream of Spring* is a sort of generalized autobiographical poem—it's not things that actually happened to me, but just the kinds of things that have happened to me and everybody—a one-size-fits-all confessional poem.

MH: *Has philosophy had any effect on your work?*

JA: No, and I haven't read very much philosophy either; I don't understand it. I took a course in philosophy in college and almost failed it. It seems to be a question of language. What I thought I understood was not what was there to be understood although I liked what I thought was there.

You see, I thought of philosophy as a kind of poetry, and I think that's where I made my mistake (both laughing). But perhaps later Wittgenstein and Heidegger are understood the way one understands poetry.

MH: *Is there any of that unknowing Zen master quality in your work or Buddhist yearning that you like or admire?*
JA: I'm not a Buddhist, and I don't believe in selflessness at all. In fact, I'm trying to find my way out of it. On the other hand, the Zen idea that whatever happens is what happens makes sense to me.

MH: *You don't name drop at all in your poetry?*

JA: I don't approve of that. The reader might not know the person you were talking about and would feel left out. I certainly wouldn't want a reader to feel left out! In fact, a critic wrote me about *Shadow Train* saying, "Well, I like it, but you have all these private references like "Penny Parker's Mistake" and "Corky's Car Keys." This critic implied that I was talking about people that I knew, when in fact, they're not people that I knew, but just people I made up. Like Wallace Stevens in his poem "Mrs. Alfred Uruguay," I try to give the impression of somebody that someone might know, not a specific person.

MH: *At your reading at NYU, you stated that you didn't care for the sonnet form and came up with this series of four-stanza, sixteen-line poems instead.*

JA: Yes, because sonnets seem to be artificially microscopic. What I object to in a sonnet is the octet and the sestet resolving it. So, if you were to flatten it all out into four equal stanzas, you would in effect be destroying the fearful asymmetry of the sonnet by making it regular and bland, the format at any rate.

MH: *You mentioned that you like Maurice Scève and his ten-line stanzas or "dizains." You said, "There's a beautiful monotony about them."*

JA: Yeah, I had a period of reading him when I was living in France, that I think was totally loony really. That was when I wrote my poem "Fragment."

MH: *Does this form help you to write?*

JA: Any form helps. With *Shadow Train* I decided I would write fifty poems of sixteen lines each, so then I knew what I had to do—right? But that doesn't mean it's anything important, or has profound significance. I want to read you a statement I wrote in an essay about the painter R. B. Kitaj. I mention Eliot's *The Waste Land* in connection with Kitaj's paintings and say: "Their contiguity is all their meaning, and it is implied that from now on meaning will take into account the randomness and discontinuity of experience, that indeed meaning cannot be truthfully defined as anything else. The gulf has opened up and art with any serious aspirations towards realism has to take into account the fact that reality still escapes laws of perspective and logic and does not naturally take the form of a sonnet or sonata."

MH: *That helps explain your approach to using poetic form. My other question is about your titles, I'm wondering how you get them.*

JA: Usually, they sort of come to me, and I think, "Gee, that would make a good title." But it's not that it would make a good title, it's a kind of opening into some space I haven't investigated yet. I keep them (titles) around and start working on them whenever I have time.

MH: *Wallace Stevens used to keep a separate notebook of titles.*

JA: I didn't know that and it's nice to know, because occasionally people ask, "What? You think of the title first!" As if this were some sort of aberration.

MH: *Why the title "Shadow Train"?*

JA: Originally, I had it titled "Paradoxes and Oxymorons."

MH: *You had mentioned at NYU that many people don't even know what an oxymoron is.*

JA: Right, and it's not too long ago that I learned what it means. For commercial purposes I thought I should change it. Then I thought, "Shadow Train" is kind of nice. The only reason I didn't like it is because it sounds too spooky, and my poems are perhaps spooky enough already. The cover is from a photograph of a city brownstone sidewalk fence in the snow that I admired. And the book is sort of like a train because the poems are all of equal length and linked up like a long freight train.

MH: *Do you sequence your poems to come out as a book?*

JA: No. Originally, I was going to have the poems in *Shadow Train* in the order in which I wrote them, then I discovered that it

43

didn't really work too well because I hadn't really got into the form until I had been doing it for a while, so I shuffled them all up.

MH: *Stanley Kunitz puts his most recent poems up front and then works back.*

JA: I always do that, too, because one always likes one's most recent work.

MH: *What is your favorite poem or group of poems of yours?*

JA: I like *Three Poems* and *Houseboat Days* the most.

MH: *Most critics find* Self-Portrait in a Convex Mirror *to be the best.*

JA: I don't like it as much as *Houseboat Days*, but it seems to get better press, especially after winning those three prizes [Pulitzer Prize, National Book Award, and the National Book Critics' Circle Award].

MH: *Was there a tendency to be as different as possible from your previous book?*

JA: Well, I guess I wrote *Shadow Train* because I had written so many long poems and I had become notorious for it, and my previous book, *As We Know*, opened with an endlessly long poem titled "Litany" and I said, "Well, maybe now's the time to try something short. There's no reason why I can't."

But since *Shadow Train* I have tended to go on and on as is my usual practice.

MH: *So, the future book of poems, which you're obviously working on, is intended to be different? [Ashbery's next book of poetry,* A Wave, *was published in 1981.]*

JA: Not intended to be, but it will be. Figure that one out.

MH: *Maybe the whole body of work is one single poem?*

JA: A number of people have considered this latest book as a long poem, which might be true. But I think my basic garrulousness is not served by this concise form.

MH: *But nothing as innovative as your long opening poem "Litany" in* As We Know?

JA: Oh no, nothing as innovative as that.

MH: *Many poets admit that all they do is to write the same poem over and over again.*

JA: Well, you do in a way, you can't escape yourself and you're writing the poem again, but you try to think up artificial ways of tricking this condition.

MH: *I think that the change also benefits the reader.*

JA: I try to vary it for the reader as much as possible.

MH: *Including a level of humor?*

JA: I think my poems are humorous, although they're not entirely humorous. Humor is important. One should represent as many different parts of one's mind's constituency as possible.

MH: *Would homesickness be an underlying sentiment in your poetry?*

JA: I guess, but I grew up in Sodus, a small farm town in western New York State near Lake Ontario, and I certainly wouldn't want to live there.

MH: *On a final note, who do you consider your favorite painter?*

JA: Vermeer. His way of recreating light. I think that light is for the painter what time is for poetry. Something that's always there that you don't think about that much. You wonder why painters are always talking about light, since it's not the only thing in the world, though as far as painting goes it probably is.
   I like the idea of open-endedness, the poem expanding itself in its reference to other poems. Vermeer puts one of his own paintings

on the wall in the background in one of his paintings, like mutually reflecting mirrors leading into infinity.

AMIRI BARAKA (LEFT) AND ALLEN GINSBERG (RIGHT) AT THE
WILLIAM CARLOS WILLIAMS CENTENNIAL READING

Interview with Amiri Baraka (LeRoi Jones)

I remember taking a cab from Newark Penn Station to interview Amiri Baraka (LeRoi Jones) to where he lived on South 10th Street. Inside, his stately house was decorated with works of African art, and in one room, he showed me his jazz collection, the most incredible treasure trove of jazz albums that I had ever seen.

I wanted to find out what he thought about American poetry in the nascent Reagan era, and how Black poetry fit within the larger context of American poetry, and what cross-pollination had takplace. He was going through a period of soul searching regarding an earlier stance on anti-Semitism. A few months after our interview, he published his "Confessions of a Former Anti-Semite" in *The Village Voice*.

His *Selected Poetry* had recently been published by William Morrow, and it was that volume that I had with me that he signed. The next time I saw him was when I invited him to read at the William Carlos Williams Centennial in Rutherford, New Jersey at the newly opened "Williams Center for the Performing Arts" when I was in charge of organizing the centennial reading. Baraka had mentioned to me how much he admired Williams.

For Baraka, that reading was like a reunion of "Beat" poets since I had also invited Allen Ginsberg and Gregory Corso and Ted Berrigan to read as well. Ginsberg and Baraka, who hadn't seen each other in years, hugged when they met, and each read their favorite Williams poem. It impressed me how much Baraka knew about Williams's poetry and how much it meant to him.

He felt passionately that if you weren't connecting to the realities of life in America that you were missing out on what is so vital about this country. He mentioned that poetry needed to penetrate this reality in order to serve the social needs and concerns of the world in which we live.

Reading him now, the poems I like best are in the books *The Dead Lecturer* and *Black Art*. The poems he was writing that came out of the middle period of his life after he had changed his name and moved to Harlem.

MH: *What do you think of these poetry workshops?*

AB: To me, that's a business. The question is creating poets; I don't think that's what they're really interested in, especially with this elitist attitude in these schools because they think poetry happens in some metaphysical way. I don't see anything wrong with these workshops, just that the majority of them are trying to push backward ideas. I'm pretty sure they're stressing form over content, tradition over reason, and similar absurdities.

MH: *Well, you've taught poetry.*

AB: But what I teach is what people have done. I try to put them in touch with writers whom I admire.

MH: *By way of exposure?*

AB: Yeah, making them read, then trying to get them in touch with themselves. In any kind of writing/poetry course, I teach that they have to abandon overreliance on things outside themselves; they have to be aware of the state of the art, but they have to abandon any kind of ready-mades or hiding their own emotions under artificial masks.

MH: *It's as if today's poetry is being written without a heartbeat.*

AB: Exactly. That's what they want, though. The official poetry of this state has to be dead, because if it were alive it would have to talk about this (gestures to what's outside)!

MH: *There's a poem of yours in particular that addresses this feeling from* The Dead Lecturer *entitled "A Poem for Speculative Hipsters."*

> *He had got, finally,*
> *to the forest*
> *of motives. There were no*
> *owls, or hunters. No Connie Chatterleys*
> *resting beautifully*
> *on their backs, having casually*
> *brought socialism*
> *to England.*
>   *Only ideas,*
> *and their opposites.*
>   *Like*
> *he was really*
> *nowhere.*

AB: Yeah, absolutely. Poetry is supposed to give you the world and if you're going to cut out all the interesting parts and deal with only what is theoretical and intellectual, then it's better just to walk or take the bus, or sit on the porch and watch things.

MH: *Your statement in the introduction to* Hard Facts *has a lot of the same feeling:*

> *"Poetry is saying something about reality. It reflects the sayer's place ... middle-class poetry which is most important to the*

American Academy, is a reflection of American middle-class life and interests, petty bourgeois social and production relations."

But doesn't this obviate the possibility of there being a need for the academic poem?

AB: Well, I'm a Marxist communist, but I like all kinds of poetry. I don't just like communist poetry. There are all kinds of people who can tell you who they are and what they feel whatever their ideology is. What I dislike is poetry that is super formal and artificial.

MH: *Are there any prime examples that come to mind?*

AB: Well sure, most of the poets who are celebrated by the American establishment.

MH: *Like Ashbery?*

AB: Ashbery is more interesting because at least his imagery is wild, although obviously, I couldn't eat a lot of that. Ashbery is interesting to me because I admire the root which is O'Hara, but there is a whole school of much deader poetry. Now I think Ashbery has been given these awards really to soup-up American poetry. It's as if the judges are saying, "OK, we're going to give this to John Ashbery to try to jack the rest of you up in order to establish a higher norm." Ashbery's imagery is wilder than the standard Theodore Roethke, John Crowe Ransom, *The New Yorker* Howard Moss shit.

What's happening finally is that you're being subjected to somebody's deadass life! And what the hell are they talking about, adjectives, nuances, some party in the East Hamptons, using twenty metaphors to describe a grape.

This country is so wild and crazy and brutal and corny and vulgar, that if you're not trying to deal with that you're missing. It's like you're not even in this world.

I think that the reality of our lives in our society is even more shocking than the headlines. You know what I'm saying. The problem with the headlines is that they tend to be shallow but the reality of this country is much more shocking. The question is, can the writer penetrate that and raise it up to a level of serious concern. The challenges are fantastic because the average rock group raises up a level of serious concern higher than the average academic poet. John

Lennon is much more interesting than Howard Moss.

MH: And Lennon was a casualty of the craziness.

AB: Of the craziness to be sure.
 The point is, you have to be able to capture that, otherwise you're not here. It's like a landscape painter: if you have to sit and be right next to this landscape and then paint us a picture of a closet! Hey, we didn't want a picture of a closet. What is this? Show me what this landscape is, what's happening in it, what do people feel in it, what does it look like, how do people talk, how do they sound, what do they do? Academic poetry cannot do that, its closet is its royal domain, because in that closet it is supreme. In the world it's just a little fat professor walking down the street who might get mugged.

MH: Definitely not the real world.

AB: It's not real. It won't reflect the folk tradition of White America not to mention all the other aspects of this culture, the Black and Latino, the Native American. It tends to be elite and right wing.

MH: Narcissistic?

AB: Yes, very narcissistic. That's Capitalism though.

MH: In advertising you can really feel it.

AB: Well, you see it's an all-pervading thing of which advertising is the most blatant. But you can go around to all these university campuses and the shit they're pumping those students full of is essentially the same thing.
 I think the artist has to demand education in the real sense of how all the shit works. Education in school is such a small particle of what this whole life is all about, and if that's all you're going to focus on then you really don't know anything. The motivation behind that trend of getting a job is understankable because the market is so competitive. Business only needs about 30 percent of the college graduates. The rest can go screw off and become artists.
 This Reagan administration probably feels artists are nothing more than a bunch of accordion players. Well look, they're going to cut those grants in half, but art itself is going to get chopped because

they're going to lay with the academics, the so-called scholarship.

MH: It could be good in a way.

AB: I think that the only positive thing that's going to come out of it is people's increasing capacity to fight back. I think there'll be a big division, too. There'll be a small group of people who'll actually show up on that other side, who'll become the Reagan's intellectual. But when do we fight back? Do we wait until we're in line with the soap and towel in our hand?

Not only are people afraid of losing what they have, they're afraid of losing what they don't have. The white middle-class wishes it were on welfare and food stamps. They really need welfare. Socially, it would be hard for them to come to that admission, but that's the reality of their situation. This society is in total anxiety. The middle-class is in anxiety constantly. The poor at least can say, "Fuck it, I'm poor!" The middle-class has to keep up the façade that they're not poor, that they're doing all right, when in actuality they're about two inches from being poor. For the middle-class, it's a question of credit cards and credit up the ass which hooks you up with your imaginary acquisitions.

MH: A lot of the war protest poetry from the '60s was good. You can replace the Nixon names with those of the Reagan administration.

AB: Oh yeah, it's real and it's obviously coming back, there's no doubt about it. The idea of Alexander Haig as the goddamn Secretary of State is in itself miraculous. What are their accomplishments except death? Well, if that gets to be it, when people have to look up to skilled murderers. That shows you where it's at though.

Well, this will be a very interesting time to be living in but I think it's very definitely going to cause sharp polarization.

MH: Can art produce the changes necessary to improve some of the conditions of society as Richard Wright thought would happen?

AB: Well, you see the question of art interested in change is that it's interested in reaching people and arming them, giving information, giving them the emotional commitment to go out and do things, or to resist, telling them the truth about the world and society, because one thing about any society like ours is that it has to be operated on basic lies, has to be. The fundamental policy of any repressive government has to be the lie. When nothing else works, lie! So, anything that cuts through the lies and actually tries to sort it out can be a weapon: what actually did happen, what is the real history of this place, who are the people running things? I think there are a lot of people from diverse ideologies who are doing something like that. Ed Sanders when he talks about his investigative historical school of poetry is very positive. To me, it's saying that somebody understands that history is a real thing and that it's not just buried in the past, but that the weight of history actually sets people in motion in whatever direction they're going. They're carrying the burden of history as they understand it. It might be total bullshit but then they're going off in a bullshit direction.

MH: *History can be a lie, too.*

AB: I think there is a real history. There is a real life that has happened, but I think that a lot of times what we get are lies as history. Any writer who is interested in giving us the real world is very important.

MH: *Lance Jeffers says that the future of Black poetry lies in continued rage and protest, and criticism and analysis of Black people.*

AB: True, that's our tradition, that's a particular tradition. I think that has to be real because that's the real condition. You see, any Black poetry that doesn't begin there cannot really be Black poetry. Then it's outside of the people's experience because there is a real experience.

MH: *Right, and it's so complex that it requires some analysis to figure it out. You just can't put it all in one group and call it "Black poetry."*

AB: No, no, poets come from different ways, different ideologies, different methods, and things like that.

MH: *Robert Hayden is still a romantic, for example.*

AB: Hayden is much closer to that kind of American academic norm, but he still has life to him, this is my view. He still has a life to him based on some kind of relationship to real people in the real world involved with real struggles. This makes it more interesting to me than the Howard Mosses and the Robert Penn Warrens. I think the main tradition of Black poetry always is connected up with Black people, and as such has to be related to their struggle and has to reflect their condition, their life, their desires.

MH: *But is there such a thing as racial poetry?*

AB: In the sense of it being a precise reflection of a group, obviously. But I think it is only that. I don't think there's any kind of exclusive area.

MH: *Is Russian poetry racial?*

AB: In the sense that it reflects Russian life, Russian people, Russian history. I think all great poetry is so precise that it has to reflect place, history, culture, precisely. And I don't think of it as mystical, it's simply the precision. The poet is so precise that he has to reflect the totality of that life that he is in. It's not just an isolated person in space.

MH: *So, in a way, it's not that poetry has to be motivated or inspired or confined to racial utterance. Hayden says that it shouldn't have to be limited in any way.*

AB: No, I don't think of it as limited, I just think of it as specific. The problem with most academic poetry is that it's abstract. Bourgeois poetry generally tends to be abstract and subjective, one person talking about the inner rulings of their own ego. But there is no one person that I know who is not in this world, and it's the world that we share collectively. Obviously, a person's subjective consciousness is the focus of what they see. It's their perception that we are confronted with in their poems, their rationalization, their rationalization of that perception, their use of that rationalization. To talk about your own inner bumblings without any connection with the world that we all share commonly is boring. So, in terms of talking about Black poetry, Black poetry is simply about Black people, their lives and history. It might have a particular accent.

MH: *You don't feel there's two schools or a gap between two forces?*

AB: Oh yeah, but that's just a class distinction. People write from where they come. Just like in slavery you would have poetry written by house servants and poetry written by field servants. They would reflect their different place in society. So that today you still have that, you have house niggers, and field niggers still.

MH: *You mean from Hammon, Wheatley, and Dunbar on one side.*

AB: Yeah, that's a house statement.

MH: *And the tradition of Hughes and McKay on the other.*

AB: Sure. I think that the mainstream has to be the majority experience no matter how it comes out. The mainstream of Black letters is the majority's experience reflected in the brain of the poet.

MH: *Who have been your influences?*

AB: A lot of influences, I've had a lot of influences. I'll say that I've been influenced by poets. Back when I was in college, I was influenced by Elizabethan poets and Eliot. Later on I was influenced by Allen Ginsberg and Charles Olson and Robert Creeley, then people like Askia Touré.

MH: *Did you know Owen Dodson?*

AB: I knew him as a teacher at Howard.

MH: *Sterling Brown?*

AB: He was a teacher of mine at Howard. Sterling taught me, Owen never did. Owen Dodson ran the theatre company. I knew he was a teacher at Howard, but Sterling Brown actually had influenced me more intellectually. It was he who taught us Black music at Howard, unofficially because Howard never allowed that. After class, in the dormitory, he would come over and teach a group of us about the history of Black music, which was very important.

MH: *That was quite a strong force having those two.*

AB: He was one of the great professors. There were several great professors at Howard. Sterling Brown was one, Franklin Fraser was another, Elaine Locke was another, Owen Dodson still another.

MH: *You've lived in other places.*

AB: I've travelled a lot, but I haven't really lived abroad very long. I travel a great deal. My main residence has been Newark and New York. I lived in other cities off and on, San Francisco for a few months, etc.

MH: *And in the Air Force?*

AB: I travelled around in the Air Force a lot sure. I've been to Africa, Europe, and Japan and to other places. In terms of long residence, I haven't really lived in many places outside of here. But I do think it important for other poets if they have the time, to learn other languages, because there are still very few translations. People think everything is automatically translated. In terms of Black poetry, there is still a great need in the world for more and better translations.

MH: *Why did you study German?*

AB: I studied German because at the time I thought I was interested in German literature, culture, history, and philosophy. Actually, my interest first started as a pre-med student. I studied German because that was one of the requirements.

MH: *And you liked the language?*

AB: Yes, and I was reading some things like Heidegger, but basically it was a requirement for school. I went past that as my interest in phenomenology developed in studying people like Husserl, etc. I became friendly with a fellow who was really into it, a Ph.D. in Phenomenology, and we became close friends, a guy by the name of Peter Schwartzberg from Munich. I liked German writers and was reading German poetry, that's how it started. That was a while ago.

MH: *Your poetry has been informed by it?*

AB: Obviously, sure.

MH: *Your poem "Hegel" from the book* Black Magic *speaks to me, especially that line, "Give me someone to talk to."*

AB: I think the poem is about finding yourself in an isolated position as far as what you're thinking about is going on in the world. Paraphrased, it expresses, "So what everybody thinks I'm saying is off the wall, but what I really need is somebody to discuss these ideas with."

MH: *Whites can read your poetry and get a lot out of it I think, in a reverse metaphor way of reading it.*

AB: Sure, I don't see why not, especially that early poetry. I think that for most intellectuals it would be pretty clear. I don't see why it wouldn't. I even think the poetry I wrote when I was a Black Nationalist is pretty clear to whites.

MH: *Well, it even transfers over to me as a white and substantiates my own personal gripe that I have with the political world.*

AB: Yeah, I don't think that it would be necessarily obscure, it's very obvious; you might not agree with it. I don't think my poetry is obscure except in the earlier stages of my work.

MH: *Like your poem, "For Halfwhite College Students"?*

AB: Yeah, I think that's pretty clear.

MH: *I guess there's no way a poet can get away from a more universal lament.*

AB: No, that's real. If it's particularized enough, it also is universal. You begin to see in that specific way that can become everyone's specific reality. Everyone's cry is that one cry.

MH: *Do you feel that American poetry is ahead of other poetry? It might be fair to judge against England for example because we share the same language.*

AB: English poetry died out at the beginning of the twentieth century. Language became so full of shit, it became a mash more than a communication. It becomes a sham, a social instance more than a real message. It becomes a social sham in the sense that it tries to fake society out with gibberish and elegant facades, when in actuality the whole goddamn world is burning, the empire is crumbling and meanwhile they're talking about—dee dee doot, dee dee doot, dee dee doot, some iambic pentameter. The American thing is more real, and what I think continues to make American poetry strong is that it still continues to incorporate so many elements. American language is not English even though people still tend to talk about English departments. This is not England. Since the end of the eighteenth century there has been an American tradition. The American tradition is fed by many streams—the Black stream, the Latino stream, the Native American stream. All of those things are bubbling in it all the time, are making it vital. When the Voice of America broadcasts, they don't try to reach the people of Eastern Europe with dull academic shit, they'll play Duke Ellington or Stevie Wonder or some salsa or country music; the real living stuff and that's what keeps the American thing alive. If they just wanted to focus on the Anglo-Saxon Harvard-Yale tradition it would be as dead as England, the empire would be dead, too.

MH: *Do you like William Carlos Williams and Charles Olson for that reason?*

AB: Oh yes, absolutely, because they're talking about real American speech. There's still a huge Anglo-Colonial mentality in socalled high academics. They still push English and English literature.

MH: *Is Black poetry even further along in that respect?*

AB: They're much further removed from that Anglo tradition. When you read Williams, you're already taking a step away from English. When you read someone as reactionary as Pound, it's clear that nineteenth-century English could not serve poetry. He was certain of that. Williams becomes stronger because Williams actually connects with the real American tradition. Ezra Pound and T.S. Eliot went back to Europe. Williams stayed here and wrote about Paterson. He knew where the essence of this country was to be found, and he knew if he was going to reflect that in literature then he had to be in tune with this culture.

MH: *I think he succeeded. He knew it was in the people around him, in the real people he encountered as a physician making house calls.*

AB: Exactly. It steps away from dead English and deals with the living American idiom. Black poetry is even more rooted in that sense because Black people have even fewer illusions about Europe and England. That stuff is just way out there and away from them, and just doesn't exist.

The best American poetry from the last few generations has not connected with the old world but has been rooted here. That's why I liked Ginsberg's poetry when I came out of the Air Force back in 1957. He talked about America.

There are a lot of Black and Latino poets who are very interesting and who have been raised in this tradition, and the main element of their strength is their being rooted in real American life. They give us this society. I'm not opposed to tradition.

Tradition is supposed to drop us off in the present. What it is supposed to do is let us know from whence we came, but it's not supposed to make us addicted to it. When you take the A train you want to get off in Harlem, you don't want to ride the subway forever.

MH: *Besides poets, what other artists do you identify with?*

AB: I'm sensitive to all the arts and I always tell my students that even if they're writers they have to be in tune with the state of the arts, all the arts, because they might be able to see some dance that will shake a poem loose in them.

For me, music is the most important, especially Afro-American music, jazz, blues. It is my own heavy source of energy and inspiration and my own historical reference. I'm inspired as much by music as by other poets.

MH: *How about painters?*

AB: Painters yeah, I love painting, but it is not as accessible. To check out paintings you either have to get books or reproductions.

MH: Getting back to poetry, in your poem "The Liar" for example, the opening of that poem reads like it could have been part of Wallace Stevens's "Thirteen Ways of Looking at a Blackbird."

AB: Definitely could be. I used to like Wallace Stevens a lot. I read him during that period a lot and loved his imagery and so forth.

MH: How do you approach the poem? I want to get some insight into your creative process. Ted Berrigan says he thinks of words and phrases first, and Allen Ginsberg says he connects words to a certain feeling that is being drawn out on a particular rhythm and cadence, and Robert Bly seems to be writing mostly out of images.

AB: I think I'm probably closer to Allen in that respect. There's a definite kind of rhythmic impulse, but at the same time, there's this desire to say something, to speak out about something. The rhythm is the way into it, the way to get it out. The rhythm is definitely like train tracks.

MH: Then you can start working in those images.

AB: Well, I think that the rhythm itself is the music of the poem, then you have to visualize the whole in order to articulate the content.

MH: You have to develop a strong ear.

AB: Yes. Poetry to me is a kind of music, and that is taking it back to its origins. It was either spoken, sung, or danced to.

MH: Have you ever thought of not writing anymore, of giving it up, abandoning the whole thing?

AB: Occasionally, I guess, but I've never believed that.

MH: I'm always amazed by writers who quit writing, Rimbaud for example, or J.D. Salinger perhaps.

AB: I don't understand that, though often you can be put in a bind by society itself. For instance, I have about four unpublished books that publishers might want to commission. They want to titillate you.

MH: *That must be more than 200 poems.*

AB: Well, they're not books of poetry. I do have about three books of poetry unpublished. Those are different. One group of poems I never even tried to publish, early poems, my first book of unpublished poems that I just keep around. Then there's some recent poetry that I will try to publish if anyone's interested. I have a book on John Coltrane that's half-finished that the editor didn't like and refused to publish. I have an unpublished novel that I wrote under commission for Putnam several years ago. I did have a jazz opera commissioned by the Paris Opera that they didn't want to produce.

MH: *That adds up to a hell of a lot of frustration.*

AB: Yeah, and that can actually put a damper on you. But in terms of poetry, no, poetry doesn't depend on that. That's my necessary form of expression. So that's not in any danger from editors and publishers. The other things can be tampered with because they do require a link with production. Not seeing my plays produced tends to dampen my spirits and has limited my production of drama. I used to write a great number of plays. I would continue to write a great many more if people would produce them, but once they stop then the desire to write them dissipates, but the poetry is safe. I know that I will be able to read those. They do conspire not to produce the plays though and it does dry you up to a certain degree, and I usually do write a play a year no matter, but the fact that they don't produce them does have a real effect. I do think that I will be able to get around that eventually. The last three I produced myself.

MH: *Is there anything harder to write than poetry?*

AB: All of it is hard to write. Poetry is easier for me to write, but the rest of it is more difficult because it takes more discipline.

MH: *A lot of people start off in poetry because it is smaller and they think it is easier and they do it more readily.*

AB: Yeah, it has its own demands, and those demands are complex.

MH: *Do you have habits of sitting down and writing every day?*

AB: When I'm working on something, yes.

MH: *Can you name a few poets writing today who hold your interest, keep you angry and informed, and make you want to keep on writing?*

AB: Well, there are a lot of poets I like, a great many. I would say Askia Touré, Lorenzo Thomas, Jayne Cortez, would be the ones who turn me on.

MH: *Do you like Gwendolyn Brooks at all?*

AB: Yeah, Gwen's poetry is good, and I think she's certainly written some great poetry, but she is not the kind of writer who revs me up. Any new book of hers I will buy, but any new book of Margaret Walker's, let's say, would be a great event. There are a lot of other poets who really turn me on and who I would look for.

MH: *Even outside this country?*

AB: Sure, there are poets like Aimé Césaire and Nicolás Guillén. Pablo Neruda and Nicolás Guillén are the Latin poets I like the most. There's a lot of third world poetry that I admire and which is very vital.

MH: *Did you know Jay Wright while you were at Rutgers? I believe you and he are the same age.*

AB: No. I knew Jay later when he was at Yale in '77. I believe he still teaches one semester there a year.

MH: *Jay Wright says he has nothing to say and no statement to make about poetry.*

AB: Is that what he says? But I think that's Jay's line. He tends to be that kind of person. He lives way up in the woods somewhere in Maine in a cabin with nothing but firewood.

MH: *Could you picture yourself doing that?*

AB: No, I'm an urban type. Newark is about as rural as I'm going to get. Up there in the woods of Maine would drive me crazy. Chopping wood, starting fires, I'm not interested in that. The more modern it is the better I like it. I'm better informed living here. I need the stimulus. I need privacy every once in a while, but I don't want to make a fetish out of it. No, this is my home, this is where I grew up.

Interview with Ted Berrigan

I remember Ted Berrigan's poetry class at Stevens Institute of Technology in Hoboken, New Jersey. I wasn't a student there, but Ted let me sit in. He played a recording of Jack Kerouac reading, and then later read a poem by Robert Creeley, and wrote one solitary word on the blackboard in giant capital letters—"Grace"—and circled it with his chalk after he had finished the poem. After class, I went with him to his office to ask him questions. He laughed when he got to his door. It had his first initial, but the last three letters of his last name had fallen off, so it read "T-Berri."

Afterwards, I walked with him down to the Path train station to the train that he took to get back to the city. I could tell from the way he was able to convey to engineering students something about the importance of poetry and how it should matter in their lives, that he was someone who lived the life of a poet. And I could tell that the students in his class opened up to him and paid attention to what he was teaching them. I hung on his every word.

I left Ted a list of additional questions that I had typed out, and he returned them to me with his handwritten replies. In one question, referencing his poem "Red Shift," I asked whether he thought poetry was a way of restructuring time. He wrote, "This question is a whole interview."

I had with me his just published *So Going Around Cities New & Selected Poems 1958-1979*. He signed my copy in his office and wrote, "For Mark, in Hoboken, after listening to Jack Kerouac together, Affectionately, Ted Berrigan."

Today, I go back to many of the poems in that collection, especially poems selected from his book, *Many Happy Returns 1961-1968*, his "Personal Poems" that he dedicated to his poet friends, poems that reveal the true intimate nature of the New York School. And of course, Ted would say, all his poems are personal.

TED BERRIGAN IN HIS APARTMENT

MH: *Do you have any students who are trying to be poets?*

TB: No, none at all.

MH: *They're in it just for the literature?*

TB: They're in it because they have a requirement. Engineers are hardheaded about taking only what they think they need. Something which I do deal with a little bit is that they don't yet understand that they're still going to have to talk to their wives and husbands and children, go to the grocery store and not just work in the lab making Napalm (both laughing).

MH: *It's like taking a segment of the public at large and approaching them with poetry.*

TB: Well, when they're twenty years old it's a little easier. They're old enough to think and young enough not to have thought too much yet. There's one who still insists that none of this stuff makes any sense. That's a common complaint, and it gives me the chance to come at it gently. I mean I'm making a little fun about the idea that anything "Makes Sense." It doesn't make much sense to me to say that if I'm made up of floating atomic particles and so is this chair,

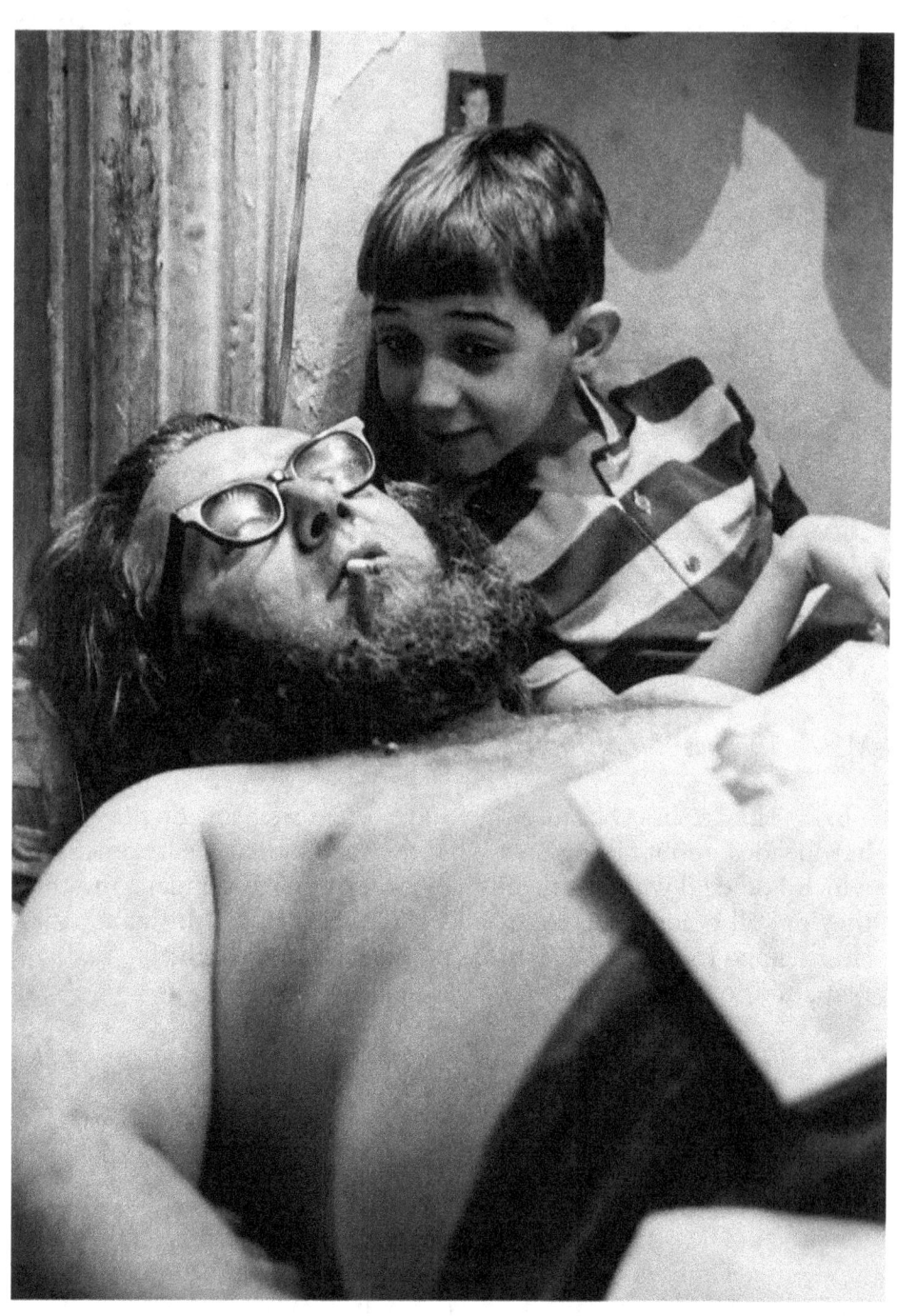

Ted Berrigan with His Son Edmund, 1983

then how come when I sit down my spaces don't fit with its spaces and I go right through? But I don't know if I'm made up of floating molecules. That's poetry to say something is made like that. Most of these students are very surprised to find out that anything has been going on in poetry since Edgar Allan Poe.

MH: *You're sort of force feeding them since they don't go off on their own.*

TB: Yes, and I'm very delicate about that in a way. I like to convey to them that no one should have to be interested in poetry who doesn't want to be. So, I'm trying to impress upon them the fact that they can't get along with just what they think they have to know.

MH: *Have you always taught poetry?*

TB: Since 1968, I've taught all but three years, and every year I've taught some part of the time and I've taught in a lot of different places: New Haven, Ann Arbor, Iowa, Chicago, Buffalo, Boulder, and Essex, England. I'm teaching full-time (Stevens Institute of Technology) here. Three years in a row in any one place and you find yourself saying the same things over and over again, and that's not much fun. I am a poet first and a teacher after that. I like teaching because I like the students; I like the people in that age group. When they like something they really light up.

MH: *I've met a few poets that just hate to teach.*

TB: Well, I can understand that. I suppose if you resent doing something you shouldn't do it. But there are days when I hate to go anywhere, when I hate to come to class. I feel put upon.

MH: *Especially if you are in the mood to write.*

TB: Well, if I was in the mood to write I'd stay home. I wouldn't come in. But I write in the evening. I consider part of my job as being visible and accessible. My door is always open.

MH: *Why do you write in the evening?*

TB: I write at night because I can be alone in a certain way and

ANSELM AND EDMUND BERRIGAN

there are no phone calls to distract me. Initially, I wrote at night because at one time I had been living in a small room with the darkness outside closing that space inside down into a particular kind of space I felt very comfortable in (thinking). I would have bright light bulbs so I could see the paintings I had; see the things around me very clearly. I was able to see my life there inside my head, and could see what my life had been like the day before when I had been outside and so forth, and that was very nice.

MH: *What do you do when you can't write?*

TB: Sleep, read, take drugs, get agitated, take stupid stances, complain, hate my friends, read Frank O'Hara, worry about money, gossip, be a generally terrible person.

MH: *Do you write at the typewriter?*

TB: I don't much anymore. I got into the habit of writing by hand after having gone to bed when it was inconvenient to get up and go to the typewriter. I'd reach for the pad by the side of the bed. As the years went by, I started keeping these journals and I started writing poems in them and that I believe got me into the habit a lot more.

MH: *Do you keep a lot of poems in your journals to refer back to later?*

TB: Oh sure, well, not too much later. I will often start a poem (pulls out a journal stuffed with clippings and photos and rummages through it), and when I start a poem, I will always finish it. Often, I think I didn't get it but that doesn't bother me. I'll just leave it for a couple of weeks and work on it later.

MH: *You're from New York?*

TB: Now, yes. I grew up in Providence, Rhode Island. I consider myself a real New Yorker though, somebody who was born and raised somewhere else and who came here by choice because it was best for my career. In almost no other city of America can an artist who doesn't really have a product that has much commercial value support him or herself as well as in New York. There are a hundred places where a poet can read for fifty dollars. In most other good-sized cities, Chicago for example, there weren't more than half a dozen reading series going on.

MH: *Is it a good thing to be close to such a large community of artists?*

TB: Yes, and it becomes especially important when you get to be my age, into your forties. You do need to live near other people your own age who are your own kind of people, just to check out your own sanity, your own ethical codes, and your own behavior. To pick you up when you're having hard times or they're having nicer times so you can see that it is not always going to be the way you're having it and vice versa. It's not even a matter of helping, but just having that kind of community. I can go to lots of university towns to live and there'll be lots of other aspiring poets around, people interested in the arts, but they'll all be twenty to twenty-five. Once you begin to be forty you become this oracle at the exact time you shouldn't be one because you don't know everything. You start feeling like you do know everything when you should be readjusting because you're into a new phase of life.

MH: *Do you think New Jersey could become a place that would be supportive of poets and their work?*

TB: In a way it seems to be happening now. It takes guys like yourself, young guys getting involved and helping others get started. It's lonely, going in your mind from let's say being a lawyer to becoming a poet. So, it's very good to create a set of activities and have contacts, things going on. There are people out there willing and happy to come to poetry readings. In any community, even small ones, it's possible to bring out a few dozen people on the basis of its being "Poetry" and "Cultural." It's always small gatherings of poets first, and then as they get better it gets stronger.

MH: *How did you start?*

TB: Pretty much the same way. I started going to this coffee house in the Village where Paul Blackburn was sort of in charge, around '62 to '64. In 1964, Paul gave me my first reading. That same year I was invited to read at New Jersey State Teachers College by Pearl Epstein.

MH: *So, you got started in your late twenties.*

TB: I got started a little late because I went into the Army for a few years in the early fifties and did my basic training at Fort Dix. I hadn't written anything before or during that period. In '57, I got out and began writing seriously.

MH: *Did you get exposed to it in schools and universities?*

TB: I went to the University of Tulsa, and by accident there were some painters and young poets around. My enthusiasm for it took a big jump by having some company. When I saw their poems, I thought, well I can do this and write as well as they can. At home my mother was a great reader and always had plenty of books around, so I picked up the habit of reading from her.

MH: *This was in Tulsa?*

TB: Yes.

MH: *Sounds like an out of the way place to get a poet to come read.*

TB: No, it's just if the universities have any money. The school I went to is famous as a petroleum engineering school; they had plenty of money (both laughing). In '58 I became aware of Ginsberg and Kerouac and those guys. But I was not influenced so much by them as I was by William Carlos Williams. He was the first poet I was reading who wasn't writing in the way that's now considered conventional.

MH: *Did you ever meet Dr. Williams?*

TB: No. I met his wife with my own wife and children. I went up and rang the bell, and with this very good friend from New Jersey, a very good poet named Joe Ceravolo. He had shown me the house where Williams had lived and he had always said that he wanted to see him and go up to the house but he had always been too shy. So, I said, "Well, let's go now," and went up and rang the bell and Mrs. Williams came to the door and I said, "We're young poets and we're great admirers of your husband's work and we came to see the house and I thought we should come up and ring the bell." And she said, "Well my husband is dead you know!" And I said, "We know your husband's dead; we came to see you." And then she just beamed at us and invited us to come inside. We played with the kids and she gave them potato chips. I knew a lot about Williams so she and I just talked mostly about his friend, Robert McAlmon and people like that. Then she showed us his writing desk and the paintings they had in the house. This was back in '64, and she was really terrific.

MH: *You were lucky.*

TB: And furthermore, there was a red wheelbarrow in the backyard which really blew my mind (both laughing). I wrote some poems influenced by Williams.

MH: *Your Sonnets?*

TB: No, they were something else. In the period I was talking about when I was influenced by W. H. Auden and Delmore Schwartz, I was still a student and I knew quite clearly that you couldn't be a poet and a student at the same time. I knew I had to wait until I got out of college and I still had some time on the G.I. Bill so I finished my Master's degree. Then I moved back to New York and got an apartment and was seriously writing and reading a lot. I wrote some poems I thought were OK but, at one point I thought, "Well now I should do what you do if you're an ambitious poet starting out." Then I decided that you must write a sonnet sequence because that's what Shakespeare did.

MH: *Did that make the writing easier? I mean having to stop at fourteen lines?*

TB: Sure, that made it easier. That's why I did it. In fact, that's why I became a poet rather than a novelist because it seemed easier to me at the time, and that's why I took up with the sonnet because it seemed to be the easiest next move. I felt quite comfortable within those fourteen lines, and I spent a lot of time taking sonnets apart and putting them back together writing imitations until I felt I understood the ways in which you could stretch out a sonnet, and how you could have things be in three parts of four lines each and have them come together in the final two, or you could have seven couplets, or how it could be eight and six lines, or you could have two of those at once whatever. And in the course of making my own sonnets I did get to where I could sometimes do two and a half at once maybe, but I was influenced probably more at that time.

MH: *Berryman's sonnets?*

TB: No, not one bit. I didn't even know about him at the time. In fact, mine and his are not entirely dissimilar but he had the advantage of being quite academic, conventional, writing in the English tradition and trying to be avant-garde, too. I really didn't have to worry about that. I was influenced more by Jasper Johns' painting, John Cage's music and Marcel Duchamp, and just took the poetry thing for granted. So, I always felt that my sonnets did more of what he wanted his to do? If that's fair. I'm quite respectful of John Berryman, but not of those poems. I feel they're too cranky.

MH: *Cantankerous?*

TB: Not so much cantankerous as odd. They're cranky the way a drunk can get. That's not a putdown at all. But I was looking, as he was, to have more than one voice in my works, but my avenues were more accessible, easier even. I was able to see what Jasper Johns was doing, and Rauschenberg. They were serious artists who were not ashamed, and they were also broke, they were not one bit self-conscious about being artists. They also came to my poetry readings and were a poet's audience as much as anybody else. I started this poetry magazine called "C" and sent a copy to Jasper Johns. He wrote back, "I like your magazine." And enclosed ten dollars, and went on, "This is for a subscription for me and for my friends, Mr. and Mrs. Frank Stella." So, I felt pretty good about that. These guys were pretty open and were all listed in the phone book, which is how I knew where to send the magazine (both laughing). And that was a great revelation to me, that when I wanted to send this magazine to other artists, just to find them there. I mean Barnett Newman, one of the greatest patriarchs of American painting right there in the phone book. I was also influenced by John Ashbery and Frank O'Hara, the New York poets.

MH: Did you know them personally?

TB: I got to meet them. Well, I met Frank in '62 and Ashbery in '64 when he came back from Paris. But I wasn't intimate. In a certain way I did go to Frank's a lot, to the parties he had and I knew him well enough to read with him at Princeton. I was a friend; well, Frank had a lot of friends but (gesturing with his arms) I always stayed about this far away from guys I admired in case they had bad character. I didn't want that to make me admire their work less. Also, I wasn't fully into myself yet. I suppose I was waiting before presenting myself until I felt I was the poet that had my name.

MH: Do you think poets have a greater need to stick together than other artists?

TB: No, (lighting another Chesterfield) no. I don't think so. You need an ally. (Thoughtfully stroking his beard.) You don't need to stick together any more or less than any other artists. As I said before you need friends who understand where you come from and where you're at and what you're thinking about. You know, what your life position might be. But any other artist will do. Still, my friends are as often painters as well as poets, and I have friends that are not in the arts either. They like to play pool. They're not self-conscious about the fact that I'm a poet, which is kind of a hard thing to overcome sometimes. I am this guy that writes poetry but I'm also just this guy from Providence, Rhode Island.

MH: *Isn't it true that painters and poets aren't together as much as they used to be?*

TB: Things are not the way they were in the '60s. There's something else going on. You can always look back. I mean the Second Law of Thermodynamics is that no matter how orderly things are, they once were more orderly, and in the future, they'll be less orderly.

MH: *Everything in a constant state of decay?*

TB: Not decay exactly. Breaking and re-forming.

MH: *Your latest book of selected poems,* So Going Around Cities, *seems to imply a certain indifference to "place" by its title. Is this true and do you have a "home" in mind when you write?*

TB: No. I am at home in my life, in my house, on the street, in cars, planes, trains, just about everywhere. I think for me it comes down to the basic place right now at the age and in my head, in the rooms that I and my family share with the pictures we put up on the walls.

MH: *Just the space your body requires?*

TB: Yeah, and the way in which we generally make that space be. We have a sense of how to make spaces be our own. Generally, the places we live in end up looking the same inside. In Virginia Woolf's term, "I need a room of my own." As any person does, I think, where one can go for rest as well as to be creative. I also need to go out of that room a lot. Whether it's city or country, I still need to go out a lot.

MH: *Has New York given you a sense of place?*

TB: Sure. I used to say that, for me, New York is a very tangible

CHRISTMAS IN SEPTEMBER

For Mark Hillringhouse

You hear that big heroic land music?
Daddy, who can stand it?
Support & preserve me, father, Oh
Humming, "from this Valley," who's gone.
Land a one could call one.
He starred, had lives, looks down:
Had a long waist he once but yet
You to look back, well he's
Snow cows. Part of a dream, she
Did she wear a hat or the
Windmill still now they buy only
Never encircled, and now I'm
other side? Get off my own land? We
were all born to die on it
With no writin' on it. But who are
In charge of this? this donkey with
A charmed voice. Elly, I'm
Being sad thinking of Daddy.
He marshalled his private Lady.

(after Alice Notley)   ~Ted Berrigan 11/5/87

TED BERRIGAN POEM AFTER ALICE NOTLEY

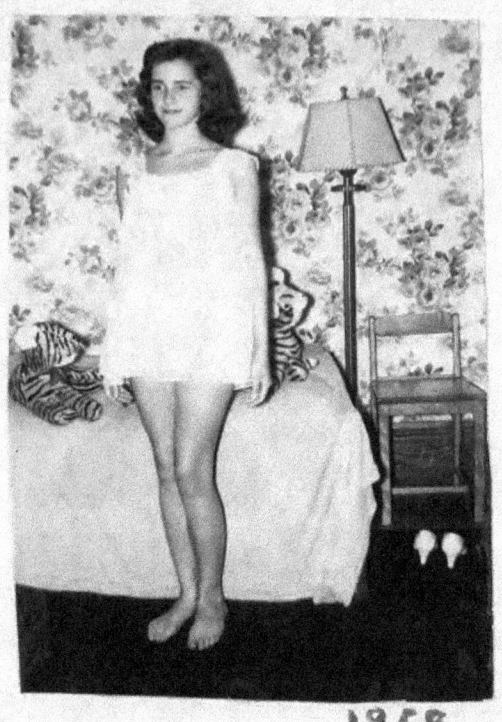

ST. BERNADETTE & ALL THAT

1958

"25 years from now I will be an orphan; married; a poet; have 3 children; one husband; the stigmata; and will be the political boss of Tammany Hall. I would rather die for love, but so far I haven't."
(P.S.: Add: "have Lesbian Tendencies") Ted Berrigan 10Sep82

TED BERRIGAN TEASING BERNADETTE MAYER

place, a very definite place, in that my poems were informed by it, and might not be the way they were had I not done my growing up as a poet here.

MH: *Do you agree that people in the city need a poet who understands the country as well and who can write both?*

TB: Oh sure, sure, but they also need somebody who understands that the city is a good place. Gary Snyder's rap about death to cities and so on is much too extreme. What Bob Creeley says is exactly right, "We haven't yet garnered all the information that is to be garnered from the existence of cities." We don't want them to be dead yet and it would be a loss, I think, to us. We're not about to solve our life problems by getting rid of cities. Given my natural choice I still think I'd like to live in a city. I think I am a city poet certainly more than I am a nature poet.

MH: *The Midwest has this space, this great outdoors. Doesn't it seem that this exterior space, this landscape, can become your mental space, and that by meditating there you can sort of live in it, by going out to it in thought?*

TB: Yeah, and I think that's good. I've read some damn nice books with that kind of space in them. Larry McMurtry's novels have that sort of Texas space in them, and you get both potentially negative sides of it such as the heat and the way that everything can seem of sameness.

MH: *Or the weather sure?*

TB: And the weather, sure. You're very aware of the weather in a very different way than you are here, because here in New York it might be very cold, just as cold as it gets in the mountains, but you only have to go two hundred yards and you're at your friend's house and you've been to seven stores and to the movies.

MH: *You internalize a little more in the city.*

TB: It's a lot of little quick moves, too. You become very quick rather than fast. People say that everybody goes so fast in the city, but it's more that everything has a sort of quickness.

MH: Do you still yearn to travel or has that urge subsided?

TB: Oh, not at all. But more now I'd like to go to the places and then live in them for a while, a few months, or whatever. I'd love to go and live in Italy for a while with my family. I used to travel and did yearn to do it too, but I love the idea of going places for a week or so then going somewhere else. I no longer am so much interested in that, it's too damn strenuous. I did do that. I did go to Rome a year ago and to Amsterdam a year before that. In the course of both those trips I went to several other countries all in like fifteen or eighteen days, but it was too damn much. I was a wreck when I came back. By this age and at the level of reputation I have when I go through with a trip like that its read, drink, smoke coke, take codeine, and get on a train, and the whole round over again, and the next thing you're seeing the poets you haven't seen in eight or twelve months and it's all reunion, party, and excitement—Good god! I mean, I'm forty-six years old.

MH: I'm thinking of a quote from Henry Miller's Big Sur & The Oranges of Hieronymus Bosch, *when he says, "And how very much the same it all is. Why drag one's carcass around? Stay put and watch the world go round."*

TB: Yeah, and I know right where he was coming from when he was saying that. The answer to that of course is that when you're younger you don't have the feeling you're dragging your carcass. You feel like you're riding a wonderful bicycle or something.

MH: Do you worry about writing the same poem over and over again?

TB: No. That's exactly what I do.

MH: When you were starting out as a poet did you have someone you could show your work to?

TB: Yeah, and that was very important for me too. It's because it's necessary to have encouragement and necessary to be in a community of interest in writing poetry.

MH: *Workshops?*

TB: No, not workshops. Let's say two or three other would-be poets who are always telling each other about books you ought to read. You know, just being enthusiastic.

MH: *What are your feelings about workshops?*

TB: I'm not crazy about them. I don't think they're very effective unless I'm teaching them, or maybe one or two other people I know. I mean I just don't think there're enough people who can teach them. It's not enough to be a poet to be able to teach. You have to encourage, to discourage, and to cultivate a certain feeling of irreverence in the students. That last point is often left out. I don't know too many good poets who are products of the university workshops. Like the University of Iowa where I taught. But I don't think they do any harm. You understand, most of these kids who go to these places, what happens to them when they graduate is that—well, they're even married or whatever, and then they go and teach English at some small college in Iowa.

MH: *Do you think it gives them some sort of false sense of encouragement?*

TB: Yeah, and then it makes them bitter that they did this pretty poetry thing like Pre-Med or Pre-Law and they get nothing for it. I don't know why they think they should get anything for it because if there's no market for your services then how can you complain that you can't make money.

MH: *Most of the great poets of this century never made any money off of it either.*

TB: Yes, but that doesn't mean you have to be against the idea (laughing). I would love to make money just for being a poet.

MH: *Rod McKuen makes a fortune off his poetry.*

TB: Rod McKuen is not the enemy though. I have no quarrels with that guy. He probably serves some purpose of some high school kids, making them at least comfortable with the idea that there is such a thing as a "Poet." I find his poetry too easy, but I don't find it offensive in the way I actually find the poetry of Marvin Bell offensive.

MH: *Or the lyrics of the songs you hear on the radio.*

TB: Yeah. Whereas Bob Dylan on the other hand at least makes me interested in everything he does by the high level of skills.

MH: *Everybody writes bad poetry.*

TB: Of course, of course. There's no way you can get away from that at all.

MH: *Right, and I'm willing to read through somebody's bad poetry in order to get to a good poem.*

TB: Oh, me too, you have to. Bad poetry is usually the result of trying to do something that some good poets older than you do that is not suited to you. You still have to do some of those same things those poets do, but you'll have to find your way of doing it. Initially you can't know whether it's suited to you to do it that way until you take some tries at it.

MH: *Isn't it true that in poetry, in the last twenty or thirty years, America has really done a hell of a lot more compared with Europe?*

TB: At least it appears so now. Certainly more than England. One can know because it's the same language. What's going on in Russia we don't know, but there's evidently a lot going on. I've talked with Yevtushenko and he said there are many young poets in Russia outside the Writers' Union. It would be the equivalent of a lot of our poets who are still kind of rough and informed but who are good. Yevtushenko is quite good. Better than he comes across in translation.

MH: *I like hearing Russian poets read. They read almost, it seems, completely from memory.*

TB: Yes. They're wonderful showmen, but we could do that that way too. That comes from the nature of the verse that they write. It is written very clearly with the sense that it is going to be read aloud. A lot of mine is written that way too, but not all. Mine has to be written with both ideas in mind. I am going to do readings out loud quite often, but lots of people who come in contact with it are only going to see it on the page. So, I have the difficult problem of trying to make it functional in both ways. It's a technical problem.

MH: Can you say anything about the inner transformation of a poet other than his formal training, something he has to go through, a kind of fire in his being?

TB: I hear you. Yeah. I think that's true. You do have to go through some fairly difficult rites of passage to become a real poet, a true poet, in that sense. But the passage is out and then back. If you don't come back you're just far out, which is not as relevant, as real as being back here. I mean, Allen Ginsberg, after all, is a little middle-aged Jewish man from New Jersey who has been to a lot of places. When he could be thought of primarily as a dope smoking faggot limp-wristed Buddhist poet. His verse was a lot less effective once than it is now, when he stands in front of any audience. Now there is this adult who is a serious man and who is full of monkey-glee and joy. Also there's his sorrow later on for his father's death. The feelings he expresses are everyday feelings, something that could happen to anyone. And Allen, because he is interested in everything then, will go everywhere. Allen believes you should use the full range of your voice when you write, and that you should be absolutely out front, straightforward, and fairly simple with your content. I believe that too, but some experiences are more complex than others. Allen simply doesn't write about those things.

MH: Shouldn't a young poet read his ass off?

TB: Sure. Just as a young engineer or doctor should read the technical journals and keep up, just as the president must read the cables from his embassies. You must do that. You have to stay on top of it and besides that, you should have a love of doing so. You have to cultivate it. Poetry is a habit. If you don't cultivate the habit of writing, and only write when you feel like it, you won't get it. You'll have long periods where you won't write that much and you'll atrophy. In that way it's like being an athlete. What's wrong with the jobs most people have is that they're one life, and at home is another life. Most people don't get to take their jobs home. They don't get to pursue them in any way except to go to them. That's no good, that's no fun. You have to be fired a little bit with the love of what you do, so that when you drag your feet on it, well it's because that's how it feels that day. Any day that I don't feel like coming here and teaching I do know that by the time I get off the Path train and come up those steps into New Jersey, already my mind will be in the classroom thinking about what I'm going to be dealing with, and that I'll be feeling terrific. On the other hand, I might get shot down in the classroom and go home feeling horrible.

MH: *Does that ever happen?*

TB: Who the hell's going to shoot me down? (laughing) I'm a good professional. I don't stake my ego on whether or not I have a good class. If I don't have a good class today I'll have a good one tomorrow. It will be above that minimum standard, and if it isn't, I'll just junk it and start doing something else. I go by how it feels out there in front of me.

MH: *Who are the poets you love to read the most?*

TB: I don't know if I could name all the specific ones. It's more like (thinking), it's more often someone that someone else mentions who they've just been reading whom they'd like to share. My wife (Alice Notley) is a poet and we kind of feed off each other's interests. My favorite poet to read is Frank O'Hara, and has been for a long time. I get a lot of magazines just because I'm a poet who has been around for a long time. So the younger poets send me their magazines just like I used to send mine, and I read them all avidly. Generally there's something good in them. Right now I'm probably in a position of being more influenced by younger poets than from older ones still living. I am influenced considerably by older "dead" poets.

MH: *It's almost an impossible task trying to keep up.*

TB: I read prose more than I read poetry. I like to read novels and biographies. Yesterday I read Abby Hoffman's latest book which was quite interesting since I was there during that time near the things he was talking about. I like to read Philip Whalen a lot. There's an English poet by the name of F.T. Prince whom I like reading very much, who's not all that prolific. He's a man in his late 60s whom I admire tremendously. I think he's teaching at Brandeis right now, having gone through the English university system and after having reached the retirement age. He's a remarkable poet. I go to a lot of poetry readings. There was one last night at St. Mark's and there are always a lot in Manhattan. So in that way I meet new poets too. Friends also drop in with new poems from time to time. Steve Carey, Harris Schiff, Ron Padgett, Anselm Hollo, Bernadette Mayer, Alice Notley, Kenneth Koch, Jame Schuyler, are all poets whose work keeps me alive, and angry. There are others.

Interview with Edwin Denby

I remember arranging by phone to meet Edwin Denby at the corner of 7th Avenue and West 21st Street. I could see him standing there waiting for me as I approached; we greeted each other and then he took me up to his top floor loft, a loft he had lived in for fifty years and once shared with photographer and filmmaker Rudy Burckhardt. The painter Willem de Kooning had once lived in the loft next door.

The sun was pouring in the large windows, and Edwin sat in a chair facing me while I asked him questions. At one point, I had to take a photograph, because of the light and the way his head cast a silhouette on the wall behind him.

On the walls were original works of art, sketches, paintings, and photographs by all his artist friends. In his eighties, it was getting more difficult for him to navigate the bustling and crowded busy streets of the city.

I had his *Collected Poems* by Full Court Press that Ron Padgett published in 1975 with Frank O'Hara's essay on Denby's poetry at the end of the collection. I also had his *Looking at the Dance,* which was published in 1968 by Horizon Press, a collection of many of his dance writings that he had published when he was the dance critic for the *New York Herald Tribune,* or when he wrote for other publications such as *Modern Music* and *Dance Magazine*. And I also had a libretto titled *Miltie is a Hackie* published in 1973 by Kenward Elmslie's Z Press with the addition of photographic movie stills by Rudy Burckhardt that were made in 1936.

As the oldest member of the New York School, Edwin didn't go around giving poetry readings. His entire life revolved around the world of dance in the city, and his dance criticism was crafted with the same attention to imagery and metaphor as his sonnets. But he was revered by the younger generation of New York poets, and his poetry captures the subtle nuances and movements of city life. My favorite section of his poetry in his *Collected Poems* is the section titled, "Poems written to accompany photographs by Rudy Burckhardt." They capture the very essence of Burckhardt's photography and give them another dimension in verse.

EDWIN DENBY IN HIS CHELSEA LOFT, 1982

MH: *You were born in China in 1903.*

ED: Yes.

MH: *How long did you live there?*

ED: I don't remember at first. I remember going back when I was about four. My parents and grandparents had been there travelling.

MH: *They were missionaries?*

ED: No, they were in the Diplomatic Corps, and my father went into business there.
But the time that I remember was the second time at age four, that was in Shanghai, and I remember it because I remember the house, and pagoda, that marvelous thing with the great big tower in the back yard was overturned outside the wall of our garden, and it was so amazing to see it lying there on the ground. I remember that I went to kindergarten in China and there was a pony and a two wheeled little wicker cart which took me and my two older brothers to school. And the great thing about it was that when you got to school you could throw the reins back into the cart and the pony would go home.

MH: *Do you speak Chinese?*

ED: No. I once thought I knew the word for milk, but when I said it nobody who knew Chinese knew what I was saying (laughing). But my father did. Later on, I always thought that I had some sort of affinity for it because Waley made such a deep impression on me as a writer and a poet.

MH: *Which writer?*

ED: Arthur Waley, the one who translated Chinese poetry. You don't know anything about him? He's a marvelous poet really and a marvelous man and his prose is so good.

MH: *So, he started you in poetry; you read him early on?*

ED: No, well, yes. I was about sixteen in college when someone gave me or I found this book titled *One Hundred & Sixty Chinese*

Poems and I read them. And because I thought I had an affinity for Chinese I went right into them and had no trouble with them at all. Much later I discovered that they were really very good poems, very well translated.

MH: Where did you go to college?

ED: Harvard.

MH: What years?

ED: It must have been in 1920. It didn't interest me and I didn't graduate.

MH: You quit?

ED: I didn't like it. At the time I was in my junior year and I was drinking a lot. I must have been nineteen and I thought it was boring.
  I had two very good friends and it was exciting in a sense because it was Prohibition time. But I got very impatient with school and decided I would rather leave than take my senior year.
  I was lucky because a history professor's mother had an old-fashioned estate in New Hampshire. Though I didn't know her or have a course with him. There were several professors who were very nice to me because I had gotten the highest scores on the college entrance exams. I had no idea why but I did. And that didn't mean anything to anybody I knew, but when I got to Harvard several professors knew it and they wondered who this creature really was, and they couldn't find out because I had no character, nothing. And I didn't seem to know anything so they thought, "Maybe there's something to him." I was doing Latin and Greek and the Latin professor said to his old friend the history professor who lived on the same Cambridge street, "Maybe your mother could give him a job in the country. It might do him some good." This was because I had said that I wanted to be a farmhand.

MH: From Harvard to becoming a farmer!

ED: I wanted to get away, and of course I never had been on a farm and had no idea what a farmhand was.

MH: *They didn't get many farmhands with Harvard educations in those days.*

ED: It so happened that she needed somebody.

MH: *But did you start writing at that age? Did you write poetry? Did you meet poets at Harvard?*

ED: Yes, I think I must have. I didn't write anything while I was on the farm because I was completely idiotic. I was quite astonished. I woke up! I had been there for five months and I thought, "I've had enough of this." So, I left and got a job in a hotel as a busboy. I needed $5 to take the train from northern New Hampshire to southern Vermont, to a place where a painter at the time named Rockwell Kent lived. I don't know if anybody knows him anymore, but he had written a book on Alaska with his son. There was something mysterious about it in my dazed state that attracted me there because I wanted to meet him. So, I earned the money. All I know was that they were very glad to get rid of me at that hotel. Then as soon as I left the hotel, I started walking past Mount Washington from the north side and I began to feel wonderful. I got to this place called Manchester in Southern Vermont. I lose my memory once in a while but somehow these things come back to me, and in Manchester I met a very nice woman poet. She was a very old-fashioned type woman poet and coincidentally a friend of the woman who ran the hotel where I'd just quit. So, I thought, I'd like to give a reading of Shakespeare's sonnets. In fact, I had given poetry readings in college to my friends of all the classics because those were the ones I liked. I didn't know contemporary poetry or anything. I wasn't even curious about it! So, the woman said, "Oh, I think that's very interesting, and I don't think we could afford to miss anything like that." So, I went to the local library and got a copy of the sonnets, came back, and asked how many should I read? I wanted to read them all, but they suggested twenty. At any rate I read them and must have read them terribly. But that gave me enough money to get to the next place because I was going home to my family for the summer in northern Michigan.

MH: *You love sonnets more than any other form of poetry; you write mostly sonnets.*

ED: I love the form because it is so clear to me, and I love the way the shape is so determined. I love the way it begins as a quatrain and builds up gradually by adding to itself in the next quatrain, and then how it comes to its emotional peak, its climax, and then subsides. And that it does still more in the third, and then I love the way the conclusion quiets everything down again, or flies off if that's the temptation. Whether or not to make the conclusion fly off and whether or not I found out about not making it fly off I don't know. I think those first sonnets couldn't have been any good at all. Because nobody ever saw them and I haven't kept them. But it was years later that I thought about it.

The form itself was such a handy challenge—no? It's like making a small table or chair. You know what it is if it's needed, but then it's up to you to do it.

MH: *And you're comfortable writing in that space?*

ED: Yes, and of course, I'm talking about afterwards when I started writing personal sonnets.

MH: *Your early sonnets are more lyrical.*

ED: Yes. Well, I don't know what that means. I say yes because I don't know. I have an image of them in my mind, but much later I knew so much more about the possibilities imaginatively as well as technically.

MH: *Were you inspired by the sonnets of Milton, Shakespeare, and Spenser?*

ED: They're marvelous. I had written a sonnet that echoed Shakespeare's passionate plea, and a professor who was a poet—Oh dear, I forget his name. Anyway, he took me to dinner and said, "Well you know, Shakespeare is not passionate." And I said, "What do you mean!" Well, he had read them the way a grownup reads them and I had read them the way an adolescent reads them, and they mean quite different things. They seemed to me to be passionate, but of course I had no idea what passion was in the literary sense. Whereas ten years later I would have known what the professor had meant and wouldn't have been so indignant at the remark. Other people in my class when I was at Harvard were much more active in poetry than I was and I sort of stayed away from them.

I knew one man who was a friend of Professor Palmer's, the one who did the Homer translation. So, he invited me to go to a reading at Professor Palmer's and Professor Palmer was an old man at that time who had led a very full life and he read very melodiously. I remember how interesting the sound was and he told my friend that I was no good.

MH: *That was nice of him.*

ED: Afterward when my friend came and said to me, "You know he said to me you're no good!" I was offended. It wouldn't mean anything to a grownup. He seemed so wonderful to me. I wasn't ready to realize that there were many worlds. But I haven't thought of that up until now.

MH: *You must have come to New York after that. After Harvard?*

ED: Yes. There's a lapse in my memory somewhere. I came to New York and lived in the Village with my best friend from college who's still a very good friend, and I still see him. He became a doctor later, but he wanted to marry his girlfriend and his family didn't want him to. There was a difference in social status and this astonished me because I was so stupid and couldn't understand those things yet. But he had a very nice father. The mother was very peculiar, a Midwesterner, who in those days were stricter about social rank. He did marry her and came to New York. We took an apartment together near where Sheridan Square is now and I think the rent was only $20. It was two rooms in a rowhouse.

MH: *What year was that?*

ED: 1919. Because that was my senior year when I came to New York. I said to my parents that I couldn't study anymore and I would rather just study alone.

MH: *And you've lived here ever since?*

ED: No. Then I went abroad. But I lived here and worked for a while at the telephone company installing phones. I did that because they were hiring people and this friend of mine wanted to go and apply for the job and he said, "Why don't you come along and just apply with me." That gave me a little nerve to do it. So, I got the job and he didn't. He was color blind. You needed to tell these wires apart. But I had to take the job because there was no money coming in so I took it for a while. Fortunately, I had a wonderful foreman who realized that I wasn't dumb and who realized that I lacked something as far as practical intelligence goes.

MH: *Mechanical ability.*

ED: Yes. He was an amazing man to know that I was perfectly willing but just couldn't do that kind of work. He would come by at a quarter to five near the end of the day to see what I had done. I'd show him proudly and he'd say, "Well that should go here and that should go there." And in five minutes he'd have my whole day's work done (both laughing). Luckily, after about a month some money came in and we all gave up our jobs.

MH: *When did your interest, your fascination with dance start?*

ED: That came when I was abroad. First it was poetry. I came to New York to write poetry instead of staying in college. So, my parents who were going to take a long trip said, "All right, here's the money." A hundred dollars a month was more than enough to live on so they gave me seven months' worth and of course it got spent. So that's why we had to take the jobs. Then we thought we'd start a school but that never got beyond the talking stage. Anyway, this friend of mine had meanwhile decided that he wanted to study medicine and discovered that he could study it in Vienna. The money it would take to study there was enough for him and his wife to live on. So, he decided to take his degree in Vienna even though he didn't know German, he learned German. And I had lived in Vienna with my parents when I was a child and so that seemed perfectly natural to me.

MH: *Had you lived all over the world with your parents in the Diplomatic Corps?*

ED: Well, it was just Vienna and China actually. But I went to school there and spoke German and read German.

MH: *At the gymnasium level?*

ED: It was the first year of gymnasium and Volk Schule before that. That was in 1914 when the First World War started. But at any rate my parents came back to America after the war had been going on for about a year and a half. I told my parents that I wanted to go to Winchester in England. I don't know why, but I heard it was a very good school. Then Hotchkiss was thought the most difficult academically.

MH: *Hotchkiss, the fancy boarding school in Connecticut?*

ED: Yes, I was sent there instead and didn't like it at all but went through.

MH: *And that got you into Harvard.*

ED: That got me into Harvard, yes. It normally feeds into Yale. But I didn't want to go where those other fellows went whom I didn't get along with anyway. Harvard was a bit more interesting and it was extraordinary to be so free.

MH: *How did you get started as a dance critic?*

ED: Oh, that's another long story. I'm sorry, these things are very complicated. As soon as I could get enough money, I decided to go to Vienna instead of hanging around New York. I hadn't any work and remembered Vienna with pleasure from my childhood. My friend and his wife were there so I went and took a room and started writing an epic in four books.

MH: *Ah!*

ED: In blank verse.

MH: *Does it exist anywhere?*

ED: No. It was silly. It was very autobiographical. En route to Vienna I changed trains in Switzerland, a girl came in with a very heavy suitcase and was trying to put it up on the rack. So, being American I picked it up and I was surprised other people didn't. Later on, I realized that only Americans did that. Europeans realize that she would have been perfectly able to do it herself or she wouldn't have been travelling all by herself, and it would be sort of pushy to help her unless she asked for it.

We went over in the train to Vienna together and she showed me the catalogue of the dancing school she was going to. In it, it said in German, "The student will have the experience of time and space." So, I said what nonsense is that (laughing), everybody knows what time and space are! I remember where it was because it was in an imperial summer castle I had seen as a child. I remembered the fake medieval castle which I mistook as real and the swans in the lake frightened me. I must have been six or seven.

So, after I got to Vienna, my friend there said to me, "Well why don't you go there, you were always interested in dancing. Go and see what it is." So, I went. I met the girl there to whom I had promised I would go to see what it was all about. I watched a class and liked what they were doing very much. The strange thing was that it was being run by an American woman. Diaghilev took his dancers there in the early twenties. I realized it had been very famous just before the war.

It was a Dalcroze type of school. Dalcroze was this Swiss educator who had invented this system to help conductors conduct in two different measures at the same time. In order to play Stravinsky, for example. Of course, nowadays conductors can do it without the least struggle. It was a giant leap at the time.

There were very few boys of course and they were doing modern dance which was based on gymnastics. Those were the first years of German modern dance which was where it started anyway. This school had a modern dance choreographer and the students came from all over the world. I went three years through that school and that's how I first learned something. Meanwhile I was really interested in psychoanalysis.

MH: *Freud?*

ED: Yes. Of course, Freud was the great idol in America. So, we all read Freud and discussed it endlessly. An American I knew, an old friend, came by and said, "Why don't you go and see Freud, you're depressed, you always wanted to see him. And he's in this town, and all you have to do is go ring his doorbell!" So, I rang the doorbell and the maid came to the door and I said, "I'd like to see Herr Professor." I learned that that was the proper way of saying it. She said, "Well, I'm very sorry but Herr Professor isn't well. He can't see anybody." And I said, "Oh!" And this woman looking at me then said, "I'll tell you, you can go to see a friend of his, Doctor Feder, who's a very good friend, and he'll let you know when Herr Professor is better and will perhaps arrange a meeting." But I said, "I don't want to see Doctor Feder I want to see Doctor Freud." And she said, "Yes, but this way you could."

Years later I said to myself who was that maid who was so extraordinarily perceptive. She saw immediately that I was not quite right in my head. At that time, I was neurotic, and she thought of this way of helping a total stranger who was standing on the doorstep asking for something impossible. I didn't even know that Freud was sick, and had been sick for a year as I found out later. So, I thought maybe it wasn't a maid, maybe it was his daughter. Of course, I never found out.

Much later I did get to see him. That was after two years of analysis with Dr. Feder who was likewise famous and respected, and Freud recognized his genius with the pleasure Europeans have. It really means something to them. That's the one pleasure there is in life, in your profession, where you can know and appreciate what a person's value is. I didn't find it for a long time here.

MH: *Did this do anything to your poetry? You must have had a lot of anxiety, or did you, maybe you didn't, about poetry and dance.*

ED: No, I think I just goofed off I suppose. I have no idea, no memories of that I was disappointed that I couldn't write my epic. I had three books of it and found writing it very dull and thought it would be more fun to commit suicide, but I never had the nerve to do that (laughs).

MH: *Thank God! But did you become a dancer for a while?*

ED: No. They thought I was too awkward but that's all right. They also thought I was bright. Finally, I found an agent. I had graduated from the school. A man said to me I could get a job in German provincial theatre. At the time they always had dance groups. I don't know if you know anything about European theatre, but it's all run by the state—opera, plays, and dance. It was always taken care of by the local King or Duke or whatever, and as the governments changed most of it was taken over by the state. There were some private theatres too, but all that was very different from competitive Broadway. The director was appointed and if he wasn't good, they'd change him. So, some of those theatres were well run.

MH: *If it's not commercial, supported by the state, does that change the nature of the performance?*

ED: Yes. It does because you appeal to the real standard of art and not the standard of what the newspaper editors can understand in a review, or what the public can take in. New York theatre understands a star but has a hard time understanding the playwright. But I did get a job in the theatre as a dancer in Germany. Again, I was very lucky because the reason I'd gone there—it's a complicated story. I went to give an audition and arrived in this town in mid-winter, a town that had an advanced theatre because it had a progressive director. I was told by an agent in Vienna that I should apply for an audition there. So, I went and said, "Here I am." And they said, "We'll give you an audition Sunday morning." They also asked me to go to their theatre that very night to see what it was like. So, I went. I was very happy and said this was the place for me.

What happened was that the lady who gave me the audition, the choreographer, was the wife of the man who had done the scenery. Well, I got to know them of course because they hired me and I got to see that they must have thought, "There's something we can do with this creature, he's not just an average person coming by, he doesn't seem like a dancer to begin with."

MH: *So, your career in dance was very short?*

ED: No, but having been brought up with modern and not ballet, I didn't know that a dancer is a special type of being. It was more like Judson Church than modern dance in those days.

MH: *You're being a poet primarily, or would you consider that?*

ED: Yes, but I didn't say no; I didn't think that I was. I thought I had been trained as a modern dancer.

MH: *Were you still thinking of poetry all during this period when you were involved with dance?*

ED: I don't think so. I was writing plays; I was writing plays in German.

MH: *Were they ever published?*

ED: No. But they always wanted to produce them. They liked them when they read them. Then they hired for the next year. Of course, this was winter and they hired for the next season.

MH: *What year was this or how old were you?*

ED: I was about twenty-three and I guess it was about 1926, something like that. I was there for a year, then we went to Berlin because this choreographer was brilliant. She did things that no other choreographer was doing. But from a theatre point of view, not from a movement point of view.

MH: *When you started writing dance criticism did you ever imagine that you would become so good at it that Clive Barnes would call you the foremost dance critic alive?*

ED: That's a lot of time after I came back to New York; after the Nazi thing made it impossible to stay in Berlin. Hitler came into power so I went to Majorca, a place where poor Americans would go because I didn't know what to do.
 So, then I returned to New York and meanwhile met Virgil Thomson in transit sometime in Paris. I saw him again when I returned here. We were friends. He was in his thirtieth year, and it

was he who suggested my writing for the *New York Herald Tribune* because their two dance critics had joined the Army. That was about a year before the war in 1938.

He suggested that I go and see this editor who was in charge of a thing called *Modern Music*. They had a very brilliant editor named Lederman who's still alive and she's still writing too.

So, Virgil had come back from Paris and knew all about music. But he was very lively and always finding people for the magazine and wrote for it. But all the young musicians wrote for it and he thought that I could write about dance for them because the only performances many of those young composers would have would be dance performances.

The music critics wouldn't go. So, he thought that I would know what they were doing and could write about it from the dance as well as the music side. And the idea would be, he said to me—I remember—"It doesn't really matter what you say because they're not interested in dance, they're only interested in seeing that their music has been reviewed." Well, that was how I started writing.

And then when Virgil saw that I had done that for a few years and he needed a writer for the *Herald Tribune* because as music editor he was in charge of dance, he suggested me. They had a very brilliant head editor in those days at the *Tribune*, marvelous man.

MH: *What was his name?*

ED: I wish I knew (laughing). At any rate he looked me over and could tell by instinct all the things I have been telling you, because he was that kind of man. He supported Virgil, who was constantly in hot water.

I remember Virgil's first Philharmonic review of their opening concert for the new season before I was on the paper. At the end of it he said, "It shows once again that the New York Philharmonic has no relation to New York's intellectual life." Of course, all the people who supported the Philharmonic, which was a sacred institution, were furious, especially the rich people who called the paper to complain bitterly to the editor. Virgil of course was quite amused because he was quite able to defend himself. The owners of the paper were very grand people socially and intellectually to know that it was much more fun this way than to have one of those acquiescent reviews that say, "Oh well, they did their best," and so on.

But I remember I used to get up in the morning to go get coffee and a fried egg and the *Herald Tribune* on the corner to read Virgil Thomson. It was such a pleasure to read first thing in the morning, one of his lively and wonderfully aggressive reviews. That was how I started writing for them. Too bad it doesn't exist anymore.

Then a young man in a publishing house said to me, "Why don't you make a collection of your reviews." I had been doing it for a couple of years, and his editor said O.K. that would be ideal when he glanced over the collection and so they published them. Somehow that got to England where Clive Barnes was a dance critic.

MH: *He thinks you're the best.*

ED: Well, he said that once. He's a very nice man (laughing). It's been quoted since. I've never contradicted it.

MH: *You went on to write books on dance.* Dancers, Buildings and People in the Streets *and* Looking at the Dance.

ED: Those were some longer articles. Some were written for *Modern Music*.

MH: *What happened to your poetry during all this time? You were still writing poetry.*

ED: Yes, I was.

MH: *Were you able to get your poems published?*

ED: No. I didn't even try, as far as I know. But I don't think anybody would've liked them. Of course, gradually I grew up and found out what poetry was about and it became much more interesting and serious to me.

MH: *What happened at the* Tribune?

ED: After a few years the *Tribune* folded (August, 1966), but there were people who preferred my reviews to others, and the reason they did was that I was modelling myself after Virgil Thomson. But Virgil was the person who taught me what it is that is worth writing about and how you go about doing it, not by telling me but by his example.

Afterwards the editor of *Modern Music,* which was a quarterly journal, who was very pleased that I was writing for a newspaper, used to call me up. About every week or two I'd want to resign because it was such hard work, and I was so dissatisfied with it. But she very nicely explained why that was good and how good that was or if it was not quite so good. And that way she kept me going for the first six months when I thought I could never learn the job. Then I got the hang of it.

At that time the Metropolitan Opera House was on 39th Street, a beautiful house that they should never have torn down, and the *Tribune* was on 41st Street, so I'd just walk across and grab a cup of coffee. And then later on at the end of the day when I was getting a little worn and stupefied, Elaine de Kooning, who had become a very good friend, used to go with me.

I could turn to her and say, "Did you see anything? I didn't. What did you see tonight?" And she'd say, "Well, I saw these green stockings so and so was wearing in the second piece that were quite interesting." (laughing) And I thought, "Oh yes!" And then it all came back to me.

It was one of those blackout businesses that you can't help if you're trying very hard to remember something. If you didn't have this tape machine you wouldn't remember all of what I'm saying.

But it was so modest what she was saying. Anybody else would have said, "Why I thought the second piece was much the best because of this and that." You know, and it wouldn't have stimulated me at all. It would have been her review and I could have imitated it, but it would have been limp because it has to occur to you at the moment. She understood that so well. Afterwards at the newspaper they loved her dearly, she was very beautiful too, besides being so sweet natured and amusing and Irish.

So, I asked whether she could take over my job for several weeks during the summer when I was going somewhere and they were delighted. And she understood Bill de Kooning very well too.

MH: *You knew Willem de Kooning before you knew Elaine?*

ED: Yes. I knew his previous girlfriend who was this incredibly beautiful Jewish girl whose name was Juliet, a very delicate Bronx girl.

MH: *What year was this? What year did you meet de Kooning?*

ED: I met him in 1936; it was the first year I was living in this loft apartment.

MH: *After you came back from Europe?*

ED: Yes. He was living one floor down in the next building.

MH: *So, you knew him for quite a long time before you ever knew Frank O'Hara.*

ED: Yes. In fact, that was one of the reasons that the poets spoke to me because I was a friend of Bill's.

MH: *What was it like; how did you meet O'Hara? Were you introduced?*

ED: I can't remember at all; it's as though I'd always known him. And of course, that's the kind of person he was if he was interested in you at all. He never asked any questions like somebody trying to find out who you were. He just took it all in. And I thought he was a wonderful poet. But I thought he was even a more wonderful man. At first, he was a swell person to have around, then I got to know his poetry better and I thought he was amazing.

MH: *Did he know you as a poet?*

ED: Yes, but you see I was always writing in this old-fashioned way and he was writing in a lively new way.

MH: *But you were much older too.*

ED: Yes, I was older. But he said somewhere, maybe it was in *Poetry Magazine*, something very nice about me, one of his great big compliments. He wrote an opinion of my poetry being very good and I was very pleased. But he was so generous to everybody. Of course, it didn't make me less happy that he was generous to other people. I realized that that was his nature.

MH: Koch? Ashbery?

ED: Yes, yes, yes, but they didn't have the same warmth and outgoingness.

MH: But you saw each other frequently?

ED: Yes, but Frank much more than the others. I didn't really make very good friends with the poets. But with Frank it was impossible not to be friends if you knew him at all. He was always interested in dance too.

MH: You were also very friendly with a lot of the artists. Obviously de Kooning introduced you to them.

ED: There too, I really didn't belong to their milieu. It wasn't that I knew a lot of them and knew them for many years, but it was that they knew I was a friend of Bill's and that I knew they were friends with Bill. I was busy with other things, and I didn't understand what they were doing until many years later.

MH: At the time you didn't realize how important that group would become.

ED: No.

MH: Were you aware of a change, a growing excitement, an enthusiasm, because you were dealing with a younger crowd of artists? Ashbery, O'Hara, and Koch must have seemed like very young men to you who were very excited and very enthusiastic about art.

ED: Oh yes. They admired Bill of course very much, especially Frank. He must have written about Bill. Bill liked Frank very much too.

MH: Did you spend time at the Cedar Tavern or San Remo Café?

ED: No. I went to the Cedar once or twice and I remember Bill de Kooning and Franz Kline standing next to each other at the bar drinking. I was sitting at a table. And it was adorable to see them because they were about the same size and they were like two teenagers having an absolutely marvelous time together. They were, of course, famous painters by that time in their own world. But the way they made jokes to each other and the intimacy between them, it's still one of my happiest memories.

MH: *What was New York like in the '50s?*

ED: Well, New York was always heavenly to me.

MH: *You love it here?*

ED: Yes. This (Chelsea) was a very quiet part of town then.

MH: *This same apartment?*

ED: Yes. Rudy Burckhardt's darkroom was here but he was living across the street with his first wife and Jacob was a baby then.

MH: *You must love New York because you write a lot about New York. Your poems, except for* Mediterranean Cities, *have a New York subject matter.*

ED: I suppose so.

MH: *Was the city better then?*

ED: It's really ruined compared to what it used to be.

MH: *You still like New York?*

ED: Yes, very much. Of course, being old and sick makes it a lot different since I don't have the nerve or the energy I used to have. It's a nuisance. But as far as I can be aware of it, I think it's still a marvelous city. It's changed a lot because of those painters really, who started the New York intellectual life. Before that it was merely literary.

MH: *A whole new dimension was added.*

ED: New York is always self-consciously theatre oriented. But they added another dimension to the theatre life, and so did the dancers, and of course so did the painters and the art dealers who were all so different from the previous generation, the pre-1930s New York art scene was totally different.

MH: *Do you know Saint Mark's Church-in-the-Bowery?*

ED: The first time I went to Saint Mark's Church was for the funeral of a friend of mine, an old man, who belonged to one of New York's first families, and whose church it had been for generations. I didn't realize that until I went in to the funeral and felt the people around to realize the presence. I thought it was an incredibly beautiful building and I had never been in it before. I was very much interested that it was one of the few things left over that was beautiful from the eighteenth century. It was very interesting that it wasn't famous.

MH: *It has a ghost.*

ED: Oh really! I didn't know.

MH: *Peter Stuyvesant's ghost.*

ED: Oh, his ghost (laughing)! His ghost would be rather noisy, don't you think? That's funny, I've never heard that. Well, before the Saint Mark's Poetry Project there was Judson, the artists of the Judson, who are now being revived in modern dance. Let's see, I think that was the Reverend Carmines. The Judson Dance Theater begun in the early '60s was housed at the Judson Memorial Church on Thompson Street and Washington Square South. There was also the Judson Poets' Theater.

MH: *Did you give readings?*

ED: No.

MH: *You don't give readings?*

ED: No, terrible.

MH: *Did you in the '50s?*

ED: I read once on the machine at Saint Mark's because they asked me to come down and read some poems, Denbyesque poems. I never wrote enough to make it feel that I belonged to their group. I mean I like them as friends and I admired them as poets, and some of them I didn't understand and some of them I did, but literature as a profession was never a part of my life. I knew that there was that profession but I never worked at it.

MH: *Who is your favorite New York poet, or do you like them all? James Schuyler? Frank O'Hara?*

ED: Oh, Frank really is the one that I enjoy reading and rereading the most. Schuyler is very brilliant and wonderfully very alive and flexible. I think he's a first-rate poet.

MH: *Did you meet him along with O'Hara and the others?*

ED: Yes.

MH: *James Schuyler doesn't imitate anybody.*

ED: No, neither does Ashbery or Koch. Those three old friends of mine don't imitate themselves the way you'd expect other people to.

MH: *Well, Ashbery keeps changing; every book is different.*

ED: He certainly does (laughing). You have to learn how to read it all over again.

MH: *Frank O'Hara changed.*

ED: Yes.

MH: *And Schuyler.*

ED: Yes, it's true, you have to learn how to read their poetry all over, as if you were starting fresh. And that's marvelous. Ashbery, after inventing so many things, can go on and invent even more. He's not nearly appreciated enough.

MH: *Ted Berrigan told me he thinks he's our greatest poet right now.*

ED: He certainly is. There's no doubt about it, is there?

MH: *But there are such strong regional preferences.*

ED: Who do they say is the best?

MH: *Allen Ginsberg is probably the most famous.*

ED: Oh yes, but he's scarcely a poet at all. He's a member of society. No, I mean he's a man alive at this time. That's wonderful (laughs).

MH: *He's so magnanimous.*

ED: Yes, and he'll be of the greatest use to people who'll be trying to find out what it was like generations from now. But we who see what's happening don't realize that. Don't you think? He's a very magnanimous man and I admire that very much, but I like poetry to be poetry, and that is just my individual preference.

MH: *Do you see Virgil Thomson anymore?*

ED: I saw him last Christmas and he had a hard time hearing but he watched closely and is very understanding. They gave him a very beautiful concert at Alice Tully Hall. He's known all the poets from the past too.

MH: *Do you still see the artist friends that you have?*

ED: They all went off in other directions. The poets are still here for the most part. Ron Padgett is lecturing tomorrow on Reverdy. I promised to go and hear it. Anne Waldman is also very interesting and very informative. She knows them all, having begun the Poetry Project which has done so much. It's amazing to me.

MH: *What do you think of this younger generation: Berrigan and Padgett and Waldman?*

ED: I think they're marvelously crafted and talented but I don't always understand them. Padgett is so witty that I get a lift just reading him. Besides, I'm impressed by him as a person.

MH: *I'm impressed by Berrigan as a person; he's very kind and generous and not pretentious. I love his poetry.*

ED: Yes, that's true. And none of them are pretentious, are they? It's astonishing.

MH: *Well, they're all serious poets and it's very hard being a poet in this culture.*

ED: Yes, and it's hard to earn a living. I was thinking more than if you were a European poet because a university would help you out in a way that they don't here. I went to a reading at Columbia University, Ashbery's, and I was amazed he read so badly. I was relieved when I thought about all that work he has to do to earn a living, but oh my!

MH: *He has two jobs.*

ED: And he was a brilliant art critic for a while.

MH: *Still is. He writes for* Newsweek.

ED: He still writes for them? I used to get it every week but I heard he'd given it up. Well, I'll have to go to the library and look them up because I liked reading them very much. What a pleasure. He writes extraordinarily well about it.

MH: *Kenneth Koch has a new book of poems coming out.*

ED: I remember him as going off in all directions at once from sheer wit. It was his play *George Washington Crossing the Delaware* with those wonderful sets by Alex Katz. Larry Rivers had asked Koch to write the play and Rivers had done a painting inspired by the old famous painting.

MH: *There were sets designed by Red Grooms for The Red Robins.*

ED: Those were extraordinarily brilliant. But it's hard to do those plays. They'll be done better someday; they'll be much funnier when people know them better; when people know how to do them. They're difficult to do because you have to do them so unintentionally. The dialogue has to be done so unintentionally and that's something that New York professional actors don't like.

MH: *Did you know Barbara Guest?*

ED: I knew her but I didn't know her very well. Of the younger poets Anne Waldman is the only one that I know really well.

MH: *When did you meet her?*

ED: I think through the Poetry Project. I used to go to the readings there a lot.

MH: *What can you say about the future of poetry?*

ED: Well, I think that Ashbery's importance as a poet will only be realized in twenty years.

MH: *Between the three of you, O'Hara, Schuyler, and yourself, you seem to write about New York the most. Ashbery and Koch are not that open about it. Ted Berrigan is, but he's a younger man. Most of your sonnets are based on New York and the action of people in the streets. I was wondering why?*

ED: Well, I learned a lot, maybe all that I know about New York from Rudy Burckhardt's photographs and movies. Because I got very interested in them, the way that you can study them and know what the texture of light and air is all about. I wanted that in my poetry. Nobody really understood the films of Rudy Burckhardt because he was trying to capture that, to make you feel as if you might be able to touch the air and the light.

MH: *Are you still writing poetry?*

ED: Yes.

Interview with Barbara Guest

It was James Schuyler who mentioned the importance of Barbara Guest's poetry to me, and I would later discover that they were close friends. When I first interviewed her, she was living on West 4th Street near NYU, in an apartment with her husband, Trumbull Higgins, a military historian, whom I met there as well. Alex Katz and Jane Freilicher canvases hung on her walls. She had just published her novel, *Seeking Air*. Ten years later, I interviewed her again, but at her home in Southampton, Long Island. At that time, she was living with her daughter Hadley. Her husband had died a couple of years prior to that visit.

Her life was very different living in such a big house a block from the ocean. She let me and my wife stay overnight. I was impressed by her art collection. There were Tony Smith sculptures on her lawn, and original paintings hanging on her walls by her artist friends Grace Hartigan and Mary Abbott. Sitting in her yard the following morning, she was delighted by the Greek music that had drifted in over her hedge from across a neighbor's yard. You could hear ocean waves crashing in the background.

She was enjoying a good period of life even though she was widowed. She was writing new poems and publishing and getting more critical notice.

And by using art as a way to reimagine her world, she worked her poems word by word, line by line across the page letting the subject find itself the way an abstract painter might. Some of my favorite poems of hers originated in this way she had of writing.

Her poetry comes out of a poetics of painterly anti-lyricism and out of personal connections to various paintings across art history, and to the painters of the New York art world, and she used figures from Greek and Roman mythology to convey a sense of time over a sense of place. My favorite book of hers is *Fair Realism* published in 1989 by Sun & Moon Press.

Barbara Guest in Her W. 4th Street Apartment

MH: Do you remember when you first started writing?

BG: In my late twenties.

MH: So you really began writing poetry in New York.

BG: I came to New York when I was twenty-three and I began to believe in my poetry, in its future. It seemed like civilization coming from the West Coast; I thought I was coming to Paris. I knew Henry Miller and he suggested I go.

MH: You mention him in one of your poems, "The Man with The Long Face." How did you know Henry Miller?

BG: Through his novel, *The Cosmological Eye*, and through mutual friends. He lived in Beverly Hills and wrote about it. So one day I went over to see him. I needed something to free me. I became freer here in Manhattan. I remember when I was living in California and trying to write like Robinson Jeffers—well, I couldn't write like him.

MH: In New York, did your close association with painters ever make you want to paint?

BG: No, I don't even make collage anymore. I was a reviewer for *Art News*.

MH: Was Frank O'Hara the first one you met when you came to New York?

BG: Yes, and I got to know Frank when I went to the Cedar Bar, an artist and poet hangout.

MH: Is that how you got to meet all the painters and poets?

BG: Well, they sort of looked me up. John Meyers looked me up. I had published a poem in the *Partisan Review*, and they all read it. Frank O'Hara and Jane Freilicher wanted to know who I was. Then we all showed up one night at the Cedar Bar. A coincidence. That was a very necessary place. We never had much of a social life, such

July 20, 1983

Dear Mark,

I have attempted to telephone you several times, but there have always been mysterious difficulties. The last time I learned that the telephone had been disconnecteed? And so you see you have been on my mind and I thank you for your attempts to locate me.

First I was in Europe for a brief time, mostly on H.D. business, and then an odd week in N.Y. and then out here. The hospital was the most sensible thing I have done in a long time. And I am delighted to tell you that the news is good, the tests were passed and I am feeling ever so much better. Now the only thing left to do is to change my life! I am going about that in the simple-difficult way of eating little, drinking nothing, and sleeping much. Whether I am so busy congratulating myself on feeling no pain, or whether the regime actually works, I don't know, but so far all is favorable.

Now the H.D. galleys have arrived and I shall have three abstemious monastic weeks of grueling, difficult work over them -- I detest going over proof. But it means the end of this long enslavement which brought me much happiness and much labor, 602 pages! I had no idea there was so much blood in it!

Have you seen the current <u>Newsweek</u>? There is an article on the small optimistic presses -- North Point and Black Sparrow in particular. About John Martin's press. I have not actually <u>seen</u> what you have now written about me, as you know. I would certainly hope to vet whatever is said before it goes into publication. Not so difficult a manoeuver as some poets who will remain nameless, but I do, Mark, expect to be presented with whatever you have written about me so that there are no flaming commas or purple paragraphs. And this means that I am sending you all my best wishes that Martin will take your book. I know, I believe, what accomplishing so many pages -- did you say over five hundred -- means to you and that you would like all that extensive work and planning to see a printing press.

Thank you for your card -- your concern -- and yes, I shall break a rule if you come out here to visit the squire of this district, and wouldlook forward muchly to seeing you.

As ever,
Barbara

BARBARA GUEST TO MARK HILLRINGHOUSE

as dinner parties. We had the Cedar.

MH: *What year was that?*

BG: 1955. The person who influenced me was Tony Smith (1912-1980), a sculptor, from South Orange, New Jersey. I knew him a long time, back when I was living on Eighth Street in the Village. And I first met him in L.A. He and his wife, Jane, who raised me, artistically speaking. He's a very seminal influence in painting and sculpture.

He would come over to visit me on Eighth Street. He had bought a Rothko painting and I told him I didn't understand Rothko and he said, "You will, you will." And of course, later I did.

Barnett Newman was a close friend of Tony's. I could really talk to Tony or rather, listen to him. I listened to him when he spoke about *Finnegan's Wake* and *Ulysses*. He taught his art classes at NYU to read *Finnegan's Wake*. He believed they would understand more about art through Joyce than through a discussion of the technique of painting.

He had a wheelbarrow and he used to carry his students' paintings in the wheelbarrow to exhibition rooms as if the wheelbarrow were part of the painting execution. Tony was probably one of the most important people in my life. He was close to Jackson Pollock and he taught me to understand what Pollock was doing.

In my book, *Moscow Mansions*, the poem "Egypt" is dedicated to him. And in *Seeking Air*, I quote what he said to me, "Time works for you." Once, when I was writing a poem, he saw the title written above the unfinished poem and he said, "Why don't you let the subject find itself." Which is a theory of Abstract Expressionism. I always remember those words.

MH: *Being part of that group of painters and poets in the fifties in New York, how did it influence you? Were you looking at each other's work, showing each other new poems?*

BG: I think it's where I found my first acceptance. I was an outsider, then suddenly they began reading what I wrote. I read at the Artists' Club on Eighth Street and artists took it up saying it was interesting poetry.

It was very curious, because we all like the same things. There was no disagreement, and we were completely alone. We were interested in French poetry. What we were writing was so totally alien to anything going on at that time in American poetry.

I worked for the *Partisan Review* for a while. I was their poetry editor—an unknown fact. I was first published by the *Partisan Review*. I sent in a poem and Delmore Schwartz liked it. I didn't even know Delmore Schwartz. It was very odd. They accepted two of my poems and asked me to come in to meet them.

MH: *How old were you?*

BG: Thirty. They sort of took to me. Philip Rahv, the editor, said, "Would you mind coming into the office to read the poems? We haven't got anybody now that Delmore's quit." But then I discovered that nobody was interested in poetry at that magazine, so I asked friends like Frank to submit poems, and other poets. Then I decided that I would like to publish a poet who I thought was wonderful—Boris Pasternak. They had never heard of him. I had to get a translation and talk the *Partisan Review* staff into printing him. I had to sit with Philip Rahv for ages and say, "Now here's Jimenez, here's Pasternak!" And he'd say, "I never heard of them." And I'd say, "Well, please publish them!"

So, I did that for quite a while. Hettie Jones was working for them as a secretary—LeRoi's wife (Amiri Baraka). She wasn't his wife then. But he was always sending in poems every week, and so was Louis Ginsberg (Allen Ginsberg's father). I would talk with Frank (O'Hara) about it, about publishing Ginsberg's poems, and he would say that he really didn't think he would fit in very well with the "Partisan Review" crowd.

MH: *Did you go in for confessional poetry?*

BG: I think all poetry is confessional.

MH: *Why do you write? Why is poetry important to you?*

BG: If you were a cabinet maker, you'd be bored if you didn't make cabinets.

MH: *You'd be bored if you didn't write poetry?*

BG: Yes, or in a continuing purgatory. I think the older I get, the more important it is to write.

MH: *Why was it important to you when you were young?*

BG: I think that was love. I think that's something that was passionate. And there's no possible way of writing without passion.

MH: *A lot of poetry I've read lately has no passion in it.*

BG: That bothers me tremendously. It's one of my tests: how much passion and how much imagination is contained in a poem.

MH: *(walking into the ground floor studio) This is where you work, the main room of the house?*

BG: Working here means that I don't use the fireplace (laughing).

MH: *Is that important to your work, having a space like this?*

BG: I only use this space in the warmer months. In winter, it uses too much heat. I can work anywhere. I've been in so many painters' studios and I envy all their space and light and so I set up here, I suppose in imitation of them. I've learned so much from painters that I might as well learn about space.
   I don't think writers put enough demands on their surroundings. It's almost as if they're afraid to do it, as if it were indulgent and detracts from the mysteriousness of their occupation. And there's always a little bit of the sense of punishment that writers have, not to deserve anything larger than a place to put pen and paper. Whereas painters demand it. They don't always get it. I read here as well and look out these windows, all of which gets into the poetry.

MH: *Now tell me, you work under these great paintings. There's a Grace Hartigan over your desk and a Mary Abbott. You have such great art in this house—Larry Rivers, Fairfield Porter.*

BG: That's part of my poetry, these paintings, because they're part of my past. This painting by Mary Abbott is a poem/painting collaboration that we did in 1961, and we did an entire series. Then of course, the Hartigan was when she was working in downtown New York long ago. I was getting ready to go to Europe and she said, "Well, I haven't finished this painting yet, and I'd like to finish it before you leave." So she painted, "For Barbara" on it. She was very generous.

MH: *Why is this whiteboard here on the floor?*

BG: I used that when I was in California. I used blackboards because the room I was given was in a building that was formerly a Chinese orphanage converted to a school in the hills of Berkeley. It was a large room with blackboards and I looked at them and thought, "This is going to put another dimension into my work because I'll write on the blackboards." As a consequence, I wrote the poem sequence called "Chalk."

When I came back here to Southampton, I still carried with me the idea of notation on a board.

MH: *So, then you move your writing from that large white space on the whiteboard to the page?*

BG: To the page, yes.

MH: *Does it free you, like a painter working on a large canvas?*

BG: Yes, exactly. I write, I find, differently on different spaces. There was a point when I wanted to change from the work in *Fair Realism*. I wanted to make a change in my work and that blackboard in that schoolroom, and the use of chalk, gave me the impetus.

MH: *What year was that?*

BG: The summer of '89. In fact, when I used the chalk, I sent the poems that I wrote to Lee Hickman of *Temblor Magazine*. He wrote back to me, "These poems remind me of Cy Twombly." Well, I had not made the connection with the idea of chalk and Cy Twombly. But I found I had a poster from the Twombly show at the Castelli

Gallery. The poster was of a blackboard on which Twombly wrote in chalk.

MH: *You saw the connection immediately.*

BG: Yes, but I was not conscious of that connection when I was writing, and I certainly wouldn't want to import his work into mine. It was coincidental. I think if you are working toward the same idea of space, sparseness and openness, you are apt to make these connections.

MH: *I see that old Kaypro computer there on your desk with the pads and the notes next to it with the whiteboard. How do you get started?*

BG: I start on a piece of paper, and I "speak" to the old Kaypro which isn't even in DOS.

MH: *On lined paper?*

BG: No, always unlined. Often, when I wake in the middle of the night, or before I go to sleep, lines will come to me and I'll write them down. Originally, I would transfer those lines onto a typewriter to see how it looked. Then it went onto the computer, not always. "Otranto," a recent poem, was written on a typewriter. It was written from notes on paper to a typewriter and then expanded on the computer and drastically edited. The computer screen is very, very misleading. It's enchanting and it makes you think you've created a movie or something. As you know, the screen is seductive, and if you're visual, it's extremely seductive. It's very good for viewing a poem, because I use broken lines. On the screen, I can get the spacing and I can visualize it more accurately than I can on the page in the typewriter. And that helps to speed things up. It's the editing that's so great with the computer and it saves so much time and energy and you don't sit surrounded by a sea of paper.

MH: *So you still begin in a traditional way?*

BG: I don't always. But I don't begin from an idea, usually. I think that the poem appears of itself. In some poems, for instance, in "Ilex," which is about Alexander the Great, the first line appeared, then the research acts almost as a damper. I did a lot of research on him. I was ill. I read all day long about Alexander. So there was the subject matter that grew. Then I translated the subject matter into my own terms. I would get a grasp of the subject in the first paragraph and then I would start writing sometimes directly onto the computer, but I also depended on notes that I made on paper.

MH: *So that's still pretty much an anchor, the page, the notes?*

BG: Then I change the notes radically.

MH: *Do you save all your drafts?*

BG: I save a lot. I'm of two minds about that because sometimes I look back and realize that was pretty awful when I was reaching for something that I wasn't able to get. But I save them out of habit. It's as if they are a part of the poem, the finished poem. These are the ancestors of the final poem.

MH: *Do you pay attention to literary forms, any traditions, or are you very open?*

BG: I pay more attention to my ear. I'm not so open as it seems. I won't pretend to say that I'm working formally. I know when things start and where they begin. Yet, I am formal in my attitudes toward poetry. But not formal in a sense that you must learn the rules. I find that I get more formal as I give myself the rules, because I am very strict with myself. I can't see writing without a pattern. Placement on the page becomes important.

MH: *What are these books?*

BG: I can't get rid of them (pointing to a row of old books on shelves beyond her desk). I sit there at that computer and I'll look up at a title and that's how I worked on the poem "Borderlands." I saw a book on Czechoslovakia after the First World War, so I got that idea of "Borderlands" as I was reading about it. These books are friends and they're helpful. And over here are art books and they're useful. I reread constantly and I continually consult art books.

MH: Which ones in particular?

BG: I was recently reading Delacroix's journal. I read it to get its toughness. Something that my poetry has to work for. And the toughness of Delacroix and the expanse of his thought are there in that book and I can enter into it when my own thinking is getting shriveled. It's like breathing. I want to stay in the atmosphere. The Matisse books, Matisse has taught me so much.

MH: In particular?

BG: Well, I bought at the Metropolitan Museum in Manhattan that poster of a Matisse that was in the Hermitage in Saint Petersburg, the goldfish. It's upstairs. I saw it and I thought, "What a painting!" I was writing a poem about the beach and the pool and the sea, and I was having a rotten time with it. It got very baroque, very full of words. I tried to rewrite it to simplify it and I succeeded, but it was not as interesting a poem and I continued to look at Matisse. We all talk about his use of color, yet, he is a very intellectual painter. He has that French mind, that direct French mind, and he taught me to think more deeply. His use of black, for instance. All painters' use of black is very interesting and sometimes the word "black" appears in my poetry and it comes from the need to put that dark space into a poem the way a painter will use black, which is composed, of course, of many colors.

MH: *That is interesting because in* Fair Realism *there's a lot of mention of black in color.*

BG: Yes, there is. In the first poem, "Wild Gardens Overlooked by Night Lights" that was the black ink of the Genji, their hair. But black in a poem gives it depth, for me. Matisse uses black frequently. Another painter who uses it is Manet. His use is incredible. Picasso discusses this use of black, because Picasso doesn't have much of a color stretch, nothing like Matisse. But he understands black in himself; he has a lot of black in his soul.

MH: Your poem "Borderlands" just came about haphazardly by just browsing the bookshelves?

BG: Well, yes, but you see, my late husband (Trumbull Higgins) was a military historian and some of these books were his and we discussed Czechoslovakia and we were in Czechoslovakia, and I have a friend who's Czech, and he's gone back there now. It's that Slavic mind that's full of secret exits and entrances you know, and that interested me, and so I applied that to the actual borderlands of the country.

(Showing me more of her house) This little room is what Hadley, my daughter, calls the tapestry room (laughs). Those are very good friends these little lambs woven into this wall piece which isn't a real tapestry. The lambs are only printed on it like the word. They have come into the poems with the medieval world they represent. Some recent poems reflect my ideas of medievality. I believe I may be looking for a time and place that is medieval. Yet the medieval age was somewhat similar to now, to events in this country.

MH: In what way?

BG: Well, it was one war after another, but it differed in that it had a secular and a spiritual foundation, the church and the king. However, the kings were fighting every minute for property. The Crusades ... actually the knights thought they were right to impose their religion and God approved of their venture. Like oil. And the medieval world got very seduced by the Arab world and they liked living over there. They had a great time and they began to live in a luscious land and did all the things the church wouldn't permit them to do. But this is a digression that shows up in my poetry.

MH: It's interesting, your attraction to medievalism.

BG: Yes, it's a curious one. It's my own medievalism, obviously.

MH: Is it something you're picking up out of the tapestry on your wall?

BG: I'm picking it up out of the tapestry and out of my own desire to remove myself elsewhere. I don't think (laughing) that I want to go to a medieval idea of heaven. Although, that might be an improvement. There are several touches of medievalism in *Fair Realism*. "In Medieval Hollow," for instance. There, New York City is an example of the medieval.

MH: *In what way?*

BG: I feel a sense of tambourines and messes of people wandering around and churches with people sprawled on their porches. The whole garble of a town which is what New York is turning into—rags and tatters and holding out hands for alms. It's very medieval. In medieval times they were searching for a solution to these tragedies and found it in wars.

MH: *The peasant invasion of the cities during the plagues.*

BG: It's the chaos. It's the people who were once knights who were lost in battle or lost all their arms and were reduced to penury.

MH: *And great wealth next to poverty.*

BG: Yes, that's very medieval.

MH: *Does Chaucer enter into any of this?*

BG: Chaucer is one of my favorite poets, a complete inspiration to me always. This doesn't perhaps show in my work, yet he is one of my cornerstones.
  Chaucer gets to the point through a wonderful control of poetry. I like his getting to the point. But he writes poetry with a language that is both musical and dry and as if poetry were a product of nature. Chaucer draws me up and makes me think of condensation and where words should be, and then he's so wise. He never preaches to you, but he hands out his common sense. It's the whole medieval world that was trembling and he sought to control it to bring an order into his poetry.

MH: *Any particular character out of the* Canterbury Tales?

BG: (looking for "Otranto" in a pile of papers on her desk) Troilus. This poem has medievalism in it. For instance, in Chaucer, there's a beautiful line from *Troilus and Criseyde* when Troilus first sees her in the church. It's similar to Petrarch and Laura, and he is so stunned by her beauty that he stares at her and so I used that "Troilus as he stared." Chaucer doesn't use the word "stare"; it's another word, but the use of Troilus came naturally to the poem and it's an instance in which I use a direct reference from Chaucer who's always at the back of my mind.

This poem, "Otranto" has a medieval overcast. A weird thing happened with that poem. I dreamed and when I woke up, I was saying, "The Castle of Otranto." Then I asked myself who had written that book which I hadn't read since college. It is Horace Walpole, the first gothic novel. It has that eighteenth-century humor that *Frankenstein* and later gothics lack.

MH: *(moving to her upstairs bedroom) Do you read up here?*

BG: Yes, I do. This used to be the desk I worked on always. I wrote *The Countess from Minneapolis* and *Seeking Air* on it. It still has a mellow, thoughtful feel and it's useful because the past comes through. I also use this room in winter. The downstairs workroom eats up too much oil, so I close it off.

"The Rose Marble Table" was the poem that was influenced by this Matisse painting (pointing to the Matisse poster from the Hermitage on her bedroom wall). I like to get the order of the day somehow settled on this desk. This is the first year since the death of my husband in 1990 that I've been able to go at my own pace, to go on writing here at any hour or any time I want to. So I am not as compulsive as I used to be about working. I think I'm not. Formerly, I had to go to a place to write and I had to finish by a certain time. Now I inhabit the house in a different way. I think this may be changing in my work. The earlier work had a spriteliness to it and perhaps more joy. As you get older there is less joy. The earlier work may have had more spontaneity. But there are other benefits now.

MH: *Do you find your thoughts changing?*

BG: Variations, censorship of emotions.

MH: *Do you write every day?*

BG: If I am into something, then I do.

MH: *Do you have set hours for writing?*

BG: I usually like to start first thing in the morning, not always.

MH: *The mind never shuts off.*

BG: No, it doesn't. The mind keeps on working on the poem all day, all night, anytime, but the process is what is so interesting. That is when the poem develops. You're always going to encounter difficulty. Once in a while a real gift—the poem just writes itself.

MH: *Has that ever happened to you?*

BG: In *Fair Realism*, it was the poem "The Farewell Stairway." That was pleasure from start to finish. I just felt I was given a present.

MH: *You wish that would happen more often.*

BG: It doesn't though. I keep thinking, why doesn't it? Well, recently I was writing a shorter poem and it went the same effortless way.

MH: *What is the longest you've ever worked on a poem?*

BG: *The Altos*, a collaboration with Richard Tuttle, is one time. The poem took a year or so.

MH: *The Altos is coming out soon?*

BG: It keeps being postponed because they decided on a different cover, and Hank Hine of *Limestone Press* is so careful to please me, and I made changes. I changed that poem I don't know how many times after I originally sent it in. The great value to a poet is in working with a painter whom you can be stimulated by. So, when I handed in seven pages, this was after three or four months, I was sent one etching by Tuttle, and I thought this poem has to go somewhere else. So the poem began to change and I rewrote parts of it. Nobody was pushing me to finish and I wasn't pushing him and everybody was accepting everybody's work and time sense. This is why the book is taking so long to get out. There were constant changes.

MH: *It's a real collaboration. It's not just you'll do your thing and he'll do his.*

BG: It came about through Richard Tuttle and Hank Hine. Richard makes interesting books. Some are very, very small, some are four or five pages of his writing or drawing. And he finds, usually, a small publisher who'll do it the way he wants it. He knows how to do it. *The Altos* is an elaborate book.

MH: *Has your poetry influenced his etching?*

BG: I don't know, ephemerally, yes. I've done several collaborations in book form such as *Musicality*, and I told you about that poem/painting collaboration on the wall with Mary Abbott.

MH: *(reading out loud from "Red Dye") "Brown eyed water was mother of pearl." What a wonderful line.*

BG: It's those Russians around (laughing) and Pasternak who inspired the poem.

MH: *And "enameled wind destroys their rope ..."*

BG: That was a present.

MH: *How long does it take you to do a book?*

BG: That absolutely varies. There is no way of saying.

MH: *A lot of the locale of this place (Southampton, Long Island) comes into your poetry. I was wondering about the changes you felt working out here in the country as opposed to Manhattan?*

BG: I relied on the city when I had the place on 94th Street. That's where I wrote *Moscow Mansions*, though I wrote some of that out here. On 94th Street I wrote *The Countess from Minneapolis*. In *Fair Realism* "The Screen of Distance" has parts that are written on 16th Street. A large section was written there but I know that there are certain parts of "The Screen of Distance" that come from living here.

The sunset mentioned in that work comes from a sunset an artist painted out here. When I first moved to 16th Street, it was very stimulating to be in a new place. The whole idea of clear space was very thrilling to me. On 16th Street, the light filtered through the room and I got very excited and it did affect my work and so I wrote a lot there and then I would come out here occasionally and a little piece of Southampton came into it. *"The Türler Losses"* was written out here.

Moscow Mansions has many poems centered here. There's one about Jimmy Schuyler who lived down the street for a while (in Southampton). You were asking me about having friends here, poets. My community in the beginning really consisted of Jimmy at the Fairfield Porter house here in Southampton. That was a "location" where I could intimately establish a connection.

MH: *Does it really matter to you ultimately where you are when you write?*

BG: No, not much, except that certain places make it easier. For a long time it wasn't easy to write here. Then I wrote in California. It's really more the spirit of the place. Your spirit responds to certain places. I reminded myself that it was good to write here and to edit in the city. But I often write here and take work back to the city. Nature's so powerful and you either come under its rule, (Guest's house was a block from the ocean) or you are under the rule of mankind in the city. I must make an unconscious division. My novel *Seeking Air* the first half was written in Manhattan, and the last half in California.

MH: *There is a lot of landscape in terms of your poetry. In* Musicality *there are those great watercolors.*

BG: That was a nice collaboration.

MH: How did that come about?

BG: By chance. I know Rena Rossenwasser who is the editor of Kelsey Street Press in Berkeley. She suggested I give her a poem for the press. Then I met June Felter, the artist, and we became good friends. She and her husband would take trips around California in the car, and she was drawing all the time. I had those drawings in mind, a moving landscape of house and field and mountain, and wrote the poem.

MH: *Just from memory?*

BG: Yes, But the experience of the watercolor is what she's declaring. Having lived in California, it's a familiar landscape to me. I just gave her the poems. I stayed in New York. There was no direct collaboration other than our knowledge of each other's existence. It was very different when I collaborated with Tuttle. I finished the poem, then she gave the watercolors to Rena. I was inspired, of course, by her work. Her work is in the poem. There was a naturalism to the collaboration and there was a respect and a certain delicacy in our relationship with each other and I think that comes out in the poem because it is a very modest book. There are several things in my poem that I'm not too happy about but it declares itself in a very pleasant manner. It's a book that you can have around (laughing).

MH: *You can read it straight through—there's only a few lines on each page. There's a lot of spacing between the lines. What were the aspects of the poem that didn't agree with you?*

BG: I don't like the last line. The whole last paragraph I think I'd do differently. It goes with it now, but it's not right. Another thing about that book is that June (Felter) goes to a swimming pool—and she used to ask me over a great deal when I was staying in Berkeley, and she would sit around the pool and she always had her watercolors with her and a little bit of that comes into the poem—not directly, but a little bit of that spirit. I think also, I wanted to pay a respect to California. I just wanted a little touchdown.

MH: *You seem to be of two places, New York and California.*

BG: I've been here so much longer than I've ever been in California. Yet, I believe it is necessary to have another place in the consciousness.

MH: *California is that place?*

BG: Yes, it is.

MH: *You mention having been a surfer.*

BG: The poem "Surfing" is in the book *Blue Stairs*. That poem is really an anti-Vietnam poem. No one knows this unless I tell them. I wrote it in Greece though. But yes, I always have that in the back of my mind about surfing (laughing) when I was young.

MH: *You've been to many countries, cities, but you don't seem to be of one place. Your locale is the locale of your mind, the paintings around you, the music you listen to, the books you're reading. So it is very hard to place you.*

BG: It's very hard on me not having a definite place. It has created a lot of anxiety. Growing up with my aunt and uncle for instance. I first lived with my grandmother. Then I lived with my parents in Florida. Then I was sent to California to live with my aunt and uncle when I was ten. So I never really had a "home." That was hard and it created unnecessary anxiety, so that I am grateful for this house as long as I am permitted to live here.

MH: *This is home now?*

BG: Yes. When I say the word "home" I almost whisper it. There's an emphasis on that word in the poem "An Emphasis Falls on Reality." There's a line that goes, "I think those people are moving in." I didn't analyze it that way when I wrote it. It was a symbol. It did have to do with "perhaps" they will move in.

MH: *Do you have music playing while you write?*

BG: Sometimes it stimulates me. *Musicality* was written to music.

MH: *Which music?*

BG: I don't want to give it away. In this last poem, "Prokofiev Plays Prokofiev," on the last line of the page, I have written several poems about Prokofiev and one is in the *Countess* ... I love his music and I love Shostakovich and I find I was playing them on my tapes.

MH: *What is it about Prokofiev and Shostakovich?*

BG: The life, the enormous life in the music, not only their extraordinary technique but their modernism, when you think about how isolated they were.

MH: *Russian again.*

BG: Again, it is Russian energy, but the music is so explorative and brilliant and takes off in so many ways. There's not any composer in the U.S. who's done this, and Schoenberg, I'm very devoted to his music. I wrote "Expectation" about him. I read a couple of books about him. He would have been all right had the Nazis not taken over Berlin. Instead, he got stuck in California and he was forced to take students who were very mediocre. When UCLA retired him, they gave him $29 a month in retirement income.

MH: *But are you taking off from Schoenberg's music in your poetry? Is it the atonalities of his music that inspire you?*

BG: Yes, it is, and it's such a stringent work. He pays his respect to the past. I'm not a musicologist at all. And now that he's become so fashionable, curious in this era, that there would be this attention since he was so neglected. Well, poetry is music, we all say it. There's no question. The self is music, just a different notation.

MH: *Yes, but it lies on the page silently.*

BG: But I hear it. Sometimes that gets in the way. I hear too much. Then it disturbs the silence. I realize silence is sometimes in my work. I will put in a blunt word or I will erase a word, or I will take any measure in order to silence music. If I feel there is too much music, I deliberately make something awkward, whereas, I know perfectly well how it could go. But that awkwardness destroys the liquidity of the line and I feel that's necessary.

MH: *That's sort of an anti-lyrical device.*

BG: It's anti-lyrical because I struggle against lyricism constantly and I struggle against my ear.

MH: *That's an interesting point. If you're struggling against lyricism in that struggle to break the lyrical flow, wouldn't that cause more tension on the focus on the sounds themselves?*

BG: I don't know. That's coming from outside.

MH: *But it is as if these "dull" words draw more attention to themselves. It's like in the non-narrative atonal music that you become more conscious of the separate notes of music and their dissonances.*

BG: I wrote a poem titled "Dissonance" (laughs) which is partly on the surface about Schoenberg. But I don't go into dissonance, because it is a great operative field and if I'm becoming dissonant, then I'm becoming dissonantly lyrical at the same time, and that can happen to me. For instance, vowel sounds and onomatopoeia and all kinds of things like that look very easy and one shouldn't be aware of them at all. I don't just think that it is a modern idea. I think the great poets who were lyrical poets like Shelley or Keats, were able to get around it. With our emphasis on language, we're taught to look at the language structure. We have taught ourselves to look at the language structure of the poem and we'll say, "No, look at that." You know, each word begins with an "A" or there's too much alliteration or something like that. I think that comes from an unsureness of the speech of the poem because we're in a sort of crisis period in poetry. It's going in a different way.

MH: *Explain. How do you sense this crisis?*

BG: Poets are taking the modern tradition further. I don't like that term "postmodern." I think it's a cheap idea. There's no such thing as postmodernism; you're either modern or you're not. "Postmodern!" that sounds like some sort of advertising cliché. To digress a moment, it's one of the reasons I'm sad about Robert Motherwell's death (he had just died) because he was a holdout for modernism in painting. He really explained it, loved it, and was its knight. Now I think painting is in a pretty bad position, but poetry is not. Poetry is really the most interesting form, I believe today. I wouldn't have said this twenty years ago. But I think it is the most interesting art form right now in the decline of painting today.

MH: *Your later poems seem to question the meaning of meaningfulness. I get that impression from the poem "Words" in* Fair Realism. *Also, there seems to be a dwelling on the failure of culture, the searching for meaning in art in the culture.*

BG: That's a good question. I don't know that I can answer it. What was it in "Words"?

MH: *The poem "Cradle of Culture" is the best example where there's a searching after a meaning in what's around in the culture. In the poem, there's an emphasis on language itself. In thinking back to your older work, then comparing it to your more recent work, there's more fragmentation. There's also an ability to bring back an image, or to make the images resonate with each other—in motifs instead of symbols. These images define themselves and give it a sense of unity, yet the poem remains undefinable and abstract (rather than try to define them as symbols). I have in mind poems such as "Cradle of Culture," "The Nude," and "Words."*

BG: I thought that "The Nude" and "Cradle of Culture" were very plain, clear poems, particularly "The Nude" which is really about many things of course. I thought it had very little fragmentation. "Words" could just as well have been called "Spoons." It doesn't matter that it was about—words, except that it details the uses of the commonplaceness of words. I'm saying that I couldn't tell you the meaning of the meaning, but in the "Cradle of Culture" I can tell you what it means. The man who appears is Miro, who is the symbol of culture. And then he says, "Surrealism detested culture, but I'm no longer a surrealist." The other person who is there is an ignorant person, a young ignorant person who is wandering around this broken-down pool which could stand for a broken-down civilization or something, but sees Miro who is suddenly the symbol of civilization. (speaking of sound) There is a misprint here (reading poem):

You called "come back Mediterranean!"
(And I'm talking about the Greco-Roman Mediterranean civilization.)

That word learned from Miro
with its heavy foot and watery
whiplash tickling your ankle where it bled.

The misprint "tickling" bothers me tremendously. It should be—I wrote, "ticking your ankle where it bled." I would never use the "l" of tickling with "bl" in bled. We were discussing earlier the sound. I would have broken that sound.

MH: *Because of the alliteration?*

BG: Yes. So that misprint bothers me tremendously. But I am talking about culture and I am talking about a person who is outside of culture. It's about learning about culture. "The Nude" is from a book I did with Warren Brandt about his pictures of the nude. His book is over there (pointing to her shelf in her studio) and the poem is in that book.

  This poem, "Country Cousins" was written right here upstairs. "Chevettes" really is a made-up word. I was thinking of "little Chevrolets." Also, I confess, the geese on the town pond.

MH: *What was the impetus for the poem, the image or the sound?*

BG: Well, it couldn't have been written without an eye, without an image, and it is the image of all these things, that the geese are in the pond. But it's really about language. It's a little rondel.

MH: *You seem to keep the poem "open" so that it never seems finished or circumscribed. It never arrives at any formal completion or thematic statement. It seems to be a poetry which creates a field of play for language. There's a lot of use of specialized language, special words, foreign terms, exotic words, esoteric words—"lacuna, apse, verdigris, scala, guignol." Then there are the foreign names—"Tűrler, Dora Maar."*

BG: Those are directly implied not as foreign words but as "Tűrler" is a watch and "Dora Maar" is a person, so they are not introduced as foreign words.

I feel that my poems always come to a conclusion. I wouldn't be happy if they didn't. They are supposed to continue into the whole book, and in that case, they may not have a conclusion. But I came to a definite end in "An Emphasis Falls on Reality." In fact, they always have ending to me and the endings often leave me very sad. The endings are rather sad.

MH: *Yes, the end of "An Emphasis Falls on Reality"—"The darkened copies of all trees."*

BG: You see, it's as if it fades; the scene fades into darkness.

MH: *We were discussing before the use of black in different painters. This poem was interesting to me also for its refrain (going back to "An Emphasis Falls on Reality"):*

> Cloud fields change into furniture
> furniture metamorphosizes into fields
> an emphasis falls on reality.

Then you introduce a narrative voice:

> It snowed toward morning a barcarole
> The words stretched severely
> Silhouettes they arrived in trenchant cut
> the face of lilies
> I was envious of fair realism.

It is a beautiful poem. There's a dream movement I really loved, a meditation on this emphasis on "reality" and what reality is and how that enters the mind or world and where does it end or begin. Then you mention "being and nothingness," appearances, different directions—motors floating on water: "So silence is pictorial / When silence is real." It's one of my favorite poems in the book. Different realities are in this poem. "The idea of real trees / willows are not real trees / they entangle us in looseness, / ... / the natural world spins in green / ..."

There are beautiful passages here: "A column chosen from distance / mounts into the sky while the font / is classical ..." There's an artfulness, too, at the same time. It's hard to describe this poem without discussing the meaning of reality or whether it has any meaning or any connection to the language.

BG: This poem is on several levels and moves back and forth, I hope, between the levels as reality does. The end of the poem, and it has an ending, the poem itself can be open-ended, but an ending occurs. It's true that some things are never completed, you just leave off.

MH: *In your poems, I get the sense of textures, and it's as if I can feel my way through your poems. I don't really have to understand them. And there's an overall sense of poetic design. It's sort of the shape of the thought within the poem. That's the form to me. The form is the shape of thought in the poem, and the design is the shape of the sound of the words. How does poetic language come to you, spontaneously or through experience?*

BG: What do you mean by experience?

MH: *The daily acquired vocabulary of your own lexicon. That language as opposed to a poetic language that may come from other places such as novels or music, or other poems, certainly.*

BG: I think poetic language comes from the same place as experience. It's not a separate activity, because if I were talking to myself in the market, I wouldn't use the same words I use in a poem. To the person who was checking me out of the market, I would have a different speech because they'd be terrified if they heard what I had been verbalizing (laughing). But my continual silent speech is the same wherever I go. I think that poetic language is ubiquitous; it never leaves you.

MH: *You mention paying more attention to your ear, and I wanted to know what are your rules for a poem, if you have any, because you did mention placement on the page as primary in importance, and I'm wondering what determines this placement.*

BG: The poem determines it. Placement is a very interesting point, because in the form, placement is decided by the poem itself. For instance, in this poem, "An Emphasis Falls on Reality," there are four lines, then three lines, etc. But they're long lines. All of a sudden, in this poem, I will change the placement. Then it goes like that (pointing open armed to a manuscript of new work on a page) and it's open. Lines are long, but they're opened. Then there'll be a shorter line, but they are spaced differently. On this page, it's entirely different, so no single page is exactly like the opening page. So that was determined by the poem itself, by what I was relating and designing in my mind, the idea. I'm not talking about the page. I suddenly wanted this and this is just totally extemporaneous what I did. I got very tired of the formality of that page and I felt that what I had to say should be broken and I should go to another line space. It's very simple and it's not simple. I could have continued to copy the exact same stanza spacing that's on the first page, and many times I have. I was very interested in working with four-line stanzas, but then I thought, I don't feel free enough in this poem. I can't quite operate in my ideas and in my words, in my vocabulary of words as I want to. So I am just going to move them out. This is not a physical thing that's done by a computer where you can twist it where you want to. This is designed this way. Each page came to me in this visual context. Nearly all my poems do change as the poem goes on. This poem, do you mean?

MH: *Is it the sense of time in the poem or the time it takes to write the poem, the narrative time?*

BG: No. Each poem decides its own self (logical) placement. It's the sense of wishing to move, actually sometimes to see it, to see the poem on a different line. For me, this works. I don't suggest that this is the way poems ought to be written. But I do like contemporary poetry that moves around, that occupies itself on the page in different ways. This is only for me. Now, as you know, you're writing the poem and you go on and on. Then suddenly, the poem takes over and you don't have any control over it. You've lost it; it's found its own form, its own personality, its own body. Often, I would have preferred to restrict a poem to a certain kind of space, but it just moves away from me and I know that it's taking control. But it has to have its own action and its own life. But in these particular poems, its own life took place in these lines. I would have preferred to have continued with a four-line stanza on every single page. And I originally wrote several of those that way until it wouldn't work.

MH: *Were you opposed to the density of the four-line stanza?*

BG: Yes, the density, because my poems tend to be too dense, I believe. One of the ways to break this density is to move the lines out and around. I would like very much just to take out indiscriminately—just remove ten words. And in "Chalk" I did. That's the way I worked on "Chalk" because I was working with an eraser. When I was writing with chalk, I could just erase it. And I felt tremendously free. Then I looked at the poem "Chalk" itself and I thought, there's a lot of words on that. I got rid of a lot of those words and there they were, they stayed there. I got rid of a lot but not all of them. I do like poetry that is very open with four words then a big drop, and it's very difficult to do because you must have a very important idea. I think that rests much less on language than it does on ideas. My poems tend more to language than to ideas.

There's a French poet, Anne-Marie Albiach, who's translated by Keith Waldrop. She's a magnificent poet, I think, and a lot of other people do, too. I read her in translation, and she, I'm told, relies entirely on Whiteout. But you don't feel that anything is missing because the idea is there. The poem can stumble on the page then pick itself up brutally. There's an enormous amount of strength in anyone who is able to use a few words on the page. It doesn't take very much strength to write long-worded poems. I'm not saying that it doesn't take poetic ability, but on the contrary, to very few worded poems, it doesn't require as much strength.

MH: *Is there any consideration for the reading of the poem in this shape, in this form, due to the spacing?*

BG: Yes, I think it reads better.

MH: *Do you still want to maintain the linear sense, the more isolated the lines?*

BG: I think, probably at this point, we should look at *The Altos*, which is going to answer your question.

MH: *Ok. This is a very large book, like an illuminated medieval manuscript, about a foot and a half across by two feet wide on beautiful thick vellum paper.*

BG: The reason I suggest looking at it is the spacing.

MH: *(laughing) It's blank! (turning pages) If I were to read this, my eye might go here. Now as I look at it without reading it, I see three areas that the poem occupies. It's like three pictorial areas if this were a canvas and (the text) seems to be fighting that linear tradition of starting on the left and moving to the right.*

BG: That's right.

MH: *It starts on the right.*

BG: He (Tuttle) changed the spacing.

MH: *Now, did the idea of spacing come after looking at the artwork?*

BG: That's why we're good at collaborating.

MH: *That's very important. There's a preposition floating by itself on the page.*

BG: Yes, because I wanted it to do that. (pointing) It could have gone here.

MH: *Then these lines (looking to the opposite page) become more traditional lines on a plane.*

BG: Yes, it brings you back. You see his take on it (Tuttle's drawing).

MH: *(turning pages) Stop here for a second. What about the timing, the spaces give you a pause. You could read these lines together. Words that are together are closer in time. These that are separated are further away in time.*

BG: Yes, that's very true. There's a separation because this is going to read linearly. This has a different sound (pointing to a group of words on the page). This is very matter of fact.

MH: *I love this (reading her lines): "An image falls/out of the faint blue sky ..." I love that poem.*

BG: It's Hank Hine's favorite, too, and I was going to take it out and he said, "I don't want to lose it!"

MH: *How do you work this out? Do you play continually, or do you have it from the beginning?*

BG: No, no, I wrote it out just like that.

MH: *Just as it appears?*

BG: Absolutely straight. I didn't play.

MH: *Now, do these three words together, did they come as a group this way?*

BG: That's right.

MH: *And the word "night" would be a separate idea?*

BG: There was no changing. Well, by now I knew it so well; it was so familiar what I was doing. But from the very beginning, it started that way, but then I wrote new ones. I threw out a bunch of them and wrote new ones. But I never hesitated in the spacing. It just seemed that that was the way it had to be. I like this one (pointing).

MH: *"coal butter" (reading her lines). That's strange. What a strange idea (Guest laughs).*

BG: "coal butter" is pretty strange. But it changes "butter" into something like a tomb. I was thinking almost of Egypt. You don't think of "Egypt" and "coal butter" as analogous (laughs).

MH: *There are so many textures at work in your poems that's why I said I could feel my way through them by touching everything you mention.*

BG: Interesting.

MH: *Everything is very tactile.*

BG: I've got a "coat" in here, but it's a "platinum coat."

MH: *(reading Orpheus-like section) That's very beautiful.*

BG: That's the end. Now, this is not going to be the colophon. For instance, there's an apostrophe here which I don't like at all. It's going to be changed physically. This is Richard's idea. He got it from the Japanese filmmaker Kurosawa, from his recent film "Dreams." Then he said, "Did you see the end when the credits roll up?" He said, "That was the greatest roll." And he said, "That's what I want in the book. So what the compromise is going to be is on a pale sheet, because you've been through the text, this is the light. Everything that happens in here (in the text) is like this in space. You know, it weighs down here and there, but it's light in space, and you come to this and you go thunk, thunk, thunk. It's boring, so Richard's lifting it up into this thin sheet and it's going to be here (end paper) the colophon is going to be on the back, in the most difficult way possible which he knows how to find.

MH: *The most expensive way.*

BG: He's a genius at that.

MH: *People may want to cut some of this out and frame it, wouldn't they?*

BG: Oh sure, well, yes, but they shouldn't (laughs).

MH: *In the book* The Altos, *the word "gestural" appears. I want to go to that in terms of a question, in terms of painting, gestural realism. The gestural manners of approaching a subject, gestural realism like Hartigan and de Kooning, and unlike Porter and Katz and Freilicher, an abstract expression but in a gestural manner in terms of approaching the subject. I find that in your poetry, you have these gestures, and it's moving in terms of gestures, not only the shape (of the poem) can become a gesture, but the shape of the poem on the page. As we were looking at the spacing on the page before in these different fields, it moves this way instead of that way. I was wondering if you could comment on that.*

BG: The only comment I could make, really make, because the word "gestural" was used in *The Altos* for a reason. I should consider more the syntax of the word. I was of course, influenced by abstract expressionism because of the freedom which is gestural. It may appear to be an influence of abstract expressionism. I don't consider it an influence now. But it's possible. It's more my temperament really to make an abrupt turn, for instance, in this last poem ("The Glass Mountain") I do this (turning the pages to read):

    Afloat on borrowed wind
We promised the raft
skin on the raft
a king
picked up boards
and flung them

And I think that's a gesture.

MH: *It's a violent gesture.*

BG: Yes, well, I think of gestures as violent.

MH: *There are graceful gestures.*

BG: They are graceful, because it is hard for me to be as violent as I'd like to be in poetry. I think that I would like more violence in my poetry.

MH: *Really, that's interesting.*

BG: I think that when you mention the serenity or something of the sort, I think that it can be controlled violence. That's like a Freudian statement.

MH: *It's almost oxymoronic.*

BG: Yes (laughing).

MH: *Reminds me of the banner the cadets had strung out across the stadium at a West Point football game that read "Managed Violence."*

BG: Is that what it said? Oh, that's marvelous. Well, I think that comes into certain people's poetry whom I admire. Leslie Scalapino has a lot of that managed violence in her poetry, and there's a lot of that in contemporary painting right now if it's any good, taken from the screen.

MH: *Is it because the culture is so violent?*

BG: No. This is just utterly practical. I wish my poetry contained a temperament of violence.

MH: *You mean shock?*

BG: Maybe shock. I try to break the evenness, but I like poetry that suddenly stops.

MH: *I'm thinking of the poet Paul Celan who appears to have a lot of embedded violence in his poetry.*

BG: You feel that?

MH: *A brutal imagery that is so brutal and startling as in lines like "Hatchet swarms above us."*

BG: That's very true. I think he's a very great poet. That violence may be one of the reasons I like him so much. Yet, it is anger, really, at his fate that he projects. I wondered how long he could keep it up. And of course, he couldn't.

MH: *His level of tension.*

BG: Yes, tension, and poetry should have more tension. That's an even better word than violence. That's something that's missing from Wallace Stevens. I think it is coming into contemporary poetry more and I admire that.

MH: *Who do you think is getting it (tension) in there?*

BG: Well, I think a good many younger women poets are working very hard at it in a nihilistic way. I think it's more a product of the times. Poetry has more to do with tension than vision.

MH: *Political reality?*

BG: Yes, and observation. Some people are attracted to that, meaning they see substance more instead of pushing it away, they see it. I think tension is extremely important. I'm glad you brought that word up. I'm going to think about it to see if I could do something more about that.

MH: *Going back to this poem (already mentioned) for Schuyler, "The Glass Mountain," the metaphor itself—mountains of glass. I had the feeling reading that and I read it a few times last night, that it's the metaphor for poetry itself.*

BG: Yes, it is. It really is. That's a very good reading.

MH: *It's a startling image, this transparent thing built out of words, brittle, transparent, translucent glass, and a mountain of glass.*

BG: This one is splintered.

MH: *It's amazing just how slippery the surface of the text is. Here, I can keep seeing changes where things could be changed, where punctuation should go or should not go. There are so many possibilities of misreading, combining words like, "clouds mohair," you do this a lot, imaginatively, creatively, uniquely, in ways in which I don't think any average poet would associate things—this disparate bringing together of two objects.*

BG: I'm bringing together two ideas. Originally, that was written differently. That whole page was written very differently, but I don't think we should do much of an exegesis of the poem. But clouds are very soft and brooding, and mohair is very stiff and dark on the surface. That's why those words are together as opposites. When I put them together, they surprised me because I thought that's so correct.

MH: *I can get a reading of that of turning the noun into a verb, as mohair is trying to become a verb with clouds as the subject.*

BG: You're using sound. It wasn't sound that dictated that. Mohair is a frightening substance. You've seen mohair chairs. It's harsh. There's something of the nineteenth century about mohair and the poem began in a nineteenth century way.

MH: *With the "king" you mean in a narrative way?*

BG: No, the "king," you have to take my word for it. He's on every page.

MH: *I'm trying to get a sense of what you mean by the nineteenth century.*

BG: Well, I think that for instance about sun parlors—sun parlors attached to a house, a glassed-in part of a Victorian house. They sometimes had a bird in them. It's my idea.

MH: *You did mention that D.H. Lawrence was one of the best poets. What makes you believe that?*

BG: I think he was for his time. I'm not saying he is for the entire world. I think that James Joyce wrote marvelous poems. The freedom of some of those poems of Lawrence's in which he is able to go to nature and the one about the snake is a magnificent poem. It's not anthologized enough.

MH: *It is a literal image.*

BG: I think he was very literal and I like his literalness which became very expansive. He could start at a literal point and expand. That's another thing about Lawrence, he's very broad.

MH: *Has he been an influence?*

BG: He's been an influence on my love of poetry.

MH: *And in his literalness, do you consider your work that way, too?*

BG: No, I don't think I'm literal. I think I try to be sometimes. I become too abstract in my thinking and then I tend to give my poems a literal ending because I've thought I've gotten too abstract. But those are poetry secrets and they shouldn't be mentioned (both laughing). It's boring to hear about how a poet does something.

MH: *Going back to* Fair Realism, *there seems to be a solitary night presence in the poems. The one I've underlined is "La Noche Entra en Calor," but other poems, too, like "Wild Gardens Overlooked by Night Lights." There are several of them.*

BG: "Shuffling Light" has that also.

MH: *Yes. I'm wondering about the psychic interest in that night world, or that "distance at the street end" that appears. It's a kind of perspective, too, on life, a view as much as it is a presence or feeling that has entered the poetry.*

BG: It's a lot in "The Screen of Distance." It's also withdrawal from daytime. It's difficult to say because it's true what you're saying of that book. There is a night world. I think it's a time I could be alone and I was drawn to that silence. If you live in the city, it's the time you get off the street. Night is magic. There's no question about that and any poet relies on magic. If you don't, the magic goes somewhere else. This last poem, "The Glass Mountain," is about a certain magic. The king is a magic king who controls destiny. A glass mountain is a magic mountain. I don't mean it in a "magic" sense. It comes from fairy tales, from the prince climbing the glass mountain, and all those figures appear at night to you when you push them away during the day. But it's curious, you see. Now I work in the morning. But then I take the night with me and deposit it on the table.

MH: *That changes something working in the daylight.*

BG: Yes, but the night is still controlling it because the day hasn't fully begun.

MH: *Your poetry often deals with loss, even in titles. Take "The Türler Losses," for example. Even your novel* Seeking Air, *feelings of losing life, losing what you can't have, surface. Also, you have an imagist's delight in objects, colors, and shapes. There's an interesting quotation about you. It goes:*

> *The poems of Barbara Guest ignore almost every convention in metrics in English and American poetry. Her poems are a search for a definable form. They're impressionistic responses. A typical poem of Barbara Guest's is a pastiche of colors, shapes, natural settings in which objects create the mood.*

BG: I don't want objects to create a mood. I want to create an object. I remember once looking some years ago at Ben Nicholson, the British painter, a few late works of his, and I thought that this is the way I'd like my poems to be. Then later, at the Pace Gallery, I looked at Agnes Martin's painting, and I wished that my poems would relate more to her.

MH: *You seem to make your poetry out of the flow of your own life and feelings. That is the subject. You mentioned before that now you have the run of the house, whereas before, you had only this one space and now you're inhabiting every room and the books are all over. You write down here in your studio; you read up there in your bedroom.*

BG: Of course, you still have to make time for the writing. It's not free time. Taking the bus into Manhattan once a week is extremely important to me, because it breaks up this sequence of time and to use that word, tension, creates a tension between city and country.

MH: Getting into this area, your lines: "Diagonals greet us those curves and sharp city verticals" is a good segue into the tension of the city from your poem "The View from Kandinsky's Window." There's a good use of perspective in that poem, in the lines, their arrangement. I see that you're using the shapes of the city, the streets, the buildings in an artful way, but approaching it as an object, yet getting distance from it. It's a nice approach to a city, and the view again from the window, that idea you're looking out onto a scene. Stevens does this frequently, this meditation to what's out there to what the scene is, then basing an imagination on it, building a new reality, a new world.

BG: This is what Frank (O'Hara) and I once talked about, how mysterious Wallace Stevens was to us. Then we started writing our own poetry, really writing it, and Wallace Stevens became simpler to understand.

MH: This passage seemed to be slightly influenced by Wallace Stevens. You might want to read it aloud.

BG: Does it really? When I wrote it I wasn't hearing him at all. [Reads from *The Türler Losses*:]

> I am content knowing loss is less.
>
> Moving into elsewhere. The way music takes
> us to boulders.
>
> These shields. Shadows secure in thunder.
>
> As boats move thick against the water, forests
> contained by sky.
>
> These are contents.
>
> Loss gropes toward their vase. Etching its way.
> Driving horses 'round the rim.

It's not bad (laughing). I think Stevens is a great poet, but I don't hear Stevens in that at all.

MH: *I was surprised to see in* Fair Realism *some changes you've made to the poem "The Türler Losses."*

BG: I was trying to tighten it.

MH: *It does seem tighter. There are a lot of changes. You've taken out words, inserted new words. Were you conscious of making it better, improving it?*

BG: I thought I was. I remember Marianne Moore's destruction of some of her poems when she changed them, and also Auden's. It's a scary thing to do, but who knows. The original is there in another book. It's something you can hardly stop yourself from doing.

MH: *Do you have ideas for stories?*

BG: They're hard to write. That's really a difficult form. I wanted to write a novel. And I think that what was wrong about the novel was that I was trying to write a conventional novel. I was trying to write nonconventional and conventional. I couldn't do it. I don't know. I can't get enthusiastic about it.

MH: *What about prose-poetry?*

BG: I've thought about it because I've written prose-poetry, but I'd rather write prose than prose-poetry. I like some of the prose-poetry very much, but it's an avoidance in a way of poetry. I think it's because when you write prose-poetry, my idea of it, is that it's idyllic to intersperse the poetry with the prose-poetry.

MH: *That's curious that you want to write novels.*

BG: I think that I would like the form. *Seeking Air* was my novel and my prose-poem. It's essentially a prose-poem.

MH: *But you'd like to continue from* Seeking Air?

BG: I don't want to do the same thing. *Seeking Air* took me ten years to write. I started collecting pieces of it, collage pieces.

MH: Seeking Air, *your novel, seemed so strange to me when I first read it. But then I began to piece the fragments together into a whole. It seemed as if your narrator was talking to herself.*

BG: Yes, because the central, the original idea, emerged from Swift's *Letters to Vanessa*. He wrote as a journal saying that "It ought to be an exact chronicle of twelve years from the time of spilling the coffee to drinking the coffee, etc., an exact telling of their little times together." I took off from there.

MH: *It seems to follow this meditation on a blue dress, a woman on a subway, and a painting by Ingres.*

BG: It's really an account of what happens every day in New York City, and about Paris, and what somebody is thinking while looking out a window, and about memory, about the collision of ideas, about coincidence, the brevity of ideas, about time, disorder, flux, etc.
  It's a New York novel but it does take you into other places.

MH: *You include annual reports, news and weather reports in the text, and other odd things.*

BG: The book is influenced by Dorothy Richardson's *The Pilgrimage*. I think she's one of our best writers. She's compared to Joyce in that she uses or relies on stream of consciousness.
  She wrote about a dental assistant whose name was Miriam, the name I gave to my heroine. When I read her in college I much preferred her to Virginia Woolf.
  But *Seeking Air* turned out differently, of course.
  Another strange thing was when I was working on the biography of H.D. I was at the Beinecke Library at Yale where H.D.'s archives are kept. Donald Gallup, the curator, brought this young woman to see me saying she was interested in H.D. and so forth. I started talking to her, and found her real interest was Dorothy Richardson. She became my assistant on the H.D. book.

MH: *In* Seeking Air, *you quote Trotsky, "Art is always limping after reality."*

BG: Yes, in my H.D. biography I use the word "reality" a great deal. The whole notion of reality disturbed her. She couldn't pinpoint it. That whole Cambridge thing of "what's real, where's the cow?"

That's why I find it very difficult to read poetry that is concerned with a subject that proceeds from start to finish. The subject ends where it begins.

MH: *Do you like to write without references?*

BG: I don't honestly think you can. Even a moment of life is a reference to yourself.

MH: *Your biography of H.D. took you ten years.*

BG: No, it didn't, only five (laughs).

MH: *That's a bit like writing a novel.*

BG: It was. It was like writing a novel. It was prose. I enjoyed the research; I really enjoyed it. I didn't expect to, but I did. I have a detective hidden in me. That's really what it is. That's why I grow impatient with biographies that don't do that detective work. I uncovered all kinds of people. But the bio, the form of the bio I chose, I felt I had to do that because there had been no biography of her previously and I wanted to make it a fairly conventional biography, I thought. I'm told it's not conventional, but I thought it was. There are biographical forms which are simply very good. If I were writing another bio, I would have chosen another form.

MH: *Did you have a model, a model biography?*

BG: I read a lot of biographies.

MH: *So you were approaching it the way you'd approach a novel, telling her story.*

BG: Yes. And you have to tell the truth. Virgil Thomson said to me, "Tell the truth no matter what." That's where I got into trouble because I really believe certain readers have preconceived ideas of your subject matter. For instance, the idolators want you to approach the subject as if she were one of the greatest poets in the world. I didn't make it fit into that scheme. I didn't make it fit into many others. Someone else told me to know absolutely where your character is at every moment if you can, which is great advice. And I tried to say what it was like in those places, in Lausanne, to describe a little of Switzerland and England in the twenties and during the war which was fascinating. And I miss that era, I miss the people (characters) I lived with in that era writing the biography. They were interesting people. They had a style that's vanished. To me, it was an event in my life to enter another life, a dangerous event.

MH: *In your preface to the H.D. biography, you mention the blue wartime editions of H.D.'s poetry which acquainted you as a schoolgirl to her poetry.*

BG: No, it wasn't the wartime poetry editions, it was the collected poems. I saw her poems first in an anthology.

MH: *She was an influence, a strong one, on your early development?*

BG: She was like T. S. Eliot. I was immediately attracted to her poetry. But I absolutely was unable to imitate her. She is inimitable, although her form appears so simple. It is really complex.

MH: *Yet, you said she was not a mentor at all.*

BG: She's a post-mentor. She wasn't when I first began writing. I didn't think of her poetry at all. But I think that working on that biography so long I learned a lot from her, not from her poetry. I learned from her life and I learned from the people she associated with and from their work, because, as I said, Pound became a familiar.

MH: *What in particular did you learn?*

BG: I learned how to work and to be selfish. She was one of the most selfish people you could encounter—a poet. I learned to keep writing. I also learned from having written the biography, how to divide my day into work. I worked hard for all those years. I wore myself out because I didn't pace myself the way I should have. George Eliot said she aged after writing, what was it, *Middlemarch*. That it was the most difficult thing she'd ever done and it changed her. And I think writing the H.D. book changed me.

MH: *You became a full-time writer.*

BG: Absolutely. And spending all that time on research. It made me very strict.

MH: *That's a valuable lesson. Are there any books that you are reading now that are important to you? You mentioned last night the Coleridge biography by Richard Holmes and the Wittgenstein biography by Ray Monk.*

BG: Yes, and I have a friend who is an archeologist and so I read archeology. I read more history now. I continue reading nonfiction. I read Handke, or Calvino, or Natalia Ginzburg.

MH: *Do you read philosophy?*

BG: The "Language Poets" refer to Wittgenstein a great deal. And I am moved by his writing, because he is a poet. We look at his carefully distributed words. I understand that certain philosophical propositions arise from linguistic or semantic causalities. If you have a clue to the language, you have a way of understanding the meaning of things or the symbols we attach to those meanings. Poets are thinking about that anyway without having to look through a mirror, however cracked. The true answer to your question is that I find philosophy very very difficult.

St. Mark's Church in the Bowery

Interview with Bob Holman and Tom Pickard

It was one of those blue sky autumn days in the city packed with tourists and locals all out enjoying the sunny weather September 29, 2018, as I walked from the corner of Houston up Bowery to East 1st St. The neighborhood was filled with fancy boutiques, restaurants, and cafés; it was not the gritty Bowery of the '70s I remember.

Bob buzzed me in, and then up three long flights of stairs to his loft. Tom Pickard was there visiting from England and Tom knew Ted Berrigan and had good stories to tell. Tom was on his way to Chicago the next day. He is known not only for his poetry, but for being an influence in the British poetry scene when he established the reading series in Newcastle upon Tyne at Morden Tower that championed the work of many American and British poets such as Robert Creeley and Basil Bunting.

Bob mentioned as we sat that we are three poets who make films. I brought Bob a copy of my recent film documentary that I jointly made with a poet friend of mine that was being screened. Bob is the co-creator of the PBS television series *The United States of Poetry*, and he co-directed the Nuyorican Poets Café which gave rise to "slam" poetry contests, and since 2002, he's been the proprietor of the Bowery Poetry Club which is on the ground floor below his loft.

Behind Bob was a floor to ceiling abstract canvas by his late wife, the painter Elizabeth Murray. He asked me what I thought the title might be. I said, "Something Phallic"—and he laughed. I loved how she used bright bold color in her work as if a dream had been painted.

Bob, who came to New York by way of Chicago, was one of the many students who came out of Kenneth Koch's poetry class in the 1970s, and he told me that Koch had influenced him toward poetry more than anything else. Bob now adjunct teaches a poetry class at Columbia called "Exploding Text: Poetry Performance."

His interest is in the oral tradition and in helping preserve the oral poetic traditions of languages around the world that are in peril of being lost. He fights against poetry becoming a silent art.

When I first met him, he was in charge of the Monday night poetry readings at the Poetry Project at Saint Mark's. Those who took workshops at the Poetry Project would often be readers in the Monday night series.

I had with me two of his books for him to sign—one of his first books, *Tear To Open* published in 1979 by Power Mad Press, and a later volume, *Sing This One Back to Me*, published by Coffee House Press in 2013. I was very moved by the poems in that collection in the section subtitled "Memory Made Real," which are mostly poems written for his late wife, poems in which you could feel the presence of her soul.

BOB HOLMAN AND TOM PICKARD

MH: *What year did you arrive at Saint Mark's and meet Ted Berrigan?*

BH: I first met Ted in Chicago before I got here to New York. I graduated Columbia University in 1970 having studied with Kenneth Koch. There (at Columbia University) I met Ginsberg, Ashbery, and other poets. I first got to New York a month after Frank O'Hara died in August, 1966. I arrived in September. But back in Chicago, there was quite a poetry scene going on at Columbia College, where Ted was teaching and had just gotten back from England

Bob Holman

with Lady Alice on his arm. There was a great reading series at the "Body Politic" in Chicago, and a great press in Chicago called The Yellow Press. I went to work at the Whole Earth Bookstore up in Evanston, Illinois and that's where the first time I started hanging out with poets.

But during my college years, when at Columbia University, I studied with Kenneth Koch, and I knew the poets around Columbia University—David Lehman was in my class taking Koch's poetry classes. But I would go to poetry readings with people like Donald Lev. These were the disaffected poets of New York—the locals—I was hanging out with local poets then, people who were in the oral tradition, who didn't want to hang out with poets who had a quote "career in poetry."

And Ted was out of town anyway during those early years and besides that the Poetry Project was just starting that year—1966. I know because I went to work for CETA (Comprehensive Employment and Training Act). I was a poet for CETA. I was officially stamped "a poet" by the U.S. Government. That was where I got paid to be a poet. It was pretty unbelievable and it started me off as an administrator. Joel Oppenheimer came in (after Anne Waldman) as the first director of the Saint Mark's Poetry Project and after it closed down from the Fed funds that ran out in '67–'68—he became a professor at CUNY.

So, a guy who had been a printer (Joel Oppenheimer), who worked in a print shop after getting credentialized as a poet, could get a job teaching at a university because there were no MFA programs yet—that was all in the future.

So how do you get to be a poet? Someone has to say you're a poet! And that was what it was like back then. We didn't have the current Ponzi scheme of MFA programs to officiate over the hundreds of poets who graduate every year.

I first met Ted over a pool table in Chicago. He was there with Paul Carroll who founded "The Poetry Center of Chicago" and who edited *The New American Poets* for Big Table Books—and "Big Table" was the "Gods" to me. Andre Codrescu's *License to Carry a Gun* came out from them, and Bill Knot's *Saint Gerome Corpse and Beans* had come out and these were going to lead me to Ron Padgett and Ted Berrigan and the Saint Mark's poets but not because I was living uptown. I knew Ed Sanders and the Fugs because I loved their music, and his Peace Eye Bookstore on East

10th Street. I hung out with my commune. I was in a commune and wrote poems for them. That's what you did. There was no need for another publishing world, although, I did get published at that point by *Rolling Stone Magazine*. I loved *Rolling Stone*. Everybody was reading it so I sent them some poems and damn it they took some and published them.

But there was Ted in Chicago—in one of the many waves of poets who left Chicago, and I was part of that. I was actually a newcomer back to New York (after my student college years at Columbia U.) with people like Bob Rosenthal (who worked as Allen Ginsberg's secretary) and Shelly Kraut (his wife). Bob Rosenthal was my good buddy. He and I wrote plays together which we produced ourselves including a play of Ted's based on his novel *Clear the Range*. And I've got photos of that—you know if you want to see those—and in fact, there's videos of that which stars Steve Carey and his brother Tom who were the stars of it, but everybody was in it—Simon Pettet, Bob, and Shelly.

So, I guess I started to hang out at Saint Mark's in the mid '70s when Ed Friedman was starting the performance series on Monday nights which would also give birth to *The Kitchen* (on Broome Street) which was starting at the same time. PS 122 grew out of what Ed did at Saint Mark's.

Prior to that, Monday nights had been open readings and Wednesday nights the feature readings—the same thing Paul Blackburn had done in the early '60s at "Café le Metro" on Second Ave and 10th Street, and "Les Deux Megots" coffeehouse also over on East 10th Street, which were the antecedents for the Saint Mark's Poetry Project.

But Ted was the guy—he just—he and Alice lived the total poetry life and visiting them at 101 Saint Mark's Place was like walking into a poem.

So, is that a good place to start?

MH: *Sure.*

BH: Maybe you want to give Pickard a start.

TP: I probably saw Ted in England when he was in Essex (Ted taught at Essex University) and he read in the Tower a few times (Morden Tower?) there was a poetry series there.

MH: *What year was that?*

TP: I've got the date on some posters I'll show you later.

BH: What years did the series run?

TP: We started this series in 1964 I think, '63 or '64. Allen Ginsberg came. The first American poets to come were Ferlinghetti, Corso, Creeley.

MH: *Is Ferlinghetti still alive?*

BH: Yes, he's approaching 100!

MH: *I hope he makes it.*

BH and TP: Oh yes, god bless him.

BH: He's probably blind. His paintings are down to black and white.

TP: Anyway, Ted would've come up when he was in Essex to give readings.

MH: *Were you a student?*

TP: No, I've never been a student (smiling). I've never graduated to that high a level of academic attainment.

MH: *Be great to have had Ted as a teacher.*

BH: Well, the story—you know—to talk to about that is Rose Lesniak. Rose is in Miami now. We just had the gathering for Barbara Barg who died in the spring and Barg and Rose, that's where I met them in Chicago who were all studying with Ted at the time at Columbia College (Chicago).

TP: That's not Rose who is married to Simon Pettet?

BH: No, that's a different Rose. This Rose is the gay Rose.

TP: I think I saw Ted in Chicago as well.

MH: *(To Tom) What was your impression of him?*

TP: I thought he was wonderful. He was funny as fuck and he had this great Irish-American humor, he was joshing and good natured and fun to be around. But frighteningly—he wasn't too bad in Chicago, but in New York with his Pepsi and pills it was kind of frightening to see.

I also saw him in—I was into my own series of drugs at the time—but we did gigs, various gigs like in Amsterdam where he read his interminable train poem which goes on and on—and the next day I was travelling with Tom Raworth from Amsterdam to get a Polish visa and we got stuck on the train and I composed that poem I referenced earlier (Tom finds the poem in his book and reads it).

BH: (laughs at hearing Tom read).

TP: It was a little jibe at Ted.

BH: Yeah, *Train Ride*—Anna Bell published that book.

TP: And when I was staying with Ginsberg on 12th Street and Avenue A, Ted was just around the corner. I remember going round to his place and he'd throw the keys out the window.

But I wrote a poem kind of like an oral history where Ted was talking about his family. I'll look it up for you later.

MH: *Ted was from Rhode Island.*

BH: Cranston—Providence. I know his poem, "Cranston City Line" or "Near the Cranston City Line …"

MH: *Do you have a favorite poem of his (to Bob)?*

BH: For me, *The Sonnets* are my favorite poems. I can teach *The Sonnets* all day long. You can learn everything there is to learn about poetry from Ted's sonnets. First, that they don't have to be 14 lines! Second, that form is constantly inventing itself.

His sonnets are the most conversational poems ever written that are also cut-ups stolen from the greats and they are poignant. How he got all the emotions into those poems—*The Sonnets*! It's nothing but art; it's nothing but art made from words.

That's what Berrigan's Sonnets mean to me. But I also love "LGTTH" because I know what it stands for (laughs). And anyone who knows what "LGTTH" stands for has to love that poem (smiling)—how the F...K are you going to find out what LGTTH stands for? You guys don't know?

MH and TP: *(shaking our heads)* No!

BH: Let's Go to The Hop!

MH and TP: *Oh (laughter)!*

BH: (laughing) And you know that's Ted—something like the esoteric Rosicrucian letters that are going to give you the key to the pentagram—LGTTH ...

And then I love his "People of The Future" epigram in his book *Nothing for You* that Angel Hair Books published in 1977 and that George Schneeman did the cover:

> People of the future
> while you are reading these poems, remember
>
> you didn't write them,
> I did.

It's because he knows he stole half of his F...ing poems and he knows his F...ing poems are going to get stolen—So just remember! (laughs) You've got to love that about Ted.

BH: (to me and Tom) What's your favorite?

TP: I love *The Sonnets*, too.

MH: *I love "Red Shift," "A Certain Slant of Sunlight," and many of his poems.*

BH: Berrigan had the Creeley tremor in his voice.

MH: *Yes, a tremor of emotion.*

BH: I didn't get Creeley. When I was going to Columbia U. and I saw he was reading at Swarthmore and I had a girlfriend at Swarthmore. So, I hitch-hiked—try doing that now—from Manhattan, from here to Swarthmore, Pennsylvania on the New Jersey Turnpike. You did things like that then—you were "On the Road!"

MH: *You'd be in handcuffs today.*

BH: So, I got there and I went to hear Creeley and then I got it because he placed the words in the air the way they're placed on the page, but he filled up all the space with emotion, pure emotion.
 And how could Berrigan take all of that and do it himself because it was the best way to do it and it was amazing. Simon Pettet also does it, Simon Schuchat does it, too. Very few will try it out, and that's the way to read a poem.

TP: He said that he cut his lines (Creeley). He actually read them like that he thought because after William Carlos Williams that's how he would've read them stopping at the end of the line, but then he realized that he didn't—leaving the words hang midair.

BH: Everybody who gives that kind of fastidious detail to Williams as if he did it—sorry, his punctuation is all over the map. It looks good; it looks like "This is just to say" it looks like the "Wheelbarrow" is crafted like a wheelbarrow. Creeley did the minutiae of the poem—Williams was marvelously observant but he was not the technician. He was a better doctor than Creeley was, but playing out the formality of the poem—good lord—nobody can touch Creeley.
 But Berrigan did the open field that nobody else could imitate like in "Tambourine Life"—he took on Duncan's (Robert Duncan) "open field" and made it sparkle and spangle. He did the one-liners, he did *The Sonnets*, he did the open field and then of course there were the F...ing genius interviews that he just made up whole cloth,

that was the thing that always got us.

MH: *He made up that interview with John Cage.*

BH: Yes!

TP: He made it up?

BH: Completely made it up.

TP: (incredulous) He forged a ... (searching for words)

MH: *Then he later told George Plimpton that he made it up after Plimpton published it in* The Paris Review *(Tom and Bob laughing).*

TP: Was Cage still alive then?

BH: Yes, he loved it; he thought it was great.

MH: *Ted gave me two postcards. One was an Alice Notley poem titled "Christmas in September" that Ted reversed. He reversed one of his wife's poems. It was a collaboration with Joe Brainard or George Schneeman and their artwork on one side and Ted's poem on the other.*

TP: He did a collaboration with me as well in a series of connected poems with both our names. We'd be talking a lot. It was the time of the Falklands War and a reactionary period. He wrote me this little poem he sent me which I published under his and my name, so I pinched one of his poems (laughs). I will show you the poem.

MH: *(to Bob Holman) What was it like when you first got involved setting up the readings and workshops at Saint Mark's?*

BH: That was right at the time when Saint Mark's institutionalized itself. We had big community meetings where everybody would sit around and decide how is a gang of poets going to become a 501c non-profit organization and what it all meant because Anne Waldman had been the quote "secretary" for the first two years the

Project had been going.

MH: *Waldman preceded you?*

BH: It was a little more complicated. Fortunately, I have to go into detail because I don't know anything else to do. The Project got its first two years of funding directly from the federal government through Harvey Silverstein who was a professor at the New School who was hired by the *Great Society* of Lyndon Johnson to do a study of the new urban poor who would come to be known as the "Hippies." So, if he's going to study them, he had to get hold of them so in order to get hold of them he thought, "Why don't we start a poetry thing and a dance thing and a theater thing and they'll (the Hippies) all show up and then I can interview them—and he did, and he paid them. Jim Brodie got interviewed ten times because he got paid for every interview. So those were the first years and they were paid for and Anne (Waldman) was paid to be (or maybe she volunteered) secretary.

But Joel Oppenheimer and the Rev. Michael Allen who was the priest at St. Mark's Parish, and I think that they were the two who were hired to be the directors of the Project. And when the federal money ran out, they left and Ted had been teaching a workshop right over here at 2nd Avenue and 2nd Street—the old courthouse building now the Anthology Film Archives. If you look at the basement, you'll see bars in the windows because those were the jail cells and the first workshops of Saint Mark's were held there.

Next, what happens, well, it was over as far as anyone was concerned the money had dried up but not for Anne. This was '66–'68. Anne said there's too much going on too much energy here we've got to do this and that was the way she was—part of her genius—so she said we'll keep it going whether there's money or not and the NEA had just started and so had the New York State Council on The Arts—and I don't know how it played in with Saint Mark's Church that they got some money—it continued and eventually— but then that's when Anne and Allen Ginsberg started NAROPA.

MH: *Ok, that's right, out in Colorado.*

BH: And all of a sudden Anne had split focus and that's when I came in in the early (to Tom) '70s because Anne was in absentia the director but she was rarely there and didn't have much to do with it, and she had handed it off to Larry Fagin who was probably the least likely director you could ever have.

MH: I think Paul Violi ran it, too, for a while.

BH: I don't remember Paul running the readings at Saint Mark's, but I know that he was involved in some way with the Poetry Center. But it was Larry Fagin who was one of the first poetry coordinators of the Saint Mark's Poetry Project, who brought his own crazy aesthetic ideas of what poetry should be, which included the kind of experimental poetry that he was writing. And he didn't work out because he didn't know how to deal with people and he wasn't a good administrator. So, Anne Waldman had to hire Ron Padgett to be the new director and Maureen Owen to be the poetry coordinator, which was right before I got involved with the Poetry Project in '77-'78 with Bernadette Mayer, and together, me and Bernadette, we ran the Poetry Project for five years.

And I had never run anything before, but I had been in the CETA artist project which familiarized me with working in a grant-funded art business. Starting out working in the Saint Mark's Poetry Project was crazy at first. I was writing press releases every week announcing that the poets who we were scheduling to read were the greatest poets in the world, but we never got any attention from the major New York newspapers. But after I left the Saint Mark's Poetry Project, and opened the Nuyorican Poets Café, and announced the first "Poetry Slams," then the major New York newspapers took notice, because all of a sudden, this new poetry format of the "Slam" became a cultural phenomenon.

And it was such a bizarre thing because I didn't have to write press releases anymore. *The New York Times* sent reporters to write about what was happening with the poetry slams at the Nuyorican Poets Café. And they were totally great readings every week with two poets who would each read for forty-five minutes and there'd be thirty to forty people who'd come every week—it was some of the greatest times for poetry.

MH: I remember the Monday night opens; I read in one; and the Wednesday night features.

BH: John Wieners.

MH: *Philip Whalen.*

BH: At those community meetings, Allen Ginsberg would come to the meetings and he would sit there and say: Ninety percent of all the Poetry Project business happens at parties; therefore, we should have more parties (laughing).

When we had the election to the board, we had a big piece of blue photographic paper, the stuff photographers use as backdrops—sky blue paper that we formed into a circle that was our voting booth ... I think I still have the book here ... I put a little book inside (gets up to look in his shelves, laughs). Here it is, this is the book (shows me) that was sitting on a little table—you went in to vote who you wanted and Steve Levine had drawn symbols for each person, so I had to put this Emily Dickinson paperback in there to give you inspiration while you decided who to vote for—the first person who went in was of course Ted Berrigan—we got one ballot that had nothing on it—that was Ted. But look what he did to the book (Bob points to cover)!

MH: *(laughing, seeing the cover)*

BH: Ted gave Emily Dickinson a goatee (Tom and Bob laughing) Isn't that funny!

MH: *I know he liked to play practical jokes on people.*

TP: And that was to vote for what?

BH: For whom was going to be on the board of directors not to be the director. There was a board of eight people—it was all poets.

MH: *I remember the first night for the opening of a poet's workshop, like John Godfrey's poetry workshop that I attended. Everyone showed up. Alice was there, Ted was there, Anne Waldman, Bernadette Mayer, Ron Padgett. That always impressed me that the poetry community would turn out in support.*

BH: You basically did this seven days a week. I keep remembering those parties in the wintertime and everybody would throw their coats on the bed, and it would be this huge jumble of coats there. And when you left you could never find your f...ing coat. It was something about the way that those coats would become like geological layers. It was really a community and we'd all go out for drinks afterwards. We'd go to the Grass Roots or it would move around or we'd go to the Orchidia for a slice of pizza which is where Phil Hartman started his Two Boots Pizzeria—they still offer an Orchidia Pizza there with five different ingredients because in memory of those days when we would all hang out at the Orchidia right down the street from Saint Mark's.

MH: *There were some Ukrainian bars and places I remember, too.*

BH: Lys Mykyta, "The Sly Fox" across the street on 2nd Avenue between 8th and 9th Streets.

TP: I remember drinking in that one.

BH: I remember Anselm Hollo going in there and then people would keep showing up we never heard from like Jack Collum—and who was Jack Collum? He became an integral part of the family at Saint Mark's. And then there were all these poets that Ted knew coming to town and to Saint Mark's.

MH: *I remember running into Rudy Burkhardt at one of the readings.*

BH: The art world hung out. Alex Katz would be at a reading. It was through Ada, his wife, that I met my wife, Elizabeth, who did this painting on the wall behind me.

Interview with Kenneth Koch

I was working at a Brentano's Bookstore, when I first picked up a copy of one of Kenneth Koch's books of poetry, *The Art of Love*, a mass market paperback edition with a Jane Freilicher cover that Brentano's kept near the checkout. It was the only book of poetry in the mass market rack.

And it was at a book party for John Ashbery's *Shadow Train* in the upstairs room of the Gotham Book Mart on 47th Street that I introduced myself to Kenneth Koch. I would go to other book parties there. I remember Koch telling a young woman who had purchased a copy of Ashbery's new book that he would sign her copy instead, which got some laughs. That evening, he invited me to come sit in on his poetry class at Columbia.

I found my way to 516 Hamilton Hall on Columbia's Morningside Heights campus, and I sat in the back by the windows. I wasn't the only student to drop in on Koch's class in Modern Poetry. The university was giving him a hard time about his allowing so many unregistered students to sit in on his lectures. I had my notebook open, and Koch, wearing a brightly colored silk ascot and a corduroy sport jacket, burst into his class talking about Ezra Pound, telling the class that Pound was the most influential poet of the twentieth century, and that he wanted to rid poetry of boring Victorian rhyme and meter and make it as clear as prose. At one point, he got up on the desk and recited one of Pound's poems and stated, "Pound didn't want to give up the beauty of past poetry no more than Stravinsky wanted to give up the beauty of past music."

After class, at his apartment across from the Barnard campus, 25 Claremont Avenue Apt 2-B, a great pre-war apartment in the Peter Minuit Building, we sat and I pulled out my questions and a stack of his poetry books. He then tested me to see if I had read all of his books. I passed his test, and he let me turn on my cassette recorder. I asked him to stand by his window so I could take a photograph and I saw the sadness in his face as he looked out. His wife, Janice, had died the year before.

He signed my copy of *When The Sun Tries To Go On* that had original illustrations by Larry Rivers, "To Mark, From Kenneth, All Interviewed-Out, New York, 1982."

LARRY RIVERS AND KENNETH KOCH

MH: *What is implied by the word "Formulalessness" that is found in the middle of your poem "On the Great Atlantic Railway"?*

KK: I used it when I was twenty-five years old. I was very happy then to be able to write poetry free from sense in an ordinary way.

MH: *What do you mean?*

KK: I had the impression I was breaking away from writing poetry in an ordinary, chronological, and rational way. It gave me more things to say, and I could say them in a more exciting and interesting way than I would have if I had to make sense all the time.

MH: *In* The Burning Mystery of Anna, *in an interview with Pierre*

Sadi Raab, you mention that a poem is a "Semi-concrete entanglement of first impressions-or nothing." Does this mean that you're against revising?

KENNETH KOCH IN HIS APARTMENT

KK: I revise a lot. Besides, that statement—well, that work, "Reflections on Morocco," in the book you mention, everything in it except the names of cities is completely false. Pierre Sadi Raab does not, as far as I know, exist. He was an invented character.

MH: *I was thinking that it might be a fantasized interview.*

KK: In that interview I think I wished to make myself seem rather pretentious. I would never actually say or write anything even like that. I was making fun of myself a little bit as a poet visiting Morocco who wished to do something in the school system. It was inspired by the fact that I did actually teach children to write poetry in Haiti, France, and Italy. When I was in Morocco the thought of teaching did briefly pass through my mind. I thought that it might be interesting to do it there but then I immediately saw what the problems would be which I put in that interview.

MH: *You don't write poetry to be instructive or didactic?*

KK: No. But when I wrote the poems in The Art of Love, I discovered that I had a lot of knowledge, and that I knew a lot of things; some true, some false. It was interesting to talk about things that I knew and to have the tone of giving advice in poetry. I hadn't thought of it before I wrote that book.

MH: *You weave a lot of very astute observations with a lot of wild-eyed looney images using word play and syntactical maneuvers to juggle your ideas.*

KK: Well, I suppose if I do that it's because I find it beautiful. I find that it's a good thing to do that with words. But you know, if you're talking about intellectual things, and about giving advice with what you call "looney images," it's because one is never just giving advice, or one is never just wise. One all the time has a body, an unconscious; one is aware of the people in the room, the lights, etc. I like to combine different parts of experience, like knowledge and sensation.

MH: *You have a lot of locations and names of places in your poetry. I was wondering if you visited all these places, or is it just imaginary?*

KK: I'm not sure if I've been to Zanesville, Ohio (both laughing).

MH: Kalamazoo?

KK: Oh, I've been to Kalamazoo. I don't restrict myself to places I've been or to people I've known. I remember being very inspired by a line of Frank O'Hara's which I read very early on. It was one of the first poems by him that I had read, a poem called "Easter," and I remember the line. It was 'The roses of Pennsylvania,' and I found that line very striking and inspiring. Wallace Stevens had used American State names before in poetry. 'I placed a jar in Tennessee'—but the line 'The roses of Pennsylvania' seemed rather different and I liked it—Bof!

MH: In the Donald Allen Anthology of New American Poetry 1945–60 *you're quoted as having made this statement—"My poetry was very much like a foreign language to me for about a year and a half." Is this in reference to your having been influenced by such French poets as Jacques Prévert when you were first in France?*

KK: No. Are you referring to the essay in another anthology that says I was influenced by him?

MH: Yes.

KK: I never was. I never liked his poetry. If I liked it, it was in a very mild way, but I never thought he was a very good poet. The poets I was influenced by were Apollinaire, Max Jacob, and Paul Éluard.

MH: Desnos?

KK: No. I don't see how anyone could be influenced by Desnos. Reverdy was a slight influence. Why I didn't like that statement in the *Norton Anthology* was that I had read about three or four poems of Prévert's and thought they had the charm of popular songs. But they never seemed to go very far.

MH: It goes on (reading from the Norton Anthology*), "Then it became under the influence of some rather demanding personal experiences, some strange substances in the air, more realistic."*

KK: Well, that's actually something I said in Donald Allen's anthology. In the first part you quoted, I was talking about my poem "When the Sun Tries To Go On," that was partly inspired by a certain experience I had reading French poetry without entirely understanding it. For example, supposing I read a line of French poetry. (Pulls out a book from a bookcase along the wall.) *'Comme c'était la veille du quatorze juillet vers les quatres heures de l'après-midi, je descendi dans la rue pour aller voir les acrobates.'*

When I went to France, I didn't know French very well, however, I sort of knew what it meant. So, the word *'descendi'* had its English meaning, descend, and I envisioned someone actually going down into the street as well as along the street. *'Comme c'était la veille'* could have been misread if I confused *'veille'* with the word *'vieille'* which means old in French, so that there might have been a feeling of oldness in *'quatorze juillet.'* And I was probably not sure if *'quatorze'* was fourteen or forty, which gave me a rather excited feeling about the 40th of July. I also could have read *'vers les quatres heures de l'après-midi'* as toward the four hours of the afternoon, since I wasn't familiar with the French way of saying things, and could almost envision the hours as four girls walking down the street. So, I would see a lot of things in these words that weren't there, and I wouldn't see some of the things that were there. Thus, I got pleasure. I felt a tremendous amount of richness of meaning without its ever really completely making sense to me.

This inspired me until I had been there for three or four months. After I came back to America, I started writing poems in which I deliberately couldn't understand what I was saying. I was trying to get that rich effect of words meaning lots of things at the same time.

MH: *Do you write in French?*

KK: I have, but it doesn't turn out too well.

MH: *Translations?*

KK: I've done some translations, but I don't do it anymore. The French poetry I have written is slightly parodic.

MH: *Richard Howard calls you the best parodist of our time. Is this a good way to get into another's poetry and open up your own?*

KK: I used to do a lot of parodies. Sure, it's one way to pick up someone else's style, to get close to their poetry. At certain times it seemed almost irresistible. I usually parody the poets whose work I like.

MH: *William Carlos Williams?*

KK: Oh yeah, I like Williams very much.

MH: *I have the feeling you don't like Whitman.*

KK: Where did you get that feeling?

MH: *From your book* The Art of Love, *from the poem "The Art of Poetry," when you write, "Or so it seems to me. Walt Whitman's 'corrections,' too, of the* Leaves of Grass, *and especially 'Song of Myself,' are almost always terrible." But it might just be a false impression I got.*

KK: It is. I like Whitman a lot. I don't like Whitman's revisions of his poems. I think he's a great poet. But I like the version of "Song of Myself" from 1855 the best. It seems to me that when he revised it, he made it syntactically more correct, but added certain things which seemed to take away slightly from its power. Though not an awful lot. I was influenced by him. "A Poem of The Forty-Eight States" in my book *The Pleasures of Peace* was written that way. There are a number of great poets who were never very good at revising. Wordsworth's first version of *The Prelude* is better in my opinion.

MH: *What teachers did you have?*

KK: I took two writing courses at Harvard. One was with a man named Theodore Morrison, the other was with Delmore Schwartz. It would be hard for me to say what effect those courses had on my writing. There never was an "older poet" who acted as my guide or mentor. I know that some poets were very much influenced by Charles Olson; Allen Ginsberg was influenced by Williams; and so on. I never had anything like that. I've been influenced by lots of poets. By Williams and Stevens and French poets, and I always liked to be influenced.

MH: *O'Hara?*

KK: Frank and John and I influenced each other, and we were all about the same age.

MH: *People have the impression that he was much older.*

KK: Oh, poor Frank, it's just that he had the terrible misfortune to die. That's what makes him seem older and wiser. But I wouldn't say that Frank O'Hara was a big influence. Certainly, I learned a lot from John and Frank. But I had the feeling that the situation was mutual. We all were inspired by each other and competitive with each other.

MH: *And painters?*

KK: Oh yes, but you'd have to ask them.

MH: *In the Donald Allen anthology that we've already mentioned, James Schuyler makes an interesting statement. He said that in the '50s it was painters like Rivers, de Kooning, and Pollock who were steering the boat.*

KK: The boat! What's the boat! Our social life was the painters. I'm not aware of my poetry being much influenced by the painters. When people want to just start talking about this so-called "New York School" they say, "Well, they were influenced by painting and surrealism." But that's nonsense.

MH: *Does that get you angry?*

KK: No, it doesn't get me angry.

MH: *Ashbery said that he didn't think there ever was such a school.*

KK: I don't know. It may have existed. It's all right. It wasn't only a school. In the beginning it was John Ashbery, Frank O'Hara, and I. We knew each other and liked each other and were influenced by each other and hung around together with certain painters. There was no credo. We knew what we liked, what we didn't like. It was very clear to us what was good and what wasn't, but it never manifested in document. And certainly, our poetry at that time in the early '50s had a lot in common. I think we got more and more different as time went on.

MH: *What inspired you to write* Ko?

KK: Byron's "Don Juan" which I read about seven years before. When I read it, I thought—God! I think it's one of the greatest poems in the English language. Then I thought about writing a poem like it. I thought about writing a long narrative poem that's funny and beautiful and lyrical. But I didn't think about it very much because I was writing other poems. I was in Europe when I wrote it finally. I was in Florence with my wife Janice who had a Fulbright scholarship to study in Italy. We were living in a little villino near the Piazzo de Michelangelo when I decided it was the right time to begin. So, I thought, I don't want to use ottava rima, which is what Byron uses, I want to find my own stanza. But I did a few practice stanzas in ottava rima, as I say in my poem "Some General Instructions" in *The Art of Love*. They were too good to give up. So, I wrote the book in ottava rima.

But I didn't re-read Byron when I wrote it. What I read was *Orlando Furioso* by Ariosto. My Italian was fairly good and again I didn't understand everything. Every day I'd read a little bit of Ariosto either before or after I was writing. What really appealed to me about Ariosto was that it was all action and almost no commentary. And I didn't re-read Byron because Byron had written in English and I knew he'd influence me too much. I like the strangeness of being influenced by a Renaissance Italian. I couldn't write too much like him since I was writing in English.

MH: *Is there any connection with Joseph Dah, the action poet in* Ko, *and Don Juan?*

KK: No, there's no connection. Joseph Dah is sort of making fun of certain crazy experiments that were going on in art at that time—action painting. But Joseph Dah carried it to an extreme point. I actually wrote the collected works of Joseph Dah, but never published it. There are only about fifteen poems.

MH: *When you started* Ko *did you ever imagine it going to the length it did?*

KK: I hoped it would. I wanted it to go on as long as it could.

MH: *How long did it take you to write?*

KK: *Ko* I wrote very fast. I wrote it in three months. *The Duplications* took years and years.

MH: *Did you find it hard going back to resume writing again the sequel to* Ko *in* The Duplications?

KK: I don't know if it was difficult to come back to the form. It was just that in doing *The Duplications* I wanted to do something different since I don't like to write things that are the same. I didn't seem to be in as favorable a situation for writing when I wrote *The Duplications*. There were a lot of interruptions. I always thought that the time I wrote *Ko* was in a way very idyllic and ideal for writing poetry since I was living with my wife and baby daughter and it was early spring and there were new flowers every day and all this wonderful weather. Then all I had to do was write, and I wrote in this very concentrated way for three and a half months. I worked from four to eight hours a day except Sunday. Sunday, I took off to go to the museums. It was marvelous. I never felt so close to nature. When writing *The Duplications* things weren't so good. On the other hand, life was full of difficulties when I wrote *Ko*, but somehow the writing was easier.

MH: *Do you incorporate the things going on in and around your life into the poem while you are writing it?*

KK: Ah ... There are certainly references to my personal life in my poems even though they're rather fantastic. Particularly in the beginning of part II of *The Duplications*, which is largely truthful.

> "After a year or two interval, in fact
> It's almost three, once more I come, dear Muse,
> To write this work, and hope it's still intact.
> And you will generously not refuse
> Your sweet assistance—which I haven't lacked
> At all till now, but had—that I may fuse
> What's in my mind and what is in the spectrum
> Of earth outside with my typewriter plectrum."

MH: *In* The Duplications, *where did you get the idea of using Minnie and Mickey Mouse?*

KK: I don't know. I don't think it had happened in my poetry before. Well, I used to read lots of books about them when I was a kid. I remember that I read the comic books and that I loved those mice and identified with them. I used to have "Big Little Books" which were all about the adventures of Mickey Mouse. Bof!

MH: *Marvel Comics?*

KK: I didn't read those until I was grown up. I started doing a comic book with Stan Lee but we never finished it because we couldn't get the financing.

MH: *In* The Burning Mystery Of Anna *it seems as if you're trying to get at some idea of place that shapes and informs one's reality, or changes the perspective. Is place important for a poet? Do you have a sense of place?*

KK: (laughs) The question's a little heavy. The question, 'Is place important for a poet,' I can't answer. I've always enjoyed travelling. I'm moved by it in the way I'm moved by poetry and people—very moved by travelling. In that work "Reflections on Morocco" from the book you mention, I'm wondering what it means to go someplace, what one really does get from it. All my poems have a secret locale which is sometimes in the place I wrote the poem, but sometimes not. The locale is New York in the poem "To Marina" from that book.

MH: *How about "Seine" in* The Pleasures of Peace?

KK: I don't know where that is (both laughing).

MH: *Must be Paris.*

KK: Must be. Paris, yes, but partly Long Island.
MH: *(Reading from "A Poem of The Forty-Eight States" in* The Pleasures of Peace*)*

"And vow that you will one day be a traveler like myself,

*And wander to all the ends of the earth until you are completely exhausted,
And then return to Texas or Indiana, whatever state you happen to be from.
And have your death celebrated by a lavish funeral
Conducted by starlight, with numerous boys and girls reading my poems aloud!"*

KK: Do you see the parody of Whitman in those lines?

MH: Yes.

KK: Anyway, travelling is one thing that has always interested me and that I haven't entirely understood and that I find exciting and that I seem to connect to words, so I write about it.

MH: *More or less as you get older?*

KK: I don't know.

MH: *Why New York?*

KK: Because my friends are here and I have a good job here.

MH: *Do you like it?*

KK: Oh, I don't know how one could like New York. I think Frank O'Hara did. You have to forget a lot of things about it to like it.

MH: *You write a lot about being in love at different ages in* The Burning Mystery of Anna, *like twenty-nine in the poem "To Marina." Are you trying to recapture that time?*

KK: That's about my love for Marina. Do I consciously try to recapture time? No. What I do is I try to—I don't know what I do when I write poetry—I mean I do know but I don't verbalize it.
    I look for either a place or a time in my life, the feelings connected with that time which is going to make something happen in language. It's just the way a painter would look around for something to paint. The painting may turn out to be abstract, but he'll

still want to go to a particular place.

I wanted to write "To Marina" because that love affair that I had so long ago seemed unresolved. I never understood why it had been so important to me, or why at least I was fascinated by how important it seemed to be. I didn't want to write about it in order to understand it, but I thought there might be a chance since it was such a deep experience, and since I didn't understand it, that I might be able to write well about it. But I remember reading about poets saying they wanted to capture the past, which is simply impossible.

MH: *So, you don't have a philosophy of time?*

KK: No.

MH: *Are you influenced at all by philosophy?*

KK: I was when I was sixteen years old; I read a lot of philosophy. I don't read much of it any more. I imagine I was influenced by Plato a little bit. I liked the dialogue atmosphere in it, but I don't think he influenced my thought.

MH: *Are you able to approach it like poetry?*

KK: Yes, except that it has a point to make. I like Spinoza and Nietzsche and Schopenhauer. I don't really like Schopenhauer's ideas but just the things he says along the way. I like to read Whitehead.

MH: *Do you try to capture the movement of the mind in the way you write?*

KK: Well, I let a lot of things come in when I'm writing. I feel that by not sticking to the subject I'm likely to find a subject I'm more interested in. I feel that whatever is in my conscious mind at any particular moment is probably not good enough for what I want to say in a poem. So, I want something else to come in, something that is not in my mind right then. There are various ways to make this happen.

MH: *You don't try to blank everything out?*

KK: No, I just write. I don't know. I've never really examined the process very closely. But I know there are all kinds of associations that I get from one word to another which then sort of attach themselves to meanings. In a particular text I could tell you what inspired what, what came from what, but even then, I don't think it would be clear.

MH: *Do you have moments of enlightenment?*

KK: I tend to get moments like that when I'm writing, yes.

MH: *Then the writing is itself the real experience?*

KK: Yeah.

MH: *Is that why you write?*

KK: I like to write. It engages me completely. I seem to find out things while I write. Sometimes I like the final product.

MH: *A revelatory sort of process?*

KK: Yes, I suppose you could say that.

MH: *Why do you tend to write long poems?*

KK: I've written some long poems alright! I've also written some short ones. But writing long narrative poems is something I like to do. It's not the only thing I like to do in poetry.

MH: *Do you fear writing the same poem?*

KK: What makes you think I'd be afraid of that! I'm always interested in writing something new. But it's true, one can't do it a hundred percent.

MH: *What is your favorite poem, or book of poems?*

KK: Oh, I have no favorites. I write a lot, and though I've published a good deal, I've only published a small part of what I write. Usually when I publish something I like it quite a lot.
  I think that to make any kind of judgement on one's early work and say, "Well, it wasn't as good." Or to say, "Ah, that was my best

work."—strikes me as being untrue. I like the poem "To Marina" in my recent book as much as I like my earliest poems. Picasso said when somebody asked him what he thought about some work of his, "I don't think an artist should be his own connoisseur." But I think he meant to say it because you can't sell any paintings to yourself.

MH: *I find something more confessional about* The Burning Mystery of Anna *than in your other books.*

KK: You really feel they're confessions, or are you just using that voguish term for the work of Anne Sexton or Sylvia Plath? I wasn't aware that I was confessing anything in those poems. I was just writing about my experience.

MH: *Closer to your emotions?*

KK: My emotions are in all my poems. I think confessional is a careless term. I don't think those poems are confessional.

MH: *You don't like confessional poetry?*

KK: I don't even know what you mean by it!

MH: *Lowell, Berryman, Plath, Sexton, etc.*

KK: No comment. It's not my favorite direction in modern poetry.

MH: *Frank O'Hara's "I did this, I did that" kind of poetry?*

KK: I adore Frank O'Hara's poetry. It's not confessional. Confession is about talking to a priest, right? It is true that in *The Burning Mystery of Anna* and "To Marina" and in a few other poems in that book I talk about my experience in a more direct way. But sometimes it's kind of sad. Yes. that's true. I started doing that with the poems in *The Art of Love*, but it's not as sad. In "Some General Instructions," and in "The Circus," and "On Beauty" I talk about my own past.

MH: *Yes. I perceive the directness becoming stronger with* The Art of Love.

KK: I think I discovered that things that have happened to me in the past are a possible subject for my poetry—or rediscovered it—because I've written poems about that when I was young, but then I hadn't for a very long time. The poems I was writing in *The Art of Love* led me into it. You find my other poems obscure because they are not about my past?

MH: *A little bit more in an emotional sort of directness. There's an obscurity about what is taking place. In* The Burning Mystery of Anna *there's more of a placement, you're placing feelings more concretely. I like it better. I think* The Burning Mystery of Anna *is your best work.*

KK: Oh well, you couldn't please me more since it's the latest work; that's good.

MH: *What are you working on now?*

KK: Well, I've written a new book of poetry which is going to be published within the next year. It's called *Days and Nights*. And now I'm writing more poems, yet another book.

MH: *More in keeping with your last book?*

KK: I don't know if it's more in keeping with *The Burning Mystery of Anna*. I think I'm always writing out of my own experience, and part of my experience as a person and as a writer now is that I wrote those poems. So, there's no way to get them out of my experience. No, it's not exactly like the poetry in my last book, it's slightly different.

MH: *You don't try to please the reader by being different?*

KK: I don't think much about the reader. There were a few readers I used to think about. I used to think about John Ashbery, Frank O'Hara, James Schuyler, and my wife Janice and a few others. I sort of absorbed them as readers in a way, so that their taste became a part of my own taste. I rarely think any more that so and so would like this or so and so would not. I used to.

MH: *James Schuyler?*

KK: Oh, I love his work very much. I've known him for a long time.

MH: *Is there any jealousy between you and your poet friends?*

KK: Jealousy!

MH: *The kind of jealousy that comes from their receiving all the awards and such.*

KK: They won them because they are very fine poets. Oh, the successes of one's friends are hard on one, but better them than bad poets. But how can one talk about such things?

MH: *Can you explain to me this idea of "The Art of The Fallen Limb" from your book* The Pleasures of Peace?

KK: Have you read any other works by the poets quoted in that essay?

MH: *No.*

KK: They don't exist. I made them up (both laughing).

MH: *That's beautiful! And you made up that essay?*

KK: Oh yes (laughs), and I fabricated all of the South American poets.

MH: *That's great, but do you believe in it, in concealing a line of poetry in a succeeding line?*

KK: I don't believe in any critical theory. I think that all of those statements that I make about definitions of poems are true in a way and also pretentious and silly. I do believe in some idea of what poetry is, but I never formulated it. Maybe I could, but something would be lost.

MH: *I was thinking that this might be an idea that Robert Bly would attach himself to very quickly.*

KK: Well, I am poking fun at what poets say about their work and about poetry, and the work of South American poets. At the same time, I find it touching and funny and interesting that poets take their work so seriously. Not that I don't take mine seriously. But they take it so seriously that a man can spend his whole life on a dozen poems just theorizing about them. It's like these Japanese "Go" players who play this game moving little stones around, and in their own country they are great men, and they have a philosophy about it!

When I was writing those fabricated essays I was thinking about certain South American poets. I had just read a dissertation by a graduate student at Columbia about Spanish and Latin American poetry. It was about their not writing very much and theorizing about it.

MH: *Spanish Surrealism versus French Surrealism?*

KK: Yeah.

MH: *Do you like to give readings?*

KK: Yes.

MH: *Has it helped your poetry?*

KK: I don't know. Sometimes the thought of giving a reading forces me to revise a poem. Sometimes it even inspires me to write one.

MH: *Do you take in the audience's reaction?*

KK: Of course! I try not to be too interested in it. There are audiences that don't respond at all. There are certain New York audiences that laugh at everything. I prefer the poem on the page. I'd much rather read than hear somebody read, usually. I can't think of any exception at the moment. I think it's useful to hear somebody read so that you can get the tone of his or her voice. There's a certain richness and ambiguity of language that you don't get in a reading. When you read a poem aloud, just as when you translate a poem, if there's more than one possible meaning or nuance of a word in the context you have to choose one. Whereas if you're reading it to yourself then you can emphasize it in all its various ways. So, I prefer to read poems in books though I like readings.

MH: *You write a vernacular poetry in the tradition of Williams, Pound, and Auden.*

KK: I don't see the connection. They write in very different ways. As for using the language that I speak, it is richer for me in associations than the language that I don't speak. 'Girl' has a lot more meaning than the word 'damsel.' It is much easier to get a sense of place and time when I use the language that I speak. Literary language mainly communicates a sense of books that one has read.

MH: *Why did you write "The Circus" in* The Art of Love, *about the time you wrote a different poem with the same title?*

KK: I had very recently broken up with my wife and I was feeling unhappy and lonely. I wasn't writing very well, and up until that time I had thought that "The Circus" was the best thing I had ever written. I wrote the first version when I was first married and quite happy. We were in Paris and my daughter hadn't been born yet. I was very inspired and wrote many poems during the course of a few months in that little Paris apartment—most of the poems that are in my book *Thank You and Other Poems*.

So, I looked back on that time as a time when I was very content with my work and my life was good. It seemed as if something new had happened in my work.

When I wrote the second version of "The Circus" I think it was the first time I had ever taken up the theme of how I felt when I was writing something in the past. I've done it a couple of times since then, as in the poem "To Marina" where I actually quote some of my old poems.

MH: *The poem is sad.*

KK: Yes. I thought a lot about the time I wrote "The Circus" and I felt sad about it and missed it. The year I wrote the first version of that poem was 1952 or '53.

MH: *You're questioning the value of writing in the second "Circus" by trying to wrap up your whole poetic career between those two poems?*

KK: Yes, I say, "I wonder what good will come of it?" What strikes me about that when I read it now is that I don't think that way anymore. It is not a question that would occur to me—What good will come of it?!

The good that comes from writing a poem is that it is just a poem. It doesn't change one's life. It can't change the past.

MH: *"The Circus" sets off a whole meditation on time. The next poem in* The Art of Love *is "The Magic of Numbers."*

KK: They're not in any chronological order.

MH: *They seem to follow nicely. Your present tone in poetry had its roots in that early book,* Thank You and Other Poems.

KK: Really? Well, that's for someone else to see.

MH: *It's more obvious in the poems "Taking a Walk with You" and "Departure from Hydra."*

KK: But it is all so mired in fantasy and there is no real sequence of events. But that's interesting that you see a connection.

MH: *What inspired "Thank You" and what gave you those crazy associations?*

KK: One thing that inspired this poem was that I had just begun to be known a little bit as a poet. People had started asking me to do things that weren't really the same thing as asking you to write poems. Once I received a phone call from the society of landscape architects. They asked me to their annual dinner. I responded by saying, "Well, that's nice but what do you want me to do?" And they said, "Well, we're going to show some slides after dinner and we've also invited a painter and a composer and we would like you to respond to these slides as a poet." It was one of the funniest things that had ever happened to me.

When I was a kid, I had fantasies like everybody else of all kinds of professions, some of which I thought would be very exciting. I wanted to be a baseball player and a fireman. I wanted to be in the diplomatic service. At the same time, they sort of frightened me when I considered the responsibility that went with those professions. Being a ship's doctor, I thought was an odd combination of mystery and escape. But also one of horrifying responsibility.

MH: *There's a level of ecstasy running through your work at all times. It comes across in your novel* The Red Robins. *There is so much action and excitement going on.*

KK: I wanted to write a novel which was as exciting as poetry. I liked using different styles. I also noticed that I could open it at any point and just read a sentence and get a very strong feel for it and get very excited by it. That is, you can get the whole sense of the dramatic situation from a single sentence, in the same way you can get a sense of a whole landscape from just a little blue and green and yellow in a de Kooning painting. You don't have to see the whole work to get a feeling for it.

I liked the idea of just suggesting a whole story. I also liked the idea of suggesting a whole lot of stories at the same time, having them all going on simultaneously at different times and different places.

MH: *When was it written?*

KK: I started it in the late '50s and finished it the year it was published in 1975. But it wasn't steady work. I despaired of it and wrote it in a very disorganized way.

MH: *I was wondering if it wasn't a spoof on people or friends you have known?*

KK: It is in no way a spoof. But of course, it is based on my experience of everything.

MH: *The majority of your poems seem to be trying to exhaust every facet of a subject. For example, the poem "Sleeping with Women" aims at covering all aspects of a single theme at all its angles and levels at the same time.*

KK: Sometimes that seems like the right thing to do, sometimes it doesn't. Occasionally I want to get in and out very fast from a subject. "Sleeping With Women" originally began as a fourteen-line poem but I couldn't find a good fourteenth line. So, for many years it was thirteen lines long. But every year I'd find that poem and think, "It's good, I'll have to finish it." Then one day I sat outside in my garden on West 4th Street and made it almost 1000 lines long but then I cut it.

MH: When The Sun Tries To Go On, *one of your earliest long poems published as a limited edition book with illustrations by Larry Rivers, gives me the sensation of dyslexia as I read it. I'll confuse words likes scared for sacred or misread syntax of entire sentences. You play with homographs or homonyms getting this highly emotional flow into the language, but you create an anti-landscape built on disparate images juxtaposed so there's no longer any reference to the recognizable world.*

KK: One strange influence on that poem was Tolstoy's *War and Peace*. I had just read it at the time. I was very impressed—moved by Tolstoy's way of including everything, absolutely everything. Usually there's the world of the novel, a world in which the action takes place. Tolstoy brought in everything. I like to be inclusive in my work, but that doesn't account for the strange language or the strange use of language. But it accounts for my feeling that I could go on and bring in everything.

A feeling I had when I wrote *Ko, or A Season on Earth* was that I wanted to bring in every pleasure that I ever had in my life. And I must have had something like that desire when I wrote *When The Sun Tries To Go On*, though I wasn't conscious of it.

I wrote five twenty-four-line stanzas of it and thought maybe it was finished, and I showed it to Frank O'Hara and he said, "Listen Kenneth, it's very good, and once you're doing this kind of thing so well, now, why don't you just go on with it as long as you can." Therefore, I decided to write 100 stanzas. So, I really owe the existence of the work to Frank.

He quite soon afterwards started writing a long poem of his own called "Second Avenue." We used to read to each other our poems over the telephone almost daily. He was a very inspiring friend to have.

My poetry had been heading in that direction for quite a while. I wrote that poem in 1953 after my play *Pericles*, in which the language is already rather pulverized. My book *Poems from 1952-53* is very strange and abstract the way *When The Sun Tries To Go On* is. I'll read you one of my early poems from that book. This one is called "Sun Out" (Koch reaches for a book on his shelf):

> "Bananas piers limericks I am postures over there, I are the lakes of delectation, sea, see you Mars and the winsome Buffalo, they thinly raft the plains common do it ice floes hit and run drivers the mass of the wind. Is that snow "H" ing at the door, and we come in the buckle vanquished distinguished festival relieving flights of the black brave ocean."

I love that way of writing, but I could only do it for about a year and a half. I felt I had discovered something completely new. Without the existence of James Joyce, Gertrude Stein, and Frank O'Hara I probably wouldn't have found it. I really felt I had a way of writing that was completely my own.

There are very few poems of Frank O'Hara's that are like that. I was a little inspired by misreading Frank's poetry. Frank always had something in mind, whereas what he had in mind was sometimes hidden from me and seemed very strange. And I think his work may have been one thing that gave me the idea of writing things that gave me strong sensations but that didn't make any sense at all.

MH: Would it be wrong to label it surrealism?

KK: Yes. It's not at all surrealism. It doesn't have a programmatic bias in favor of dreams, chance associations, and the unconscious.

I wrote "snow 'H' ing at the door" because it's more impressionistic and sensuous. Snow sounds like H to me. After I wrote it, I realized that a door has an H shape on it with the cross bar. I liked the image. And when I wrote, "When we come in the buckle of vanquished distinguished festival," I didn't know what I was saying. I liked the sound of it, but afterwards it seemed to me like the reflection of a group of people in a belt buckle.

When people wrote about John's and Frank's and my work, they'd say about the New York School that it was influenced by surrealism and abstract expressionist painting, but those became clichés.

MH: In Auden's warning to O'Hara he says, "I think you must watch what is always a great danger with any surrealistic style, namely of confusing authentic non-logical relations which arouse wonder, with accidental ones which arouse mere surprise and in the end fatigue."

KK: You could also warn people about the style of Alexander Pope. If you do something well you do it well. One tries as hard as one can. As Frank O'Hara said, "You don't turn around when someone is chasing you and tell him you were on the track team at such and such a school, you just run like hell." If a terrific poet like Frank O'Hara is using what Auden calls a surrealistic style, he's not going to change his style and write rational poems because Auden gives him a warning. Of course, I don't see O'Hara as a surrealistic poet at all. You can tell how little a surrealist Frank is by reading his poem "Sleeping on The Wing" where he talks about dreaming and going to sleep and escaping from the world in a perfectly rational way. But his concern for a friend brings him back to reality. That is not at all what I consider to be the surrealistic program. What the surrealists discovered has become just a common part of what a lot of poets use now.

MH: *I like Andre Breton's saying, "Le document pris sur le vif."*

KK: I like many things about surrealism but I wouldn't describe my poetry as being such.

MH: *Al Poulin in his* Anthology of Contemporary American Poetry *says, "Koch writes the kind of poetry Kafka would have written had Kafka a greater sense of humor."*

KK: I'm very grateful to Al Poulin for thinking that I'm a funnier writer than Kafka. Kafka had a tremendous sense of humor. I don't know what Al means. I guess my work makes him laugh more because the humor is not as burdened with nightmarish anxiety. But if you read one of Kafka's "Parables" where he sees these people in a tremendously deep hole and he yells down to them, "What are you doing down there?" And they yell up, "We're digging the pit of Babel!"—Kafka's constantly funny. I'm flattered that Al Poulin thinks me funnier.

MH: *Paul Carroll too.*

KK: He thinks I'm funnier than Kafka?

MH: *He says you're our greatest comic poet.*

KK: I don't think being comic keeps one from being serious at all. It keeps one from being solemn.

MH: *Is there a conscious move to change to find a new poetry?*

KK: I've always been interested in trying new ways of writing. That's caused me a little trouble too with readers and critics because my style does keep changing, but I've finally decided that that's just a part of my style—it changes. I don't know why it changes; new ways of writing enable one to say new things.

Interview with Bernadette Mayer and Phil Good

I hadn't seen Bernadette in over thirty-five years when I pulled up to a converted former church in East Nassau about twenty miles southeast of Albany, on November 10, 2018, that she shared with her partner Phil Good. Phil had been out earlier getting firewood ready for the winter. The main room, the former sanctuary, was spacious yet cozy, and Phil sat on the couch by the window and Bernadette sat in an overstuffed chair in the corner. I set up my camera and turned on the video recorder.

I asked her questions about her time as director of the Poetry Project, a position she held for all the years that I attended the readings and workshops. She amazed me with her story of seeing a ghost one night while she was alone in the church and it was late, and with her other story of her confronting the drug dealer who was selling dope at the readings. I loved hearing her infectious laugh at some of these anecdotes.

Bernadette, besides being an experimental poet, was also a photographer who came up with some amazing photo projects. She blended those two arts, like her project titled *Helens of Troy* where she looked up every Helen in the Troy, New York phone directory and set about taking each one's portrait. Or her first photographic work titled *Memory*, an early multimedia project she started in 1971 where she took a 35mm roll of photographs every day for a year to capture every moment of her life.

She asked me to go upstairs to check out the rooms that she used for her workshops. People would stay over for the weekend poetry workshops that she ran and sleep on the beds upstairs. When I had finished my interview, she invited me to stay over, but I wasn't able to, but I offered to take her and Phil out to dinner and they suggested Jackson's Old Chatham House about six miles away. And that is where I drove them down Route 13 to the restaurant.

I brought with me two of her early books of poetry for her to sign. The one was titled *Poetry* published in 1976 by the Kulchur Foundation, and its cover is a drawing of a row of New York brownstones by Bernadette's sister, Rosemary. Her other early poetry book was titled *The Golden Book of Words* published in 1978 by Angel Hair Press, and it has a Joe Brainard cover drawing, and a photograph on the back of Bernadette sitting on a windowsill in her New York apartment taken by her former husband Lewis Warsh. It is the last poem in that volume that resonated with me given how Bernadette has had to struggle ever since her stroke. The opening lines read:

> Be strong Bernadette
> Nobody will ever know
> I came here for a reason
> Perhaps there is a life here
> Of not being afraid of your own heart beating

MH: *In 1983, at Saint Mark's (Poetry Project), what happened between you and Ted Berrigan?*

BM: We were like kids playing who could be the meanest (laughs).

MH: *Because I never got the story. What I got from Ted (Berrigan) was a postcard with an angry poem directed at you.*

BM: Lewis (Lewis Warsh was Mayer's late husband) published *The Sonnets* and Ted and Lewis agreed that Ted would sign a certain number of copies of *The Sonnets* so that we "United Artists Books" could sell them and use the money to publish unknown young poets.

So, I thought that was a great idea and so did Lewis, but unfortunately what happened was that Ted took the books to the Gotham Book Mart and sold them and took the money. As a result of that, he and Lewis had this argument because Lewis didn't feel that that was fair.

So, the whole argument had nothing to do with me, except that

BERNADETTE MAYER

Ted made Alice (Ted's wife Alice Notley) feel that we had to take sides. You know how people are in arguments, they feel that they have to be on one side or the other. And Alice, whenever she was walking down the street, because we still lived in the same neighborhood, she would see me and she would cross over to the other side.

MH: Really!

BM: So that she wouldn't have to pass me. Now, I really didn't understand this fully at the time why this was happening. I figured that maybe Alice felt that she had to be on Ted's side, and that side meant "side of the street" literally (laughs). So that's what happened. So, then I called Peggy (de Coursey), who is a good friend of Alice's, several times. In fact, I harassed her and said, "Why is Alice doing this to me?" until Peggy got tired of listening to me and she said, "Alice is just jealous." Now, that made absolutely no sense at all to me. But that is all I know.

MH: *I remember a reading Ted Berrigan gave at Saint Mark's when you were the director of the Poetry Project and you were in the audience while Ted was at the podium and he said your name in an angry way.*

BM: The other thing that Ted was angry about that he expressed to me was that how could a woman like me be the head of the Poetry Project—This is unconscionable. It had to be a man. (Anne Waldman and Eileen Myles both had turns as directors of the Poetry Project.)

MH: *But it was Anne Waldman before you.*

BM: I understand everything about this. I'm just telling you what he said.

MH: *Doesn't sound right.*

BM: It was totally crazy.

MH: *Then after you left, Eileen Myles took it over.*

BM: And when Ted died, I got a letter from Ron Padgett saying, "I know what it feels like to have somebody die who's really mad at you." So, apparently, Ted was really mad at me maybe because of the Poetry Project thing or maybe because of the publishing of *The Sonnets* by Lewis. It's hard to know.

MH: *Yes, he was in a bad state, too, taking all those pills.*

BM: And getting angrier and angrier.

PG: I was pretty young when I saw him at a reading and I didn't know who he was and he was heckling someone, and I thought, who let this Hell's Angels guy in here.

BM: (Laughs.)

PG: He was very peculiar.

MH: *And he was very imposing in stature this big man with his beard and long hair.*

BM: He did look like a Hell's Angel. And there is this chapter of the Hell's Angels on 3rd Street between 1st and 2nd Avenues not far from the Poetry Project. I remember all those weird poetry readings I'd go to and there'd be someone heckling and later you then discover that the heckler was an important "Beat" poet. (This is a reference to Gregory Corso heckling Robert Lowell at a Poetry Project reading.)
 Did you interview Alice (Notley) for this whole thing?

MH: *Yes.*

BM: And she didn't say anything about any of this.

MH: *No.*

BM: You didn't ask her?

MH: *No, I didn't ask. I could go back and ask. Maybe I should.*

BM: It might be worth it. I have no idea what her version is.

PHIL GOOD AND BERNADETTE MAYER

MH: Are you still in touch with Alice?

BM: No, I've tried to be but she doesn't respond. She sent us a couple of her books and wrote a few nice words in them, but no real correspondence.

MH: Do you like her poetry?

BM: Sure, yes.

MH: Does she like your poetry?

BM: I assume.

MH: Did you like Ted's poetry?

BM: You know, when I read Ted's collected poems it was like torture for me because I kept feeling as I got through the book—angry Ted, angrier Ted. It was hard for me to not realize that and I was horrified, but unfortunately, I knew that part of Ted was the drug addicted Ted.

MH: *Yes, the Pepsi and the pills. I almost always never saw him standing up, he was always lying on his back.*

BM: He had a bad back.

MH: *I love his Sonnets. Did his Sonnets influence you, the idea of doing a book of sonnets?*

BM: I thought it was a great idea that poets should write sonnets. But yes! Did you ever write a sonnet?

MH: *One or two. I'm a very slow writer of poetry. I'm lucky to get three poems a year.*

BM: Laughs.

MH: *I write mostly articles, essays, and reviews.*

BM: Why do you think you write poetry so slowly?

MH: *I don't know. I don't give myself poetry assignments, or try to write a poem a day. They only come to me naturally meditatively as part of a slow process of working out an idea. I recently got a poem out of trying to cancel my Hulu subscription in my frustration of not being able to reach anyone by email or phone so I had to get a new credit card so that they couldn't keep charging me. Poems come to me out of left field.*

BM: I like how you said "come to me out of left field."

MH: *Getting back to Saint Mark's. Bob Holman told me that you and he started at the same time running the Poetry Project. What was that like?*

BM: It was fun working with Bob.

MH: *How did you split up the work that had to be done?*

PG: Didn't you tell me (speaking to Bernadette) that Allen Ginsberg made fun of you two?

BM: Oh yeah, Allen (Ginsberg) came into the office one day and we're all busy working at our desks and he said, "What are you guys doing here! All you have to do is run a reading series what's the big deal!" (Bernadette laughs)

PG: You (to Bernadette) did the Wednesday night program.

BM: Yes, the Wednesday night that was the feature reading.

PG: And what did Bob (Holman) do?

BM: The Monday night open readings.

MH: *Those Wednesday feature readings were great, as I remember.*

BM: They were.

MH: *I still remember Jim Carroll's punk performance poetry reading, and Philip Whalen reading in his Buddhist monk's robe, and Robert Creeley. All these great poets from all over the country and usually it was a packed audience. You would see people in the audience like Rudy Burckhardt and Alex Katz, photographers, painters, other artists.*

BM: Jackson Mac Low would always sit in the front row and he would write in his notebook all throughout the reading, and there were people in the audience who thought he was being rude. So, I had to explain to them that writing during a reading is the highest form of praise and not rude at all.

MH: *Rudeness would be sitting in the front row eating a submarine sandwich.*

BH: (laughs) Yeah, right!

PG: Jim Brodey was another heckler in the audience. But Bob (Holman) was considered "Co-Director."

BM: I don't remember what his title was.

MH: *You guys had titles!*

BM: It was for the board that we had these titles.

MH: *Bob mentioned the board and the election to the board. That was a funny story Bob told me, poets electing board members.*

BM: (laughs)

MH: *How important was the audience reaction?*

BM: I didn't notice the audience reaction as much as I noticed the reading itself. I was always really impressed when I heard John Ashbery read for the first time before I was director. He just had this piece of paper and he kept his head down and read from it, and I thought to myself, well, if Ashbery can do that I can do it, too. He was so great. But the readings themselves were fascinating to watch.

MH: *You learn a lot. Were there poets that you regretted having there read?*

BM: Oh no, I never regretted having any poet, except André Codrescu, who was really rude about his reading because he wanted me to get his check before the other poets read.

MH: *So, he could leave.*

BM: Yeah! And I said "No! I'm not giving you your check."

MH: *Good for you.*

BM: (laughs) I forgot who the other reader was, but why wouldn't he listen to another poet? A very interesting story when I was working at the Poetry Project, we went through a whole thing where a lot of the poets were becoming drug addicted to heroin and there was a guy selling heroin every Wednesday night. We had a little staff meeting about what to do and I said, "I'll do it." And so, I took this guy to lunch.

MH: *This drug dealer!*

BM: Yeah. I said to him, "You have to stop selling heroin to the poets."

MH: *That was brave of you.*

BM: Totally brave because he put his hand on the counter in the luncheonette and he was missing a finger, and I think it was a message to me that if you're going to do something like this to me, he might cut my finger off. It was totally scary, but it worked and he stopped selling heroin at Saint Mark's. Both Tom and Steve Carey had become addicted to heroin and Ted (Berrigan) tried it.

MH: *Whenever I saw Steve Carey ambling down Saint Mark's Place he was always in bad shape.*
Was there a poet or reading that stood out for you that was memorable from all the readings?

PHILIP WHALEN AT ST. MARK'S: BERNADETTE MAYER SEATED BEHIND ON   T

BM: I had two favorite readings and I liked so many. One was when we had Mahmoud Darwish the Palestinian poet read and he was so amazing, and the other was Philip Whalen and I was so amazed by his work that I invited him over to my house for dinner and it was great to have him as a dinner guest.

MH: *I was at that reading and I remember taking his photograph. He seemed like a very jovial kind of man. I remember he signed and dated (April 19, 1983) my copy of his book,* On Bear's Head.

BM: He was. I think he was embarrassed by how much I loved and revered him.
And I loved it when Larry McMurtry read because I wanted to make it possible to have prose writers as part of a poetry series. I must admit that the group of people that listened to the poetry readings was off-putting, I felt to myself often, and to the readers because they were so serious and judgmental, and I've talked to a few readers about that and they found it so, too. We wanted to be a whole bit more possible to make a joke, right?

MH: *What was rewarding about running the Poetry Project?*

BM: It was 9–5 work, but what could be better than working for poetry? You live your entire life for that, and it was all very satisfactory, except for some of the mean people.

MH: *Poetry politics?*

BM: Raising money for the Poetry Project involved some really strange situations with local politicians and them I would never go near again.

MH: *Local city council district politicians?*

BM: Yeah, people would say, well, you know, if you fuck this guy, he'll give you some money. And I would say, Oh my God! Is that really what it is about!

MH: *Unfortunately, there is that side.*

BM: In part, yes, but you don't have to go there. That local district politician's name I won't mention. He should never have been a city councilman.

MH: *Did you have to deal with church people at Saint Mark's?*

BM: I had a great relationship with the Saint Mark's Church Archivist. Remember when the church burned down?

MH: *Yes. (In 1978 the main sanctuary burned and the roof collapsed and many of the original 1799 stained glass windows were destroyed. The church was built on the site of Peter Stuyvesant's farm known as the "Bouwerie," a Dutch word for farm. Peter Stuyvesant is buried in the church's cemetery.)*

BM: Because of the fire and the restoration of the church they had a catwalk scaffold from the Poetry Project office all the way to the other side of the church and in order for me to get to my office, I had to cross over this catwalk. So, I was doing it in the middle of the night one time (working late) and it was tricky about turning on the lights as you really couldn't turn on the lights until you got to the other side. So, I'm thinking to myself, "Oh my God! What am I doing here in the middle of the night alone. I am trying to be careful while walking across the catwalk and I encounter the ghost, the great ghost of Saint Mark's Church!"

MH: *Peter Stuyvesant? Peg Leg Pete? (One of the ghosts at Saint Mark's is supposedly the ghost of Peter Stuyvesant who had one wooden leg, the other ghost is of a woman in a white dress who sits in the sanctuary or stands by the main door.)*

BM: No, no, a woman, it was a woman. And I thought, Wow! How amazing! I wasn't scared. She was a great ghost to encounter.

MH: *I always heard the story of the ghost of Peter Stuyvesant, the first governor of New Amsterdam, who could be heard walking with his peg leg across the floor.*

BM: I know that story. But I walked to the other side and turned on the lights. The ghost was gone. The next day I went to the church archivist who was my friend and she showed me a picture on the cover of the *Daily News* from years before of this same ghost looking exactly the same, and so I thought, "Wow!"

MH: *Did the ghost speak to you?*

BM: No, it made a noise when it appeared but it didn't speak. I wasn't scared; I was honored. I was also friends with the rector (pastor) of Saint Mark's, David Garcia. He took me to McSorley's Ale House on 7th Street. He said that's what you have to do if you live in this neighborhood. I was also friendly with the bookkeeper at Saint Mark's, Linda Frances, who was a painter. I was very honored to have worked there.

MH: *Were there ever any money problems for you at the Poetry Project?*

BM: Oh yeah, big time. I invited Ernesto Cardinal (1925–2020, Nicaraguan Catholic priest who advocated "Liberation Theology," a blend of Christianity and Marxism. Cardinal worked for the Sandinista Government as Minister of Culture in the 1970s and is a major Latin-American poet) to the Church but not to read because he had sent me a letter stating that he needed an invitation letter to come into the United States as an excuse to get through customs as a result of his politics. And so, I figured that this was something I could do for an international poet as the director of the Poetry Project. When he arrived at the church all of his security people were up in the gallery with their guns. It was scary. The next day, at my apartment, the IRS shows up, knocks on my door, "Can we come in?" I said, "No!" I've been in trouble with the IRS ever since, but not anymore. They forgot about me (laughs).

Through the Poetry Project I got paid ten thousand a year and I never filed my taxes. The fee for each reader was $150 which was miniscule, I felt. It should have been five times that. We asked for donations at the door and the suggested donation was $5, but it was whatever anyone could afford. And if you were broke, you got in anyway. For a while, the poet Jim Carroll was working as cleanup, sweeping the floor, putting away chairs, and he would get hold of the donation box and steal the money that was taken at the door and he would steal it all.

MH: *He was addicted to heroin.*

BM: Yes.

MH: *What do you miss about those times?*

BM: What I miss most is being surrounded by poets all the time. You could run into poets just by walking to the corner on a street and you could put together a magazine right then and there by going to all the poets who lived nearby and gathering poems and then you could go to someone's apartment who had a mimeograph machine and run it off the mimeograph. So, I miss that. I don't miss the fact that no one can afford to live there anymore, not poets anyway.

MH: *The gentrification was just beginning then.*

BM: Yes.

MH: *Do you think that you having been in your position as Poetry Director of the Poetry Project, that that helped in your development as a poet?*

BM: I don't know.

PG: I think that you had already written a lot before you were director (1980–84).

BM: But getting to know all these poets up close definitely helped. And more like my attitude to the world of poetry was developed at that time. And I was so glad that all these poets were in the same neighborhood, and that I could have access to them, and there'd be all these little dramas and intrigues of all the poets' personal lives.

MH: *Who are some of the poets you miss?*

BM: Well, living up here I miss pretty much everybody.

MH: *Up here, in the woods on a lake, it's quiet and peaceful and it's as far as you can get from the city.*

BM: As you get older, it gets hard to live in the city. I found it impossible after my stroke. And I wanted to be in a place where I could grow things and have a garden and see trees. But now we have this problem with ticks.

PG: Lyme Disease. We've both had it.

MH: *Really, both of you!*

BM: Oh God yes.

PG: Poets will visit from the city. Cliff Fyman comes up sometimes.

BM: Cliff comes in the winter, but most visit in the summer.

PG: They're all afraid of the winter up here. It's like Siberia (Phil and Bernadette laugh). I was working on the firewood pile today with the chainsaw.

MH: *How did the two of you meet?*

PG: I went to the School of Visual Arts in Manhattan to take journalism and Bernadette came there to give a reading with Lewis Warsh (ex-husband). And I had already gone to these poetry workshops before at SVA and I sort of knew Bernadette already and she gave me the old mimeograph machine and Bernadette got me an assistant's job to go to Naropa University in Boulder, Colorado. (Founded in 1974 by Tibetan Buddhist Chogyam Trumpa as the first Buddhist-inspired academic institution to receive regional accreditation, Trumpa asked Allen Ginsberg, Anne Waldman, Diane di Prima and John Cage to start a poetics department and they came up with the name—The Jack Kerouac School of Disembodied Poetics.)

MH: *Is Naropa still running?*

BM: Yes, we've both taught there.

MH: *Ok, so that is how your two worlds came together.*

PG: I was trying to make a profession out of journalism to support my poetry and I got that idea from Ed Sanders (who championed the idea of "investigative poetry") whom I met through Bernadette at the Poetry Project. Ed would give those great performances. But when Bernadette had her stroke, we had to get out of the city. I gave up my job as a journalist. I'm a blue-collar guy and I'm still trying to write poetry.

MH: *You've both had successes as poets and you're experimental in how you approach poetry.*

BM: Yes, but there's no money (laughs)!

PG: You have to win the big awards and prizes to get any money.

MH: *Bernadette, if you could go back in time to the Poetry Project is there anything you would change?*

BM: Quite a bit about the Poetry Project itself, especially the "two-year rule." I would definitely change that—the rule was that a poet could only read once every two years because there were too many readers. When I was director, someone said to me, "We can't have white male Jewish readers anymore."

MH: *Allen Ginsberg!*

BM: (both Phil and Bernadette laughing) That person was so stupid to say that. The other thing I would change is to make it affordable to live in that neighborhood, but how I don't know. Bob (Holman) at his Bowery Poetry Club once proposed buying a hotel and running it for the poets so that they could stay inexpensively like in a residence for writers. I would also increase honorariums.

MH: *What do you miss?*

BM: One thing I miss living in the East Village back then was the shopping. There were all these little shops and stores, it was like France. And with your backpack you could peruse dozens of shops within a couple of blocks and buy fish in one, meat in another, bread in another, and fruit and vegetables in still another. There was this one place on 8th Street we used to call the "Fruit and Vegetable Museum" because their produce was so perfect and unblemished but pricey. There was a "Thursday" store only open on Thursday where you could buy eggs and they had apples and some other items all supplied from a farm upstate. And there were so many great inexpensive restaurants, bars, and cafés. I miss them all.

MH: *I was reminiscing with Bob (Holman) about the Ukrainian bar we all used to go to.*

BM: The Sly Fox—it's still there I believe on Second Avenue inside the National Ukrainian Home.

MH: *That's the one!*

Interview with W.S. Merwin

It was John Ashbery who told me that I should interview W. S. Merwin. Ashbery thought Merwin was an important poet even though he wasn't part of the "New York School." But New York was important to Merwin, and he lived in the city and taught at different colleges in the city and gave poetry readings uptown and downtown. At the time of my interview he was lecturing at Cooper Union, and like Ashbery, he won most of the major poetry awards and honors.

He was very fond of Ted Berrigan, which surprised me, and I was surprised by how Merwin was affected by the news of Berrigan's death in 1983, which he wrote to me in a letter.

It was with his fifth book published in 1967, *The Lice*, very much an anti-Vietnam War book, that helped me to understand how very close to nature Merwin was as a poet, and how in *The Lice* he was mourning the passing of that animal world of fellow spirits. He was raised as a Presbyterian; his father was a minister, but he had been a practicing Buddhist for many years.

On December 14, 1982, he invited me to come see him at his top floor apartment, 27 Waverly Place, in a triangle-shaped pre-war building on 7th Avenue near Saint Vincent's Hospital. After the interview he took me up to the roof to show me the view in what I liked to think of as the "groin" of the city with all the avenues funneling into the narrow part of Lower Manhattan. I took some photographs of him while we were on his roof.

I had recently been to hear him read from his new book, *The Opening of the Hand*, and I was moved by a poem he had written for his father titled "Yesterday." It's a father-son poem that gets to the heart of what it means to love and not want to be with someone you love at the same time. His reading helped me appreciate the run-ons and enjambed nuances of his fluid punctuation-less style. The only other poet to convert me like that after hearing him read his own work was Robert Creeley.

The shades were drawn and the room was semi-dark, and Bill, as he liked to be called, sat in a large over-stuffed chair in the corner by the window near a grand piano. On top of the piano were piles of letters unopened and stacks of manila envelopes a couple of feet high. He saw me staring and said, "Those are all unanswered letters and correspondence from poetry editors and magazines." Unlike some other major poets, he didn't have a personal secretary and he did all his own correspondence.

W.S. MERWIN ON HIS ROOF

227 Waverly Place
New York, NY 10014
Oct. 5, 1982

Dear Mark Hillringhouse,

    Sorry to be so long getting back to you. I appreciate more than you would believe your discretion with that number, and beg you to throw it away. On the other hand, I think an interview is a fine idea, and would be happy to meet again. Fridays are generally good days, if they're any good for you. I teach Friday morning at The Cooper Union, until 12:30, and am free after that. Maybe we could meet at my office there; leave a message with the secretary of the Humanities Department if that would suit you.
    We're going down to Ocean Grove again, too, before the weather turns, we hope.
    I'll look forward to hearing from you: a note here, or a message at The Cooper Union. If Friday's no good, another afternoon could be arranged. I hope you have a good time down at the Quaker Inn - we certainly did.

                Best,

William Merwin

I love the idea of the Williams Center and would be delighted to read there.

W.S. MERWIN TO MARK HILLRINGHOUSE

MH: *Who were the poets you were discovering as you were growing up?*

WM: The first poets that I really read with pleasure were Shakespeare, Milton, Shelley, and Keats. I was fourteen. The first writer to really turn me on was Conrad. The first modern poet I read was Lorca. From there I jumped into Pound and from there into the rest of the twentieth century. The first modern poets I read were all involved with translation, perhaps because my favorite teacher in high school was a Spanish teacher. Wonderful man. As a result, I fell in love with Spanish. I continued Spanish when I went to college. While I was there, I went to visit Pound, who suggested that I translate Spanish ballads, since I was very young and had no subject for my own poetry. He urged me to work every day.

MH: *It probably helped you with the techniques of writing;* A Mask for Janus *employs very strict forms.*

WM: It's probably stricter than it need be. I was very aware then of poetry being a matter of tensions in the language, and that seemed to me to have to do with the forms. I think there's an unhappy situation now on the part of students who have started to write, and who have very little acquaintance with the forms of poetry.

If you read the "Waste Land" and listen to it, you really think Eliot is writing in iambic pentameter, but there's not a single line of iambic pentameter in it. The ear is playing against a form that it hears in the background. Once you no longer hear any form in the background there's nothing to play against.

MH: *Why do you suppose that so many young poets are ashamed of writing poetry with rhyme and meter?*

WM: It's a matter of fashion. They've been shamed out of it by everybody from Pound and Williams down to Bly. Rhyme is not native to English and I don't think that rhyme is necessarily germane to the writing of good poetry. But in itself, it's neither good nor bad. There are a lot of wonderfully rhymed poems in English and possibly there will be again. Bob Dylan wrote some wonderful rhymed lyrics.

James Merrill uses rhyme with great mastery and effect, as though it were natural.

MH: Would you say that American Poetry may be broadly characterized by its movement away from French and English symbolism to the objectivism of Williams, Zukofsky, Olson, and Creeley?

WM: I really don't know. I've never been much interested in literary history. I also think that one tends to describe causes in terms of effects and vice-versa. I don't know whether it was moving in that direction anyway, and the development of that movement was the form it took, or whether it was really those poets who moved it. I think the real independence came in getting away from the poetry of Britain. I don't mean contemporary British poetry. It was the poetry of the Georgians and the belletristic bellowings of that period that were deadening. Yeats is not the enemy.

But since the '50s, the influence of England just hasn't existed. One reads a certain amount of contemporary English poetry now but not very much. Oddly enough, the South American poets have been heavily influenced by Whitman. I think there are a great many poets of my generation who have learned from him secondhand. I read Whitman, but I don't think I write necessarily from the Whitman tradition, as Allen Ginsberg does or as Williams did.

MH: Critics have labeled you a neo-classical writer, based on your first three books.

WM: Well, those are big words and wonderfully vague. It's like saying "Surrealism" about somebody's poetry once you begin to have difficulties with its metaphors.

MH: You've been labeled a surrealist, too. Critics even call you an ultra-surrealist and have compared you to a poet like Phillip Lamantia. Of course, Breton thought that he was the only true American surrealist.

WM: At least Breton tried to define what surrealism was. Many people who use the term have no idea what it means or where it comes from.

MH: But why did you write so many of the classical forms?

WM: I was trying to learn how to write. The strongest influence, at the beginning, was really medieval poetry. I felt I had to begin at the beginning, so I read the troubadours. The two poets whom I really fell in love with were Francois Villon and Dante. They were the reason I stuck with the Romance Languages, and both of them believe in form not being a hindrance but a great help. Baudelaire, who was also accused of being neo-classical, said that if you find the forms of poetry are consistently getting in your way, you're probably not a poet. What those forms are is something each poet has to find out, by reading, writing, listening. And that's true whether you're an Olsonite or whatever you conceive the forms of poetry to be.

I've come to be conscious of a tension in language itself, something without which you don't have poetry. Poetry happens at some point between two poles. The one is music, formality; and the other is conversation, spontaneous formlessness. We speak more or less in sentences and we derive what we know about grammar from the way we speak rather than the other way around. And anybody's writing moves back and forth between those two poles.

You will also have people who will tell you you should be all the way over at one pole or the other, but you can't stay in such a place. You can't let go of the other pole. If you do, you have tension and no poetry. I think Williams was a very formal poet and the best formal poems, such as Villon's, are extraordinarily free. You have a feeling that they happen quite naturally.

The formality of music and the randomness of speech: the one is always playing against the other. You can take any line of Alexander Pope or any line of Williams, and you can hear both poles. One thing that's happening among students, at least the ones I've talked to around the country is that the sense of what a line of poetry is has become very dim. There are students writing poetry without any sense of why they end the line where they do. I don't think it can stay that way very long. I think gifted poets are going to get unhappy with that situation and start doing something else. Maybe they'll get more formal, or more lyrical.

MH: *At Princeton you had the opportunity to study with John Berryman, what did you learn from him?*

WM: He was very rude about the poems that I wrote and that was probably a big help. I was a senior. I don't even know whether it was a course; I can't remember. But I know I used to go up to him regularly with poems and he would be very caustic about them but he would also be very instructive. He and R.P. Blackmur were the two real teachers.

MH: As a young poet in the '50s starting out, what did you imagine you'd be writing at the height of your career?

WM: Can anybody imagine things like that? It was inconceivable, it still is. I think that I thought I was going to write plays. I did write plays and the delusion took me to England and back to Boston on a play writing grant. I was very stage-struck back then. My feelings about the theatre in the '50s were very different from what they are now.

MH: How would you characterize the author of A Mask for Janus?

WM: That's a hard question. Well, he was younger. But I'm not even sure if that's true. I began to think, that after I turned thirty and began to get older, that I was getting younger. The oldest part of my life was when I was in my twenties. I was serious about more things than necessary. The world of the university then was an old man's world, and its gestures, tones, and mannerisms were old men's gestures. It seemed that you couldn't know anything until your hair was gray.

I can remember R. P. Blackmur saying, "Don't worry about getting more degrees." I think he said that because he had not lived freely as he wanted to. He felt tied up and trapped by the university. He thought the important thing was to get out.

MH: You've certainly avoided that trap.

WM: I never wanted to live in the university setting. I like visiting universities because I like talking to students. This year I've been teaching one course over at Cooper Union and I like that a lot. It's no great distance and I don't have to be involved with academic politics or administrative duties. And one wonderful thing about teaching there is that the students are not lit. students. They're from other disciplines, such as architecture and engineering, and they've taken an elective course in poetry. They've made an assumption that poetry is something worth paying attention to.

MH: Going back to your early books, why are there so many dark and moribund images?

WM: Are there? Pasternak said, "That's what art is: making life out of death." Around the time I turned forty, I noticed to my surprise, that a lot of things that seemed to be disparate interests that I had for years, all of a sudden were part of the same thing; they all came together. And when I look back at those early poems, and remember the person who wrote them, I realize that it was harder then to make connections between my immediate feelings and the forms of writing. Writing seemed to be at a certain distance from my immediate experience. It always is, of course. I think the idea that writing is an immediate experience is one of the great romantic delusions. And one goes from year to year trying to bring those two things closer together; finding ways of doing it. The idea that you do it by just being "spontaneous" when you're seventeen, doesn't happen. Any more than a dancer can do that by being "spontaneous" at seventeen.

MH: But you didn't really answer my question. I can give you an example of one of your early somber images from the poem "Carol" in A Mask for Janus, *that goes, "And white sheep lying like tombs?" There are plenty more like it, "And, when will darkness bury me" from the poem "Heron" out of the same book. Your first three books are saturated with death and darkness.*

WM: Well, I was very young. The young are obsessed with the idea of death.

MH: According to Robert Pinsky in The Situation of Poetry, *your true subject is the nature of loneliness or separation, the lonely burden of consciousness.*

WM: I think it's fair enough. I think that's why we speak, isn't it?

MH: Out of loneliness?

WM: Well, out of a perception that our own consciousness which is singular, is something that we want at the same time to share with somebody else. The paradox is in the impulse itself. The language with which we speak and articulate our own solitary and unique experience, is something that is conveyed for general use by making it public and part of the language, which belongs to everyone.

MH: *Pinsky goes on to say that your poetic process is romantic, your way of getting there dreamlike, involving silence, extreme romanticism, pursuit of darkness, pursuit of silence.*

WM: I don't know what the definition of romanticism is on which that's based. Silence, I think, underlies every real perception. It involves articulation. And I don't think I pursue darkness; darkness in the twentieth century involves only keeping your eyes open. I really think poetry is involved with being awake. I don't think that contradicts what I take as fact, that what we're awake in is a dream. So, if you're talking about poetry having to deal with dreams in that sense, I absolutely agree.

MH: *Your background is Presbyterian; your father was a minister. How did this influence you?*

WM: One happy way was growing up hearing the King James version of the Bible. I knew parts of it very well. That's something I'm grateful for. Then, of course, there was the whole puritanical guilt-ridden Protestant world which my father came out of and which was very oppressive. His mother was a very severe literal-minded fundamentalist Methodist, to whom even Presbyterianism was suspect.

MH: *How did they react to you, their son, the poet?*

WM: It was very baffling for them. They didn't know what to make of it. My mother wanted me to be a professor. She couldn't understand that I could shrug off such an opportunity.

MH: *But you won the* Yale Younger Poets Award *when you were twenty-four. They must have been elated at the news.*

WM: I suppose. But they didn't know where to fit it into their scheme of things, then. They did later on. They lived long enough to be very pleased by the books, and attention, and proud of them. My father would have been very happy had I gone into the ministry. He was unhappy that I abandoned the Christian church, but he never tried to force or impose his will on me.

MH: *Have you lost those beliefs, or did you ever have them?*

WM: Oh yes. I left. First, I rejected Christianity for myself, when I was in college, and groped my way back toward it many years later with no success. The form of Christianity that most attracted me after I grew up, was Greek Orthodoxy. I liked very much the fact that it had a living contemplative tradition. But I couldn't have stayed very long with it, partly because of the role of women, the attitude toward them altogether, in the Greek Orthodox Church.

MH: *What about Christian mysticism: Jacob Boehme, Saint John of The Cross, Meister Eckhardt?*

WM: Oh yes, they're very attractive, but then Eckhardt was excommunicated. The theology for which the divine is the altogether "other" is something that I can't quite take.

MH: *Now you're a Buddhist?*

WM: I am? What's a Buddhist? Was the Buddha a Buddhist?

MH: *I also read that you wrote hymns for your father.*

WM: I was five years old. I illustrated them, too. I remember drawing Jesus standing in a boat out in the middle of a lake. He was actually preaching on the shore.

An influence I'm most grateful for comes from the power of the language of the King James Bible. The new translations may transmit a series of intellectual concepts that are closer to the original, but something essential is lost. Which includes a recognition of the role of the language itself in the experience it embodies.

MH: *You do employ a lot of religious motifs in your early work, and some you've never let go of; you've carried them with you. How would you explain that?*

WM: I wouldn't. But no doubt I was still trying to incorporate those metaphors which were still very much with me, and trying to find out if I could make them embody experiences which were my own, or to see how close I could bring them to my own experience, to see whether I could use them.

If I had used Greek Classical Mythology, I think I would have thought it extremely literary and deliberate. I think the same thing would have happened if I had arbitrarily taken something such as a Celtic or Scandinavian Mythology, although I found them both very attractive. I also didn't feel that I had any right to use American Indian material. I was speaking in a European language.

The fact that we are so far from coming to terms with the American past is one of the great psychotic flaws in our culture and in our literature. I don't think that any single one of us can resolve it. I don't feel, however, that just by deliberately using American Indian Mythology we're any less literary than if we used Greek Mythology. But we should never acquiesce to feeling that that distance is OK, and become indifferent to it. The distance is part of what we are—that unknown thing.

I just remember talking with someone last week about the "final solution" of the Jews in Europe and what a nightmare that was. And with reference to that I was saying that one of the reasons why the Vietnam War still seems so baffling is because it's part of a process that we won't acknowledge our role in, which is, the destruction of native peoples. It began with the English and the Spanish in the New World, and it's still going on.

MH: *How did you get a job tutoring Robert Graves' son?*

WM: I had been tutoring in Portugal after I got out of college and had gone traveling that summer on my vacation, so I went straight to Majorca because I wanted to see him. While I was there, the person who was supposed to be tutoring Graves' son William, wrote and said he couldn't come. So, Graves said "Would you like the job?" I said, "Sure."

MH: *Did Graves look at your poems and give you advice?*

WM: Yes. I was working on *A Mask for Janus*; it was about half finished, but I wrote a bunch of it there that winter.

MH: *That must have been a strong influence.*

WM: Stronger, I guess, than I realized at the time. I was consciously resisting it but I think it probably influenced me even so. I worked on one of the appendices for *The White Goddess* that Graves was editing. That's what I was doing there when the letter arrived from the tutor.

MH: What was Graves like?

WM: Very imposing. Nobody I have ever known was remotely like him. Immense energy. I haven't gotten around to writing about Graves yet. Maybe I'll do that one of these days.

MH: *How do you come up with a subject: I'm wondering if it is more visual or aural?*

WM: I think it's both. Gerald Stern and I were talking lately about this phenomenon of hearing things in language when you didn't have any words for them. Hearing sounds, like that, has always been a source. I think a poem begins in sounds, in words; it doesn't begin in ideas. It can begin with a subject, but I think that's risky. Usually, for me, it begins with the sound, a rhythm, or a sense of something, then suddenly the subject appears in it like a whale surfacing.

MH: *This is from "On Open Form," an essay in the anthology* Naked Poetry, *by Berg & Mezey: "Merwin believes poetry regularly reverts to its naked condition where it touches on all that is unrealized ... In his own poems, Merwin is trying to achieve something that would be like an echo, except that is repeating no sound."*

WM: When it's described in that way it sounds very calculating and abstract. I think that the basic activity for me in poetry, and I feel it's probably the one activity in everyone's poetry, is listening. What it is you're listening for is exactly what you're finding out. Listening to the sounds of words which are related to a kind of experience, which are experience in themselves; and the resonance of the words has an excitement which one recognizes.

Everything in words is, to some degree, "about" something, and everything in words to some degree "is" something. But one of the things about poetry, more than in any other form of writing, is that it's the use of language that characteristically "is" something. That outweighs the aspect of it that is "about" something. That's what makes it a primary use of language rather than a secondary use of language. The more a poem seems complete in itself, the more it becomes closer and intimate and yet finally elusive. I'm really convinced that the kind of poem I want to write is not a matter of pursuing darkness. The thing behind all the poems that I care about, mine or those that anyone else has written, is the part of them that doesn't know. Poems arrive out of not knowing. You use everything you know to write a poem, but the poem itself comes out of what you don't know.

Interview with Howard Moss

I wrote a letter to Howard Moss at *The New Yorker* and got a letter in reply a week later. Even though I didn't think of him as part of the "New York School," he was, in his position as poetry editor of *The New Yorker* for nearly forty years, at the very epicenter of the New York literary world. And he was influential in publishing poets like Schuyler's first book, and publishing poems by many of the poets of the New York School.

He lived in an old brownstone on 10th Street in the West Village. An ancient wisteria vine covered the outside front all the way to his third floor. His apartment had a wooden deck out back overlooking a garden courtyard below. His living room was floor to ceiling books. During the interview, the phone often rang and it would be Mark Strand or May Swenson, or any number of "New Yorker" poets.

I met him once at his office and I couldn't believe how tiny it was. There was a small desk against one wall and three walls of over-filled bookcases. Moss introduced me to Chuck McGrath who was taking over as fiction editor. He mentioned an embarrassing moment when Editor-in-Chief, William Shawn, was introducing Czech novelist Milan Kundera to the staff at *The New Yorker* and Moss didn't know who he was. And he told me that Shawn once submitted a poem to him and he had to reject it.

He invited me to his summer home in East Hampton a couple of times where I continued the interview. A baby grand piano dominated the front of the living room. On the wall was a framed broadside of an Elizabeth Bishop poem. His house was set back from the road in the pines. He mentioned that Edward Albee lived next door. I took his photograph and made him cross his arms and lean back into the wood siding of his house. He looked natural that way, relaxed and free from the daily annoyances and interruptions at *The New Yorker*.

One time, Moss invited me to attend a LAMBDA meeting at McFeely's Tavern at 11th Avenue and 23rd Street. I may have been the only straight person there. After the meeting the assembled

23 March 1982

Mr. Mark Hillringhouse
100 Prospect Avenue
Hackensack, N.J. 07601

Dear Mr. Hillringhouse,

Thanks for your letter. I would consent to being interviewed for the book you have in mind, though I wonder if my work as a poet fits in with the poets you mention. I *am* a New York poet but not certainly of any school, and what I would least like is to be discussed as a critic and editor in a book discussing other people's poems.

Actually, I think it would be interesting if *some*one cut across the phoney divisions, the little crammed pigeon holes poets are shoved into. When I was collecting material for "New York: Poems," I found poets of very different stripes who had a feeling for the city that others, maybe equally good, just didn't have. The poets who *did* were as diverse as O'Hara, Lorca, Kees, Schuyler, and Blackburn.

It is too bad about Schuyler (to put it mildly) because I think he has one of the truest senses of the city I know.

I thank you, too, for the good things you say about my work in your letter.

Sincerely,

Howard Moss

27 West 10th Street
New York, N.Y. 10011

HOWARD MOSS TO MARK HILLRINGHOUSE

group walked a couple of blocks to the Joyce Theatre on 8th Avenue and 19th Street to see the Feld Ballet. The New York art world, I would realize, had a very strong gay network of men and women from around the city who were very influential.

My favorite poems of his are in the collection *Buried City*. Moss in his later work became less formal and more open to free verse, but his gift as a poet was his way of transforming personal moments of his life without being confessional into meditations on love and loss.

The last time I saw him was when he invited me to hear him read with Mark Strand at the Guggenheim Museum on November 4, 1986. I had a copy of his *New Selected Poems* which had just won the Lenore Marshall-Nation Prize for Poetry which he signed for me. He had also just received the Academy of American Poets fellowship for "distinguished poetic achievement." He died the following year in September at age sixty-five.

MH: *What are your opinions on language-centered writing, poems as fields of speech, where the language itself is the focus?*

HM: I think that question should be answered in the same spirit in which Whitman discussed free-love. He said, "Free-love? Is there any other kind?"

In a poem, language is always the focus. For me, there is a relation between language and experience. In fact, one of the great interests of poetry is that very connection. The notion of language as being "non-referential" strikes me as faddish and a dead end. The French, where I think it comes from, are very good at turning writing into nothing and then congratulating themselves on having contributed something to the avant-garde. The connection between language and experience is primal and ancient, but every writer is interested in what language brings to experience on its own, adds to experience, you might say.

Language is in the unique position of being that medium through which experience is expressed and also of being an experience in itself. That's a far more complex process than pretending that it's "non-referential." What language brings to a poem only happens in the actual process of writing the poem, where the words and phrases bring up new associations, new possibilities. So that it's im-

HOWARD MOSS

possible for me to think of any poem that isn't language-centered. It's a bad term.

Actually, what I think you're describing happened in painting first, and in music, too. I think a better way of saying it, if I understand it, is that kind of art where the medium itself is the subject, so to speak, rather than being used as a tool for representing something. Connotation, say, in words, as against denotation, the imagination, or whatever you want to call it, as against direct experience.

But terms like that are all vague, and, to me, suspect. You can paint a canvas and explore it as you go along and the canvas may have no relation to anything but itself. I think people may try to do something similar in language, but it's not really possible. It's relevance to anything becomes problematic. The essential point in poetry is its connection between language and experience because there is a connection between experience and words. You can pretend that words don't have meanings, but they have etymologies that drag along their inevitable connections to meanings and history. Of course, you can pretend that language isn't language.

MH: *You mean by not pretending that a word is just a mere proxy for an object?*

HM: Well, it's not only that words are not mere proxies for objects but that they belong to two dissimilar worlds: logic and music. Grammar doesn't stand for an object and music doesn't denote anything. Poetry is always attempting to do the impossible: to turn non-verbal experience into words. What is the point of "language poetry" since poetry is already dealing with an impossible task: to put what cannot be said into words.

Poetry isn't music, but it's musical, and therefore what it's really doing is taking language as meaning and language as music and doing something not ordinarily done—using both for another purpose. Poetry gets at the archaic and real non-verbal substance of the self through words.

MH: *You wrote in an essay that there are three basic types of poetry: the associative, the meditative, and the narrative, and that there are combinations of those. You wrote that Ashbery fits in the meditative-associative category, "As if the 'Deep Image' had found a philosopher." Where do you place yourself?*

HM: I would put myself in a certain associative category but mainly I'm a narrative poet. I'm interested in the story, especially the implied story. That's something different from narrative in that there's no strict beginning or end. Its action is that of a small play. I sometimes see poems as small plays.

MH: *There's a dramatic element.*

HM: A dramatic element, yes, but a sequel of secret dramas.

MH: *You go on to mention in your book of essays,* Whatever Is Moving, *that the narrative form depends much less on the first line.*

HM: Much less than a purely lyric poem, yes. In a narrative poem you have something like the problem of a novel—how to begin? What's the best way to begin a story?

MH: *But your first lines seem very important to the rest of the poem. An example, the opening line from your poem "The Old Poet": 'I have forgotten how the book once read ... ' Or, from your poem "Shorelines": 'Someday I'll wake and hardly think of you ...' These lines are interesting in that they could come right out of the middle of a conversation.*

HM: Well, I think the first line is very important, but because I wrote that essay people think I think it's more important than perhaps I do. I was hoping to write two more essays to go with it, "The Middle Register" and "The Last Word."

MH: *Do you prefer concrete over abstract?*

HM: I prefer the concrete over the abstract. I like the concrete in the sense that I prefer stories that begin, "Sonia crossed the river but she didn't go home" to stories that begin, "The clouds were breaking into a tumult of light."
    Chekhov is the master of this. The miracle of Chekhov is the plainly spoken thing still retaining its lyricism, meaning, and ambiguity. Lesser writers take eight times the space and rarely manage it. In Chekhov, details are concentrated and brief. The moon never shines on and on, it just shines.

MH: *In your poem, "Notes from the Castle" you're describing boredom and contemplating it, turning it into this anxiety of existing. The "Castle" is the "I" of the poem. I think a key line is: 'We knew we were going to be stuck with ourselves ... ' And there are certain details that you might pick up on when you're bored with yourself, such as: ' ... the wind had a touch too much / Of motivation, an annoying way / Of exactly ruffling the same oak leaf / As if it were practicing a piano trill; / All day, repetitive birds, far off, / Were either boring themselves to death / Or drunk on instinct, doing their thing: ... '*

HM: "Notes from the Castle" is a poem that uses the word "castle" both in the most mundane sense of the word, such as, "A man's home is his castle," and the idea of the brain or the mind as a castle, which is Saint Teresa's idea, and one Jean Stafford used in her story, "The Interior Castle."

There is an interior castle and a literal house and a specific plot of land. The mind is sending out messages from where it finds itself. The "I" of the poem is definitely the "Castle," but the word "Notes" is meant to have two meanings—communications from the Castle and musical notes, as if someone were playing a musical instrument.

MH: *It seems though that in these new poems published in 1980, you've moved very far from your earliest books,* The Wound and the Weather *published in 1946, and* Buried City *published in 1975, and, that you have changed a great deal. It also appears that you're getting more political.*

HM: I only printed three poems from *The Wound and the Weather*, my first book, in *Selected Poems*, because I couldn't find others I liked. I was very young when I wrote them—twenty-four. But there was, even in my first book, a sort of political sense.

MH: *Your sixth book,* Second Nature, *published in 1968, is very different.*

HM: *Second Nature* was a big change for me. My first five books were romantic and lyrical. *Second Nature* is where everything changes. Political poems, I believe, should be kept within the bounds of the truly experienced. I'm afraid of falseness if I speak of things that I don't know. I can't speak for migrant farm workers, but I can support them. If I wrote about them, I'd be embarrassed at my ignorance.

MH: But in a poem, you can be strident in tone, or bellicose, and let out anger. A number of your poems in Buried City, "Cold Water Flats" or "Memories of Lower Fifth," for example, have this anger over seeing New York change.

HM: It wasn't only seeing New York change; it was seeing New York wrecked. There's quite a difference. When you see very good buildings torn down just out of greed ... when I think of Pennsylvania Station, then look at what replaced it ... that whole area has been destroyed.

MH: A line from "Memories of Lower Fifth" goes, 'I loved them once, those towering hotels / On Lower Fifth, where I imagined lives / Far richer than those lives turned out to be ... ' Are the experiences real in "Cold Water Flats"?

HM: They're real and transformed, like everything in poetry. I've been in so many cold-water flats, and knew someone who was holed up in one for a long time and afraid to come down. But the experience of the flat was a composite of many experiences and looking out of windows. The title is a play on words in any case because it goes to Cape Cod and then switches to music—the word "flats" is tying this section together—apartments, tidal bays, musical signatures.

MH: It's a wonderful description of the life imagined or experienced vicariously.

HM: It's not quite imagined or experienced. It's observed, then reimagined.

MH: (quoting the poem) ' Two windows always face a tiny square / Of neon signs and grass ... / And downstairs somebody is always home ... '
    That's a curious detail.

HM: It's true in tenements. There's privacy in the sense that you can be completely isolated and lonely at the top, in your own apartment, but there's always somebody in the house downstairs. At least, that's true of the Italian section of Greenwich Village.

MH: I'm moving chronologically now. The early work in The Wound and the Weather, seems so precocious written at a very young age.

HM: My first book has so many poems in it that seem to be a combination of Auden and Stevens. It had never occurred to me consciously that anyone could bring them together. But I think in an innocent and naïve, stumbling way since they were the two poets who were enormous influences on me, I sort of amalgamated them.

The thing about my poems, if I may say so, is that I studied music seriously as a child—the piano and theory, all the way up to four-part harmony and the beginning of counterpoint. And my poems, from my point of view, were always like music, like musical compositions. And so, when you asked me that first question about language and experience, I would say that writing my poems is more like the composition of music, or a substitute for it. It's as if I were writing a sonata in words. It was heard in the ear first. Many of my poems, particularly the early ones, were matters of sound.

MH: In keeping with the sound of your poems, your poem "September Elegy" from your fifth book, Finding Them Lost, there's a beautiful mix of sounds in the play of "s" and "d" in the opening stanza:

> The dead undo our sleep so they can rest.
>   Their August vanishes: the beachy dreams
> Of sea grass, naked limbs, the stuttering wave ...
>   Yet contra-indicated bodies move
> On space ... the summer sprays, the water birds
>   Depart, but some things never disappear,

HM: How well you read those lines. I wasn't conscious of the interplay of those sounds, but I think the way the sounds connect the meaning is one of the most important elements of the poem. Anyone who didn't sense that wouldn't hear the whole effect of the poem.

MH: *Kenneth Koch said something interesting to me. He said that he preferred reading quietly because he could read with all different sorts of nuances and inflections and intonations at the same time.*

HM: I read quietly, too. The thing at a reading is to forget about yourself and simply take the poems as a text or a composition or a score and try to play it. I don't like dramatic readings.

MH: *Do you like to give readings?*

HM: I do, yes. Unless something goes wrong. Not enough light, no lectern, no microphone—it happens all too often.

MH: *Richard Howard writes, "It is the experience language encloses not the language that encloses experience that Moss is after."*

HM: The distinction is a muddy one to me. I'm after both. I read a lot of poems that aren't "language centered."

MH: *An example?*

HM: Computer instructions aren't language centered, or scientific texts. But the idea of a poem not being centered in language is the same as saying music isn't centered in sound. I think something else is happening. Painting has become a significant part of poetry in the last thirty years. So, a lot of poets who are painter-oriented are not necessarily musical. Though it so happens that someone like Ashbery is both, luckily. But that is what distinguishes Ashbery from a lot of other painter-poets who are not musical so they never really become poets.

MH: *Can you give me an example?*

HM: Let me try to give you an example.

MH: *I was going to say painters who wrote poetry—Marsden Hartley.*

HM: Marsden Hartley is a different case. I don't mean painters who write poetry. I mean poets influenced by painting. The New York School, for instance: O'Hara, Ashbery, Koch, and Schuyler.

Schuyler is musical in a special way I try to explain in my essay "Whatever Is Moving." I think Schuyler is also an extraordinary prose writer. I love that novel, *What's for Dinner*. I think it's a marvelous piece of work. Schuyler is so ... well, there's no one like him because it's very straight writing and yet it so transcends itself all the time. No one else quite has that peculiar talent of sounding like a diary and yet not losing the effects of lyric poetry.

MH: *When I read your essay on Schuyler, I said to myself, "Howard Moss almost seems to envy his style of writing."*

HM: If I envy anything, it's his ability to pull disparate things together, to unify.

MH: *Feats of association.*

HM: Exactly. To keep that long poem going, "The Morning of the Poem," is a sort of miracle because there's nothing much to it except that everything has happened. Very few people can take (so many try) their own lives, and make such good work out of them. Mostly, they write dreary or terrible journals or grocery lists or junk. But Schuyler has managed to transcend the fact and not lie, and that's why there's something very childlike about him and very wise.

MH: *O'Hara had that quality, too.*

HM: Yes, I think Schuyler has more of a connection to O'Hara than Ashbery does. Ashbery is much more philosophical and European and big. I think in Ashbery you get the night thoughts of a truly original imagination.

MH: *In thinking about O'Hara and Schuyler, they seem to be the most "New York" of the "New York School" poets.*

HM: I am not part of that "School," but New York is one of my natural subjects. And, it seems to be a natural subject to certain poets such as Weldon Kees and Paul Blackburn, for example, and not to others, even though they may write about it.

I grew up in New York. I was born in Manhattan and grew up in Rockaway Beach. My family lived three houses from the ocean and my life was very much a city and an ocean life. This is very hard to explain to other people, that I grew up on the ocean but lived in New York City.

MH: *Your poetry tends to meditate on the nature of things. In your poem, "Venice" from your second book,* The Toy Fair, *published in 1954, there's a fear of beauty, of what is in reality, the absolute. When you deal with those topics, they are usually poems of place.*

HM: Going to a place that is different makes you more aware. "Place," my sense of it, would be just the opposite of the way I think Eudora Welty uses the word "place," where she means a writer writing out of the "Place" born, bred, known, lived in, etc. A saturation. I mean "place" in the sense of being transported. Elizabeth Bishop wrote about questions of travel. They bring up questions about everything, whether where you were and where you are are really where you should be. Travel opens up possibilities, and possibilities open up poems.

Everything is transformed and yet everything is familiar. Being both ordinary and magical is the whole point.

MH: *Your poetry has a fixation with water and shorelines.*

HM: Because I was brought up near the water. I think one should live near something limitless—the ocean, the desert. To me, the ocean is endlessly exciting, the life in it, and of it, of endless interest. It's always the same and always changing. Strangely, out in East Hampton, I live in the woods. I'm about a mile from the bay and about five miles from the ocean. But I go there for that bigness and endlessness, the secret life of it. I'm hardly the first person to be fascinated by it.

MH: *It's a recurring theme in your work this being at the edge of some absolute using shorelines.*

HM: But also my whole notion of sexual development is connected to the beach, to where I grew up. Everybody is an adolescent someplace. That place is crucial, especially to a writer. It is the place where I had discovered my first sexual desires as a teen. Then, when I discovered poetry, my adolescent experiences that I couldn't express, there they were suddenly, in poems. So, there is that strong visceral connection that drew me to poetry. When I was in high school, I used to read Edna St. Vincent Millay in the library. I fell in love with poetry then, as I loved music; they seemed very close.

But what you mentioned earlier is of great interest to me and that is good nature writing, and nature writing has always fascinated me. I touch on it in the essay I wrote about J. Henri Fabre titled, "The Incomparable Observer." He approached nature with the openness and wonder of a child, which is how I believe one should approach nature. I am impressed by Fabre's obsession with minute detail when it comes to observing natural phenomenon, and how his sense of discovery unites the naturalist and the poet in him. He felt that Darwin's theory of evolution left too many mysteries unexplained. And, I like his writing for the same reason I like emotional honesty in poetry, and for his ability to combine the mysterious in nature with very mundane and factual scientific details.

MH: Many of your poems are one-page rhythm poems, well rhymed, in short stanzas, stanzas of five, six, or seven lines in block form.

HM: I think too many poets, and this may possibly come from reading so many at *The New Yorker*, are long-winded bores. So, I may have compressed too much. I do think that poetry is a matter of compression, but many poets tend to gas on and on. What is well said is well said. I think the point, if you're a writer, is to say something well, and to say it as briefly as possible. When you have something as big to say as Proust and Tolstoy you can afford all the room in the world. But most poets are not writing definitive books on time or on war and peace.

MH: You don't wander all over the page as some do.

HM: I find that a lot of poems wander off in the middle, that the writer is distracted by something, interested in a sudden turning in the road, and never comes back to where he left off. Dylan Thomas used to describe each poem as a universe. And everything in a universe has its place. I agree with him.

MH: *You do some very complex things with juggling words almost sestina-like in your poem, "Magic Affinities."*

HM: Well, "Magic Affinities" uses the same words three times in different sequences and arrangements. Actually, I made up the epigraph because I felt the reader needed to be clued in to the overall idea right from the start. I thought the easiest way was to provide a quote the poem was based on. I made up the epigraph's author, too, naturally. I can't remember what I called him.

MH: *"George Tremplar." Kenneth Koch makes up whole imaginary interviews.*

HM: So does Mr. Borges. Anyway, I had this idea of writing a poem where you could never use any word that hadn't already been used in the section before. But each time it had to sound different and be in a different context.

MH: *Do you like the form of a sonnet or sestina?*

HM: I did write one sestina which I hate. But I did make up a form in a poem called "The Falls of Love," which is like the sestina. The sestina seems to be endlessly flexible. I love Ashbery's sestina about Popeye, or Elizabeth Bishop's "A Miracle for Breakfast." Sometimes, I've written poems like "The Persistence of Song" which, halfway through, start to go backwards line by line.

MH: *I was going to mention the poem "Gravel" as an example of a form that I love. I love the shape and I love the way it changes shape. Your groups of three and four lines or more are very self-contained, in equilibrium with twists that are virtually metaphysical.*

HM: What I like to do are variations on a theme or a subject, to wring as many changes as possible on one thing. Once you get a basic notion that is rich enough to take that kind of treatment, I vary it—"Gravel," for instance, tries to exhaust all the possibilities of one particular notion.

MH: *What was the notion in "Gravel"?*

HM: The notion is something that I usually try to write out in the first line. I think a notion is already inside you and has already been concluded and you simply find it. My poems usually come from a single line which I consider the "given" or the "gift." I get these sometimes when I wake.

MH: *Is it always the first line?*

HM: No. It can sometimes be the last line. It doesn't depend on where it is, but that it's the "given." It often comes when I am in motion, moving, walking, riding in a taxi, a bus, a car. I don't know why but I suspect that after having left my moorings, I'm sort of open to whatever is happening inside.

MH: *That's curious—motion as meditation. Everything is in motion though.*

HM: The point of motion is that you're freed from the stationary; you're free from what ordinarily preoccupies you, so that you are in a state of receptiveness.

MH: *You mentioned that you get these "givens" when you wake. What importance do you place on dreams?*

HM: I place a great deal of importance on dreams but they haven't been very useful to me. What has been useful is another thing, which may be the ends of dreams; I don't know. Say, waking up in the morning and having a line.
    Titles usually come to me in the daytime. Sometimes it's a misheard word or phrase. I think that things that are misheard, or not in their proper sequence are springboards for notions or ideas.

MH: *In the poem, "At the Masseurs" from* Buried City, *you get into some stream of consciousness.*

HM: I don't really get into stream of consciousness, except maybe by the end. I revise a great deal. In the new paperback edition of

Buried City (1982), which has just come out, the poems "At the Masseurs" and "Buried City" were changed quite a bit. I always keep the poem in some kind of formal connectedness. I often think of poems as movies or plays. I think you start writing and keep watching as you go on writing and revise so everything has relevance to what comes before. I often think of "At the Masseur's" as a kind of script. The revision in the new edition of *Buried City* makes it much clearer because I ended it with a dancer the first time and now I've ended it with a sculptor.

The main idea of the poem is that your body is being sculpted by a masseur. That's why all the Roman statuary enters into it. The poem is meant to bring together the sensual and the sublime.

MH: *I was going to say that you give the reader a poem made up of separate moments. Movies, too, are made from still pictures. And thinking about what you mentioned earlier about movement-meditation, that driving in a car goes by as if it were a film, doesn't it?*

HM: Yes, it does, you're right. If you're in a taxi, say, and the taxi is moving, what you see outside the window is purely random, except for the buildings, but even all of life, everything, is random, and that is useful. Even the randomness of not knowing what street the taxi driver is going to turn down is random. Once the process begins, it is like a film. You don't know how it is going to end.

MH: *Which brings me to a poem you wrote titled "Movies for the Home" from your book* Finding Them Lost.

HM: It's a poem about time, and each stanza ends with the word "are" bringing the poem back to the present. It's a poem based on a car trip I took across the United States. The notion is that, as you go forward in a car, those places that were always in the future on your map suddenly become the present and then close behind you as they become the past. But when you show movies of the trip, the whole process—now in the present—unrolls in a kind of perpetual present. What once had a past, present, and future, is now all in the past yet capable of being revived in the present—which, too, will soon become the past. The process, in short, is endless. It's a poem about memory, really, and it was difficult to do. I don't know if it comes across. I think when I hit on the device of ending each stanza with the word "are," I was a long way to achieving what I was after.

MH: *It has a very strong elegiac tone.*

HM: I think it's a natural mode of English poetry and a natural one for me, but to have everything past and mourned can get tiresome.

MH: *You did mention that the "meditative" form was slightly elegiac.*

HM: I think it is.

MH: *It seems that your next book, your sixth,* Second Nature, *you have gotten away from the short lyrical terse stanza, and that you've internalized more, and there's more prosier parts to your poetry such as in "Drinks with X" and "Ménage à Trois."*

HM: Actually, *Second Nature* was the first dramatic book where there are many more voices, characters, people, monologues, dialogues, and so forth. I had been writing plays and the plays influenced the poetry. I decided that that was what I should start working on—dramatic situations. So that was one of the big changes.

MH: *Another big change is your book of light verse titled* A Swim off the Rocks.

HM: Well, I had been writing them for a period of about thirty years and keeping them out of print because it had been considered such bad form to write light verse. I was not only under a "cloud," being poetry editor of *The New Yorker,* but the idea of writing light verse as well! I thought people would say, "Well, what do you expect from the poetry editor of the *The New Yorker*!"

But I thought the hell with it, this is what I want to do and so I did it. And I thought, "Well, I'm not going to be intimidated by it." So, when my editor, Harry Ford, said, why don't you do a book of light verse, and others said, why don't you put those poems together, I finally thought, "Well, why don't I?" So, I gave them to Harry Ford at lunch one day and that afternoon he called me to say he'd love to publish them. That was the fastest a book of mine has ever been accepted.

MH: *Do you feel that too much of contemporary poetry is overly serious?*

HM: No. That's not the problem. The problem I find with lots of contemporary poetry is that an ordinary incident is presented to the reader and then, at the end of the poem there's a pretension of a mysterious and enigmatic conclusion. No work has been done on them. It's simply as if you were given certain facts and then those facts were meant to have an unearned, enlarged significance. There's an irrelevant summing up—I was sitting at home drinking beer all afternoon, and guess what, I saw an angel fly into the room—there's disparity between the triviality of the poem itself and the great catharsis you're supposed to feel at the end. All it means is lack of strategy, lack of work, lack of thought.

The poet who really knew what a poem is all about was Elizabeth Bishop. There are no non-poems in her work, not one single poem which isn't a poem. And by that I mean if it starts here and goes there it has exhausted its possibilities. Most poems don't. They make stabs at it. Of course, I've seen some marvelous poems. I try to take them as an editor. But I see so many that are botched, that vaguely suggest an intention and there's no real preparation for it.

Imagine a play just before its final curtain. All you've seen so far are a group of people around a table sitting down to have dinner. Then somebody comes out and does the end of *Hamlet*. It might be unintentionally funny but it wouldn't be a play.

MH: *You mentioned that as an editor you try to take marvelous poems, poems that aren't "botched." Do you read all the poems that come into* The New Yorker *at 25 West 43rd Street?*

HM: No. Sometimes, there's a thousand a week when I return in the fall in September to my small office that is barely big enough for a desk. I have a full-time reader, Vicki (Vicki Karp), and she shows me everything addressed to my name, and we go over whether I'm going to read it or if she is, and I'll ask her to give me an opinion on certain ones, or if she finds anything good, and then she reads the whole pile, baskets of anything she finds. But I guess the trouble with that is we're hardly pressed to publish unknown poets since meanwhile all this other stuff is coming in from poets who have signed "First Rejection Rights" contracts with *The New Yorker* who have to have their work rejected before they can send it on somewhere else. These are the poets such as Marvin Bell or Bill Merwin, or Phil Levine, or Tony Hecht, and James Merrill and Joseph Brodsky, or Derek Walcott and Tess Gallagher, and then from England and Australia and Canada. It's a way of guaranteeing that *The New Yorker* gets quality poetry.

I'm sick of reading poems that might as well be prose or sound like jazzed-up shopping lists. You read poems for some kind of excitement of language and a poem that doesn't have that isn't very interesting. I can understand experimenting with language. Williams is very different from Stevens, but they're both of very great interest simply in terms of the language.

I think that poets are afraid to be musical and they're afraid to be grand and afraid to use the resources of language. Melodrama and sentimentality are the enemies, but sometimes feeling goes by the board as well.

Poetry for me is an endless swim. I can't conceive of life without it. It's so much a part of me by now. But sometimes I get terribly sick of it because I read so much bad poetry and I see how people approach poetry by trying to extract things from it that are not there. Then there's the pettiness in the world of poetry, the "ickiness" of people's ambitions. Obviously, there's not enough to go around, and as I say in this review that is coming out in *The New York Review of Books*, there's this kind of scrimmage for reputations. It's really unpleasant, and sad, because the satisfactions in poetry can't be from making money, and they're not doing it for the work. It's a very small pond to have the kind of ambitions many poets have to be sort of movie stars. And I've seen enough of people's bad behavior being poetry editor of *The New Yorker* for thirty-five years. Certain poets treated my heart attack as if it were a personal affront to their literary careers. It was as if I had inconvenienced them by being out sick and their poems weren't getting published.

MH: *You come out of a generation of poets all born in the 1920s who had no idea what the poetry world would turn into—poetry writing workshops at every college, the MFA in Poetry!*

HM: It has sort of saved English Departments from going under, yet English Departments are very hostile to poets. That is, they won't give enough money to the department because they are threatened by poets, yet what they are teaching after all is writing.

When I went to college, professors were teaching the history of ideas in place of teaching the work itself. Literature is writing; it is not history.

The most extraordinary, well-educated people, are people who read for themselves, people like R. P. Blackmur who never graduated college, or Elizabeth Bowen.

When I went to the Iowa Writer's Workshop for a reading and as a guest lecturer, I found some very talented poets. It was an extraordinary class. Here's an example of who was there in my lecture: David St. John, Tess Gallagher, Larry Levis, Michael Ryan. So, people blame the MFA for grinding out mediocre poets and obviously not all those who attend are going to be writers, but some do. But on the other hand, all the people who have Ph.D.'s are not going to be scholars. At least I think if you're teaching a writing class and you know the students are not going to be writers, and you always hope they are, what you can teach is how to read, because most students don't know how to read. Most students in my experience in writing courses haven't read. They are unaware of what is out there. They don't know Wallace Stevens. I taught a class at Barnard in poetry and none of the students in class had heard of "Sunday Morning" and it was Elizabeth Hardwick's class, a prose class. She went on leave and I took it over and made it a poetry course. So, my first assignment was for them to read "Sunday Morning."

MH: *What do you think will happen to the business of poetry?*

HM: In poetry, I don't know. There are too many poets. That sounds like such a snobbish and terrible thing to say, but actually, they all can't be poets. When poetry organizations list thousands of poets as members, it's absurd. Obviously, out of the thousands, only a few have rare talent. The rest are making their own waves. I receive all kinds of magazines as a poetry editor, which are printed using state and federal grants, etc. Sometimes there's wonderful work I come across that I would have never seen otherwise.

Poetry has for most, the immediate satisfaction that you get something down on the page, you send it off to something called

"Milk Can" and it's printed, there's your name, maybe you get a free copy, then you're launched, and then someone does a chapbook and you have twelve poems or eighteen, then you get another little grant, but then there's the bitterness that comes from not getting reviewed.

If you see the list that the American Academy of Poets puts out every year of books of poems published, and people think books of poems aren't being published, they're crazy. They come out in thousands. It's a cottage industry. But the poets you really watch, who are really interesting, I could list them on a single page. They're well-known because they persist and they're good. Take that book titled *The Incognito Lounge* by Denis Johnson, which I like, was a complete surprise to me. You think you see everything but of course that's just another delusion. Brad Leithauser sent me a poem which I'd like to publish and Katha Pollitt who is actually at *The New Yorker*, and Sherod Santos. There are a lot of young poets I admire. I think a poet like Mark Jarman is awfully good and getting better. I think David St. John is sort of in a stasis at the moment, but is a wonderfully gifted young poet. Stanley Plumly is another.

America is extremely rich in gifted poets, and at the same time, there's also thousands of bores, just like there are thousands of actors and thousands of people writing screen plays, and some are very good, but there doesn't seem to be many gifted playwrights.

MH: *Speaking of playwrights, what makes you want to write a play?* The Palace at 4AM *and* The Folding Green *seem to be wonderfully contrasted in your book titled* Two Plays. *The one is comic and the other is tragic. Were they deliberately juxtaposed?*

HM: It was deliberate to publish them together, but I've only written three plays. *Folding Green* was staged in 1958. I remember sitting with Frank O'Hara somewhere in Cambridge over coffee. Frank was involved in the Poets' Theatre. It would be wonderful if there were a "Poets' Theatre" again. It was begun in 1950 and William Carlos Williams and Thorton Wilder were original founding members, as were Edward Gorey and Alison Lurie. It is where Dylan Thomas first read "Under Milk Wood" in 1953. It burned down in 1962. So many great verse plays were staged there—Archibald MacLeish, Samuel Beckett. [side note: the "Poets' Theatre" was resurrected in 1986 until it closed in 2004.]

MH: *What was O'Hara like sitting with him over coffee?*

HM: He was witty and delightful company to be with, but I didn't know him that well. Our paths crossed from time to time in the poetry world.

MH: *Getting back to the plays, and good theater, is there anything like the Poets' Theater in New York which is the theater capital of the world?*

HM: Well, Broadway is hardly the place to see good theater. It's all very regional today. Poets are still writing plays. Ashbery and Koch have written plays. Tess Gallagher has written one.

MH: *What were your influences in writing* The Palace at 4AM?

HM: *The Palace at 4AM* was influenced by Albee's *Tiny Alice* and I dedicate the play to him. *The Palace ...* was first read at the Playwrights Unit Theatre on Vandam Street in 1968 by Ruth Ford, Paul Roebling, and Paul Sparer, and was later staged at the John Drew Theater in East Hampton in 1972 starring Beatrice Straight, Christopher Walken, and Dean Santoro, and directed by Albee.

MH: *In the beginning of that play, you don't know where you are.*

HM: That's the idea. It's really about the jealousy of an older man and a younger man and the destruction of a relationship of two people not being able to flee a certain fate which they themselves are creating. The main idea is taken from Oedipus that there's a sickness in the city, and the play is the purification of that sickness.

MH: *The Folding Green addresses that theme of jealousy between ages, between certain people, but as a farce. There's more humor especially in the Ouija board scenes.*

HM: It needs to be performed by actors who can do it comically, and it's not very dramatic. It would require a very good director. *The Folding Green* was about money. It seems to parody the lives of the rich. I've never seen it performed the way I have imagined it.

MH: *What gave you the idea of the Ouija board, James Merrill?*

HM: No, this was way before Merrill started using the Ouija board for poetry. I got the idea from Jean Stafford for whom the play is dedicated. She always used the Ouija board. I tried it once with James Merrill. This was just to try it. Nothing happened. Merrill has created this wonderful vast structure, if you believe him, by using it to write poetry. *The Folding Green* was written purely tongue-in-cheek.

MH: *There are charming elements to it. Everything is green, the curtains, there's a folding green table.*

HM: I think it's when people lack a real sense of drama, what you fall back on is the motif, so the unity of that play does depend on that "folding green."

There are three plays that I've often thought should be brought together in a book—*Oedipus, Hamlet,* and *The Seagull.* And they each have a relationship of the son with the mother which is somewhat sexual, and in each one the son is destroyed, and the mother is, too. And the mother by implication in *The Seagull,* can't imagine how she's going to live. *The Seagull* is my favorite play. And so, those three plays are from such different eras, yet they have such strong connections to each other.

MH: *Is O'Neil a playwright you like?*

HM: He really isn't. He's someone I admire enormously. *Iceman Cometh* and *Long Day's Journey* are extraordinary plays, but sometimes, there's something embarrassing about the dialogue, but then there's this power.

I like Arthur Miller's *The Crucible* and a little one called *A Memory of Two Mondays.* It came out in two one-acts. There's a British playwright that I like a lot whose name is Edward Bond who wrote a play titled *Saved.* And there are all these British playwrights I like, and the British see theater all over and they see every kind of theater, and English acting is so superior because they're trained classically being from a long tradition. But, in other ways, American actors are marvelous because they're always transcending their material. They're really better than the plays. They really make out of nothing something.

I thought my plays lacked poetry strangely enough and my poems lacked drama, and since I had been working on lyrics for so long, the plays helped me. So, I began to think of creating characters, because it's about creating characters and the geometry of the stage, and the formal excitement of a play that in two hours you have to tell a story which has in itself a beginning, middle, and an end. Dialogue and conversation are completely different. You have to write dialogue as scenes like conversations, and yet, it is going in a direction. So, it's like having a conversation two hours with someone that when the curtain goes up, you know nothing about the characters, and two hours later, someone has either killed himself or someone else. It's time duration and that peculiar problem of how to tell a story using nothing but dialogue. In a way, it has something like the compression of a poem.

I was in group therapy, and the people I encountered in group therapy gave me the idea, and that was the first attempt to bring character to life. I was so used to talking about myself in therapy, and the idea struck me that I could talk about characters in the same way. The idea of character other than oneself was very liberating to me.

I went to the Actor's Studio on West 44th Street and I took a playwrighting class and a lot of good writers were in that class. August Wilson attended. It takes seeing your work on the stage which is so different than seeing it on the page. I was lucky when they first read *The Palace* ... it was Paul Roebling and Ruth Ford who read the play, and Christopher Walken was in it and I had Edward Albee as director. I used to go to the rehearsals then I got bored because the actors are learning their lines and scenes and doing retakes.

MH: Is the writing of a play that different in terms of the struggle to create?

HM: Just giving an existence to characters, you keep thinking about them, like what would they be doing on Monday, the Monday before your play starts, and the play is all plotted out. *Folding Green* I thought I had plotted it out and I had three separate plots, but when it was staged in the Poets' Theatre in Cambridge, it had a different plot.

Elizabeth Bowen has an essay that discusses when you're writing a novel, that the early parts almost invariably have to be recast as you go on as certain things change. In a play, I always found the end much more difficult.

MH: *Some may envision the end first.*

HM: Well, I did, but it was wrong. I have a new play that I have the last act for the ending but very little in-between. Elizabeth Bishop used to have a large board on her wall where she had lines of poetry with gaps in different places and then she filled in as lines came to her.

MH: *Describe your process.*

HM: Mainly, I get a notion or I overhear someone and I write it down.

MH: *In a notepad?*

HM: No. I have a notebook but I don't carry it with me. Bill Merwin, I know, carries a little one with him in his pocket wherever he goes.

MH: *You mentioned knowing Auden. What other famous poets have you met?*

HM: Auden and I never became friends. We had known each other for many years. We were acquaintances but never became intimate. I've met Elizabeth Bishop several times. I met Dylan Thomas when he was in New York to give readings. I met T. S. Eliot once at Frederick Morgan's (founding editor of the *Hudson Review*) house, and Eliot talked about … he had a passion for cigarette lighters, and he had bought a lot of them in New York that day, and it seemed to me he talked mostly about cigarette lighters, which was a great disappointment. That often happens. He was probably shy and embarrassed and there he was, it was all sort of small talk. That's how I remember him.

MH: *You should write a book of your recollections of meeting these great poets.*

HM: I was thinking of that, but I don't think all of my recollections could be told. Sometimes you know too much. For instance, so much has been written about Dylan Thomas' drinking you'd think he was nothing but a drunk. Now, he was a drunk, but he was a thousand other things. He was a fascinating person; I thought him a charming person when I met him, and generous to other poets. He told wonderful Welshman stories and he was never boring to be with. But I'm tired of the impressions one gets. I mean Sylvia Plath did nothing except commit suicide, and Robert Lowell was always very ill.

And I knew Robert Lowell, but we never became friends, I think mainly because Jean Stafford and I were close friends—she was his first wife and they were estranged. I was very fond of Elizabeth Hardwick as well, his second wife. Lowell I don't think liked me particularly and I was never crazy about him. There was a thing he had about *The New Yorker* I believe. I don't know, he always said he was going to send me a poem every time we met and then I stopped asking, as much as I loved his poetry.

Weldon Kees I knew very well. I think he's a wonderful poet. He used to play the piano, wonderful jazz songs he made up which he would play for me and he had a very bass voice, and Weldon was a painter. I think he, speaking of neglected poets, is a marvelous poet, superb, maybe the best poet in a way who wrote about New York.

Randall Jarrell wrote to me occasionally saying he'd send poems, and he'd write to me about Chekhov about whom we were both taken. I knew John Berryman, but not well. I knew Roethke, but only saw him when he came to the city, we'd have lunch. I met Charles Olson once because when his *Call Me Ismael* came out, it was the same year as my first book *The Wound and the Weather* came out in 1946.

Most of the poets I know as friends, we don't talk about each other's poetry, unless it comes up, but it's a great relief if it doesn't.

MH: *How do you get over dry periods?*

HM: Well, they're cyclical, and then suddenly they revive themselves, like love affairs, when you've had a long love affair you lose interest in sex after three years, and then if it's a good love affair, it revives itself, it comes back enriching and different. But sometimes, suddenly, you read a great poem and your interest is revived, or you go back and read John Donne, or you read good prose. Sometimes just reading Sir Thomas Browne is enriching and stimulating.

MH: *Do you write mostly in summer when you are off from* The New Yorker?

HM: No. I write all year. But a lot of my poems come out of my house where we are sitting now such as "Aspects of Love" or "Notes from the Castle." I am between the ocean and the bay almost like it was when I was growing up in Rockaway Beach. There was the ocean on one side and the bay on the other, and here it's the same, and I live as you can see in the woods under all these pines and oaks. I had the pool built in the back so that I could swim every day since my heart attack. I try to walk every day for a mile. I like to walk around the tidal pools. It is so level here. The house is so open to the natural world that at night I watch the stars. I feel I could reach up and touch them.

MH: *What is your favorite book of poems of yours?*

HM: *Buried City.*

MH: *That's unusual since it's not your latest book.*

HM: I know. It's the one before. Actually, it is my latest since it's been revised, re-edited, and republished.

MH: *How do you feel about revising published work?*

HM: Well, it's really continuing a process in a sense, the very process by which the poem was created, and then if it's published, and I later realize there's more I could do to improve the poem, then I will.

For instance, in "At the Masseurs" it ended with the figure of a dancer when I realized later that was a very Yeatsian image. Secondly, it should have ended with a sculptor because the buried image is the person who is being sculpted by the masseur and so that is the connection, "the Medici" that I reference in the penultimate stanza. I'm looking for consistency in my work. That's just one example. Then, I cut part of the first section because I felt it went on too long, that it stopped the action, the flow of the poem. So, I took out three lines, then two lines were turned into one. Sometimes, in a poem, the narrative tale gets in the way of the movement. I prefer the new version. I don't believe poems are always finished, even if they are published in books.

There are certain poems that I will never touch, like "Chekhov" for example. But in "At the Masseurs" I worked extremely hard for a long time in revising that poem, but if there's a new selected or collected edition of my poems, maybe it'll change again.

Robert Graves revised his work and every single change is remarkably right. It was damn good to begin with and he made it even better.

MH: *Kenneth Koch felt that Whitman's revisions to* Leaves of Grass *weakened it.*

HM: I agree. The 1855 is the best. I think that Marianne Moore's revisions were a mistake, and Auden did some terrible revision. And Elizabeth Bishop never reprinted that wonderful poem called "Changing Hats" and that may have been because there were people still alive who may have been offended.

A lot of early work poets change as they age which I believe is a mistake. Wordsworth, for instance, ruined a lot of his earlier poems. But I also think that there are poems that are improvable. Painters often repaint canvases, and just think of musicians.

MH: *Who are your favorite poets?*

HM: Elizabeth Bishop obviously, and of course, Stevens, Yeats, and Auden. I would add James Merrill, Anthony Hecht, Joseph Brodsky, Derek Walcott. I could include Schuyler and Ashbery in that list. There are so many. I like this poet Les Murray from Australia that we recently published.

I find Auden endlessly fascinating. Even if you forget about him for a month or so, when you go back, you forget how wide his range is, how rich he can be, how many things he touched on, and how limited so many poets seem by comparison.

You can dip into Auden anywhere and come up with something enriching and marvelous.

Interview with Simon Pettet

Simon and I were born the same year one day apart, he British, me American, and we both came to the Poetry Project at Saint Mark's Church because of Ted Berrigan.

Simon took Berrigan's poetry classes at the University of Essex in England in the early '70s when he was a student there, and I took Berrigan's poetry class at Stevens Institute of Technology in Hoboken, New Jersey in 1980.

I remember meeting Simon at the Poetry Project, and hitting it off in our discussions of poetry, and I remember once being with him and his wife Rose in their 12th Street "Poets Building" apartment and talking all night all those years ago.

His interest in the "New York School" paralleled my own interest, and Simon's work on this school has produced several important published collections such as a beautiful book containing photographs, and an interview with Rudy Burckhardt, the Swiss-American photographer and filmmaker, and a collection of the *Selected Art Writings of James Schuyler*. And he is the author of several critically acclaimed volumes of poetry.

Simon's poetry captures the city, its quick movements and its intimate gestures. His lyrical poems are often Zen-like, and sometimes somber but often joyous, and full of meditative flashes of wonder.

It felt like going back in time, seeing Simon again in that same apartment. His apartment had walls of books and photographs of many of the New York poets on his walls, along with signed prints and posters. At the end of talking with Simon, he walked me over to where Ted and Alice used to live—101 Saint Mark's Place—and to the restaurant next door. How different it was. "I don't recognize this city anymore," I said to him, and he replied the same.

Simon's poetry has a clarity and a texture that creates juxtapositions and contrasts. There's a silence he captures. Reading his poetry is like entering this other realm, like stepping into a

SIMON PETTET

botanical garden off a city street, of seeing the world in ways that connect the reader to the mystery of time and place.

MH: *How did you arrive at the Saint Mark's Poetry Project?*

SP: In college I was interested in American poetry and I was already writing poetry and I studied American Lit. as an undergrad and that's how I met Ted Berrigan when he was teaching in England at the University of Essex.

Ted and Alice (Notley) came to live over there, and Ted taught courses at the university in Wivenhoe Park, Colchester. And this American poet whom at the time I knew very little about was to be my tutor. It was 1971; I was a freshman. I remember buying a little book of his poems titled *In The Early Morning Rain* at the Compendium Bookstore, a hip independent bookstore that specialized in avant-garde writing in Camden High Street in London. So, I had some idea of who he was when I met him.

Ted had very unique teaching methods and presence and charisma. I befriended Ted and Alice and she was pregnant at this point with Eddie (Edmund Berrigan) and I wanted to go to the States after I finished my studies and I realized I could get a grant to do a Ph.D. and Eric Mottram who was my teacher and an important literary figure and expert on American poetry, happily agreed to sponsor my endeavors.

So I got this grant that got me to New York City for a year and I had never even been on a plane before. I'm twenty years old and I was going to do my thesis on the New York School poets and painters, and when I get here, I start writing a history of New York instead of just the '50s and '60s. I was writing about earlier artistic schools prior to the New York School, but my focus was too wide so I didn't finish my thesis.

So here I am in the city not doing my thesis and I knew Ted and Alice were living on Saint Mark's Place in the East Village, and also my friends Helena Hughes and Marion Carey (married to the poet Steve Carey). So, Helena and Marion were living on 2nd Street (they were fellow students at the University of Essex) and my first night in the city I crashed on their floor on my first day in this new country. I had arranged this before I landed. I truly didn't know anything about New York City, or even anything about American money, a fiver, a ten, no notion of how much that buys you.

MH: *There are no women on our bills.*

SP: (laughs) That's a very good point. So I spend my first night at their place in a very different part of the East Village back then. I needed a place to live and in those days, you would get the *Village Voice* and a whole roll of dimes for the pay phone and you'd get up super early because everybody's doing the same thing and you'd call the numbers in each of the classifieds. So, I was doing that and I go to visit Ted and Alice, and Ted, as you know he was like the mayor of the East Village, said, "Why don't you go over (as he called it) to the 'Poets' Building.'"

So I get to the building on 12th Street and was told to go see Michael Scholnick whom I didn't know. Michael was a poet and a sweet soul and it was a terrible tragic story he died so young for no reason he just keeled over one day and that was it, and he had a little baby girl who's now in her fifties. Coincidentally, I was just talking to Bob Rosenthal (Allen Ginsberg's former secretary) the other day about Michael who was a sincere poet and teacher. So, I come here to this building and I open the door and Michael Scholnick whom I've never met, has been tipped off by Ted that I was coming by. Michael introduced me to the then landlady and Michael says to her, "My friend Simon is looking for an apartment." I don't even know what rents are going for in Manhattan. And she says there are two available, the one we are in now, and one that's furnished, and the furnished apartment was like $175 per month and the unfurnished $120, and I'm thinking no-brainer, I'll take the unfurnished. And so I move into this place.

In those days, you would get foam from the foam shop on Canal Street for your bed. I brought with me *The Selected Poems of Frank O'Hara* that I got from writing to the publisher stating that I was this young poet and I need the book, please send! I didn't even offer to review it. And lo and behold, a brown envelope arrives with the Larry Rivers original cover (Vintage Press edition, Donald Allen ed. 1974) and in my unfurnished apartment I have O'Hara's poems, a few tea bags, and some clothes. It's like I'm squatting. But now I have a place to live and I've only been in this country for forty-eight hours.

And now that I have this place thanks to Ted and Michael, I'm sitting here, an Englishman, and I'm going to make a cup of tea. This is how you ground yourself. I don't have any milk and I have no idea who lives in this building, so I walk out into the hall and think I'll just go borrow a bit of milk from a neighbor. So I go up two flights, don't know why two flights, and knock on the door which turns out to be Allen Ginsberg's apartment though he is out of town. But who answers the door is Denise who is Peter Orlofsky's girlfriend then, and Denise's sister, Rose. When they answer the door, they've stopped playing their punk band rehearsal. So Rose says, I'll get this. So Rose comes down, and that's how I met my future wife. She was still married then, but later returns with her son after she gets a divorce.

But later that night, Allen Ginsberg returns from Russia with the poet Andrei Voznesensky, and they're going to Max's Kansas City (Union Square and 17th Street) to hear this band "Eddie and the Hot Rods." And so here I am in a banquette table at Max's with Voznesensky and Ginsberg and my beautiful future wife Rose.

MH: *This is more than your average vacation.*

SP: No kidding! So from then on both in the poetry world and the rock and roll world being in this part of the city—I mean I could have been in any other part of the city—but this is where Ted was, so consequently it becomes my new home and I have a wife and a stepson.

MH: *Instant family.*

SP: Instant everything!

And so the business of finishing my Ph.D. I mean, I could get into the NYU library to research, etc., but that project got occluded by virtue of my life and it became an issue of legalities of staying in the country on a student visa. I had to renew my visa so I married Rose so we could stay in the US and so my simple short answer to your simple question—my initial appearance in New York City was this getting off a plane in 1978 and being in this apartment ever since and it has been over forty years of my life.

I've always been a poet and it was the reason I went to university in the first place so I could study American poetry and literature, but today, everybody's a poet like everyone with a smart phone is a photographer, and now there's these vast MFA programs turning out poets left and right. And there's two responses when one asks about being a poet: One is of amazement and the other is of "What do you really do?" Since being a poet is strange and exotic to most people. And now with writing programs at every college and university it's like saying everyone can be a poet. I think that poetry is an incredibly private thing and a blessing at the same time. So I say I'm a writer because to say you're a poet seems a bizarre thing to walk the earth and be doing.

MH: Your poems are well crafted so you've learned how to craft a poem, not everybody does.

SP: And it is because that's what I work at and what I've been able to do all my life is to function as a poet. And Ted, I think, gave me permission to live the life of a poet, and that's the validation one needs. So I've sacrificed a lot and it's not like I have this other life with a nice job and write poetry on the side. I don't have children; I don't have money. My life is lacking in profound levels. And at the same time, as a poet in this society, I don't have much choice. Since that's what I do, it's of the highest importance to me that I'm not faking it. I'm not deluding myself either. I live with the real existential fear that I won't be able to write another poem again. And I'm not prolific in the sense that I've lots and lots of poems.

I'm a lyric poet and I do believe in a muse so when I say I'm a poet, that's a recognition of the existence of poetry as being a vehicle for the poems that come from me.

MH: *Do you keep journals or notebooks that you come back to later for material for poetry?*

SP: I don't have good organized notebooks. I don't keep journals in the sense of a daybook or diary. I keep notes. If I get an idea for a poem, I'm going to write the first line right then. My poems often begin with a phrase. It's this notion of the muse in the old-fashioned sense of inspiration. I understand the dynamic of discipline versus spontaneity in writing, but I'm writing all the time, but I write without a schedule.

And after I've written, I will leave it alone for a while until I come back to it again and my relationship to what I've written will be completely free from my ego. Ninety percent of what I've started is not going to be good.

MH: Handwritten?

SP: Yes, handwritten first, then I will word process and in the process I will add.

MH: *Your poems evolve slowly.*

SP: Very much so. That book, *Hearth*, is over twenty years of work, and there isn't another one waiting that size that is ready for publication. In a negative sense, I start worrying that that's it, but then I'll write another poem, and I'll be grateful. I have this jealousy of prolific poets—Alice Notley, for God's sake, has written reams of poems in a torrent of terrific poetry! And the anecdote I always used to be stuck with was this Hemingway notion of if you're a writer you get up at 6 a.m., go to the typewriter, or the computer these days, and compose on that white page. My poems are short and lyrical.

MH: *Brevity is refreshing.*

SP: It's how I write and I can sustain an emotional register to a certain degree in a short form because I'm not a narrative poet—they're lyric poems.

MH: *Yours is not the poetry you find coming out of the MFA.*

SP: It does have to do with this business of forty years of working as a poet and my life's reality is embedded in that. What happens is I write it down and not at six in the morning on a schedule, but when the gods so decree.

MH: *Ted Berrigan famously wrote at night.*

SP: The older I get the harder that is, but at night the phone isn't going to ring, now it's the text messages. The writing residency I had in California was so great because I was given a studio to work in and meals were given and I didn't have to worry. But because of the shortness of my poems and the fact that when I'm writing it's coming out in line form and if I've got the first line down, then hopefully I'll get the second, and if I've got two lines down, in the process of writing, I will get three and four. So, whatever is there is going to sustain itself until it doesn't. And that explains why I would've possibly stopped the writing of the poem. So, when I review the poem later, I'll say, now that's a real poem.

And with the distance of time, it's possible to edit and make changes, to extract the poem if you will, from its unfinished terrain. It's really a dangerous thing to talk about; I always feel the danger of blowing it by articulating the process. It is magic. There's another cliché. To me, poetry is magic.

MH: *Did this inspiration ever come from anybody in this community, from hearing a reading at the Saint Mark's Poetry Project, or from meeting other poets? And how important is that world for you, going all the way back to the 1970s, being at Saint Mark's, living here in the "Poets Building" a couple of doors down from Allen Ginsberg?*

SP: I can answer that in a possibly surprising way which may not be necessarily what you want to hear, and let me think this out clearly: To be a poet is an incredibly solitary enterprise, and the solitude and the weirdness of that is the primary thing, and so the notion of a "poet community," the friendship and camaraderie and all that, and in the writing workshop cliché you can only give examples, you can't teach anyone how to write poetry, so when I say that all my life I've been a poet, I'm saying what an amazing, far out, and extraordinary life and blessing. Also though, how sad that I have no children as part of that life, and I'm not being a downer when I say that, but the nature of the solitude and that experience, is by virtue of the life that I live and I feel incredibly blessed. In fact, the older I am, the more far out my continued existence is to me, this kid who moved from England to the East Village in the 1970s wandering around the city and it's not those days anymore.

MH: *John Ashbery writes you a wonderful blurb on your book of poems,* As a Bee, *and calls you a "... pillar of the St. Mark's Poetry Project, the core of all that is New York about the New York School ..."*

SP: Yes, my engagement with the Poetry Project is true, and I am grateful that Ashbery wrote that, but I already had my own world of solitude that I was trying to address as a poet living within that community. So, when Ashbery wrote that which was flattering, it is not true, thank you John! But I'm thinking I'm not a Saint Mark's "pillar" of the community. When that book came out, it wasn't even reviewed in the Poetry Project Newsletter which is kind of interesting because it speaks to the very point I'm making about Saint Mark's. It was reviewed later on in the newsletter with Stacy's (Stacy Szymaszek, former director) involvement.

MH: *Was it a younger generation thing?*

SP: It was generational. But on a deeper level the community how it works in this way in this East Village now, this conflates several things. One, as you were saying before, the nature of the neighborhood back in the day in the period we were referencing, was an absolute community of folks, of poets turning out their little magazines and all this has been written about and documented in essays and books. And it lives in our memories as we were participants in it and so I'm not denying anything in that and certainly in various later manifestations when that low-rent lifestyle disappeared. It was great then to have youthful friends and friendships and working together with such a weird thing as poetry and mimeo magazines and poetry readings and it all made for a bond of engagement.

And as a poet, your community extends far beyond that notion of contemporary poetic souls but to Sappho or to Shakespeare who make up a part of my community. As for my contemporaries it's a little interesting and complicated for me because coming from England I didn't have a poetry buddy like Ron Padgett was to Ted Berrigan. From day one, my experience of poetry finally had to be mine. So, what was interesting when I had come to New York City and to right here to fall into the middle of this poetry scene, is part of the pleasure of America at that time. In England, you are dealing with history and class and power structures. Being here freed me from all that and how lovely and liberating that was. Being English and being in America, I didn't have to explain myself. You can be whatever you are. So the poetry community and Saint Mark's and till this day—of course it's gone through many changes, and I've watched it change over the years going all the way back to Ted Berrigan who as you recall placed himself very masterly at the center of Saint Mark's as the "Emeritus."

MH: *He was the pillar.*

SP: Yes, and significantly for them he wanted both the authority and at the same time not to have to do the gig. Allen Ginsberg was the other "Emeritus." And when I talk of community, I want my poems to communicate to the audience and the audience at Saint Mark's is pitched that way. That's the mythos of it that we are this East Village community but in my personal experience it was Bernadette (Mayer) who was the first director who gave me a reading and recognized me as a poet. I mean, Ted, too, did, but in terms of reading at Saint Mark's I don't want to sound sour grapes—they had me read with some other poet. Bernadette was the first, and then Ed Friedman when he became director had me read and Ed was always a fan of my poems. So, when I read for him, he pissed me off because he said, "Are you going to read any new poems?" And I always think that my poems are not time-based, and I'm annoyed by Ed's asking. So, at that reading I read only new poems.

So, I'm not a true participant in this communal scene—I'm outside that—I'm more ubiquitous. I'm grateful for the respect of my peers, and as in the poets who wrote blurbs for my books, they are saying true things. They're not just being generous in their comments, it's that they know the poems.

Increasingly, as years go by, I hope my poems can reach people. Poetry readings are not an egotistical desire to stand in front of an audience and have people think that you are great, that's truly not it. They're extremely important transmissions so the more various your audience, the better. The Saint Mark's audience is famously not your typical audience and I remember Lorenzo Thomas saying what he loves about reading at Saint Mark's is that he can read his new work. It is a unique audience, and apart from the Peter Stuyvesant history and the story of his ghost haunting the church, that this is a really far out place to read. There's that book of Anselm Berrigan's of all the Saint Mark's interviews and all those poets are part of that constellation.

A little bit of history. So, after Bernadette, Jessica Hagedorn comes in out of nowhere with no real experience as a director and she lasts a couple of months and that made me realize that wasn't my community—no disrespect to her. Then Eileen Myles comes in, and there were a lot of changes in the Saint Mark's poetry world. And Eileen was vehemently making the point that I'm making stating, "I'm a poet not a bureaucrat." And I got this to some degree from Ted this business that poetry is not only an identity but a vocation, and Eileen and several poets influenced by Ted and I include myself there in some ways, too, took that stance. And so, Eileen gets the gig at Saint Mark's and I was on her side for all this, and I watched it all go down. She completely blew it—she missed the Ford Foundation meeting for the grant. And her response was, "I'm this poet, what do you expect."

MH: That's why you need administrators.

SP: Exactly! And then Ed Friedman comes along and amazingly saves the day, otherwise Saint Mark's was totally going down. It was inches away from the end, and because Ed was such a good administrator, and he also had the poetic chops and the friendships, he was the longest serving director in the history of the Poetry Project. Then Ed, finally, after so many years, changed the bylaws and they get a new guy—Anselm (Berrigan) who didn't want the position, but everybody sort of pegged him and indeed he had the background and the soul and he was young. So, he took over and he did remarkably well in trying to get younger people involved. And then Stacy Szymaszek took over from Anselm and the spirit of the place devolved into gender politics, and as director, instead of doing the featured poet introductions herself, she let others do it, her friends. And the energy then was increasingly about gender politics as indeed it was in the changing culture surrounding Saint Mark's.

Then this new guy takes over, Kyle Dacuyan, he's young and has worked as the manager of Literary Outreach & Activism at PEN America. He's got the bureaucratic chops, and he feels privileged and honored to be the new director and he set up this reading with Eddie (Berrigan) and Charles North, but then added another poet, and I'm on Charles' side in this, Charles didn't want there to be a third reader, and so declines to read. So, this new director was learning on the job.

MH: Well, there has to be a period of learning on the job.

SP: Absolutely. I hope that my poems when I read to an audience, can transmit the experience I'm telegraphing directly from what my experience has been, even if it's a poem that I've written to Rose, my deceased wife. I want it to carry the emotional register that I feel so that it has resonance with the audience. My wife (Simon remarried), who has studied and who is degreed in psychology, has used the phrase "limbic awareness" as a term for this phenomenon. So, my poems should register limbically/emotionally before you even realize what has transpired.

MH: *What poets are you reading?*

SP: I'm an eclectic reader and because I'm a lyric poet, I'm interested in small poems, so I'm interested in the great haiku poets. I read a lot of Japanese and Chinese poetry. I'm reading Charles Olson's collection of his letters, too. My poetry is a poetry of distillation, of course Charles Olson is the opposite of distillation. And the other thing which has always been a feature of my poetry is that my poems have always been chiseled and self-contained and short. And my speech is very different (laughs) being that I am very verbose. And like I said, I don't want to be so animated and I love concision of speech.

MH: *Well, you're not a laconic American. You have that wonderful trans-Atlantic British way of speaking. And it has been a pleasure to listen to you talk.*

SP: That is kind of you to say.

Interview with James Schuyler

I received a letter from Schuyler dated February 2, 1983, and in it he asked me to call him at the Chelsea Hotel, 222 West 23rd Street, writing, "About one in the afternoon is best for me."

I took the "A" Train from 42nd Street and exited at the 23rd Street platform, and walked to McFeely's Tavern on the corner of 11th Avenue, and called him from a public pay phone. I wanted to see the urinals in the men's room that Schuyler mentioned in his poem, "Dining Out with Doug and Frank" that he described as: " ... the three most / splendid urinals I've ever / seen. Like Roman steles ... " The Chelsea Hotel was a couple of blocks away, a hotel made famous by the Welsh poet Dylan Thomas's dying there. When I got to the Chelsea Hotel, the desk clerk sent me up on the elevator to the 6th floor.

Schuyler sat in overstuffed armchair against the wall between two windows overlooking 22nd Street. Above his head hung a small cityscape of a New York brownstone by his painter friend Darragh Park. He pointed to the ceiling and mentioned that I should talk to modernist composer Virgil Thomson, who lived a couple floors above him and who knew all the poets and painters and musicians. "He's losing his hearing now that he's in his nineties, and he told me he loves it! He can tune out the street noise and just listen to the music inside his head."

Schuyler chain-smoked Benson & Hedges and kept a cigarette burning the entire interview. When I asked him long, detailed questions usually involving glowing criticism he would respond with, "Yeah, right." When I'd mention some of the things other poets who had high praise for his work wrote in essays about him such as Howard Moss, he'd say, "Good old Howard." When I asked him if he ever got tired sitting in his room all day he said, "I get tired of looking at that building across the street." When I asked him what he did all day, he quickly replied, "In the morning I read the *Post*, and in the evening, I read the *Daily News*."

In looking around his meager yet heymish quarters, I noticed that he had a photo of John Ashbery in a frame on his end table by the sofa. It was my photo that I took of Ashbery when I interviewed Ashbery the previous year. I had given my photo to Ted Berrigan. Schuyler told me that Berrigan gave it to him. (Berrigan had interviewed Schuyler a month or so before me. According to Schuyler it was Ted who did all the talking.) I was annoyed that Ted had turned around and re-gifted my photo.

Because Schuyler suffered from mental illness, he almost never gave readings. Near the end of his life, he gave a rare reading at the Knitting Factory and five hundred people showed up. He lived the last fifteen years of his life at the Chelsea, and was cared for by a number of friends and volunteer young poets from the Saint Mark's Poetry Project who brought him supplies and cooked his meals. When I was there, the Irish poet Helena Hughes was cooking lunch for him. He died in 1991 of heart failure.

MH: *You equal Chekhov and Elizabeth Bishop in the way you handle detail, in the way you incorporate so many details from your personal life into your poetry.*

JAMES SCHUYLER

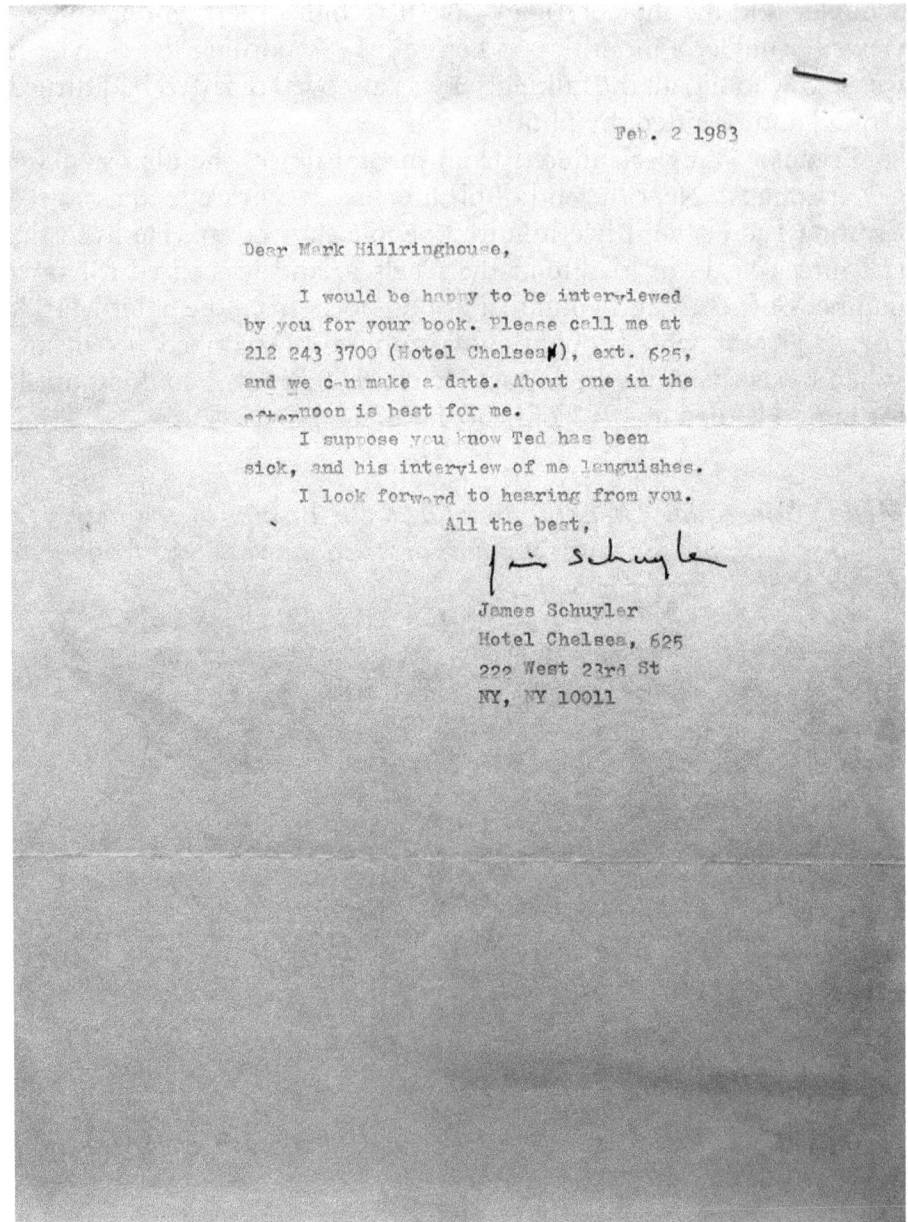

Feb. 2 1983

Dear Mark Hillringhouse,

 I would be happy to be interviewed by you for your book. Please call me at 212 243 3700 (Hotel Chelsea), ext. 625, and we can make a date. About one in the afternoon is best for me.
 I suppose you know Ted has been sick, and his interview of me languishes.
 I look forward to hearing from you.
  All the best,

  James Schuyler

  James Schuyler
  Hotel Chelsea, 625
  222 West 23rd St
  NY, NY 10011

JAMES SCHUYLER TO MARK HILLRINGHOUSE

JS: I've always liked looking at things and I'm very attracted to writers who share that infatuation with things, such as Elizabeth Bishop and D.H. Lawrence (in his poetry) or Walt Whitman and Boris Pasternak.

MH: *Would you compare yourself to Frank O'Hara?*

JS: I don't think I write like he did. Well, I think Frank's poems are often more like diary entries than mine are.

MH: *You seem amazed by the small wonders, so many improbable miracles that the world contains, like that raccoon you write about in your longest poem, "The Morning of the Poem." How do you feel about the waking day, how do you handle it?*

JS: That's a hell of a big question (laughs). I spend a great deal of the day reading, that's how I handle it. At night, I watch TV. What I write about a great deal of the time is something immediate that I see, or something I think about that I've seen.

MH: *Nature?*

JS: I miss nature living in the city. I lived in Southampton, Long Island, for twelve years, and I liked that very much. I get bored looking at that building across the street.

MH: *Where did you grow up?*

JS: I was born in Chicago where my father was a newspaper man. We lived in a little town called Downer's Grove just outside the city. When I was very small, we moved to Washington, D.C. and we lived there for a while and in Chevy Chase, Maryland. When I was twelve, we moved to Buffalo, New York. Two years later we settled in a little town just outside of it called East Aurora, where my brother and his family still live. My parents were divorced when I was quite young. I was very withdrawn. My homelife was very chaotic. I really didn't fit in and wasn't very happy growing up in East Aurora. No, it was more that I didn't fit in with the crowd in high school who were very athletic-oriented. There wasn't anyone like me who liked to read books and who was interested in art. I had a couple of buddies, but my best friend lived in Buffalo and we didn't see each other very often. He's in my poem, "The Morning of the Poem"—a guy named Bernie.

MH: *What's your religious background?*

JS: Well, I was baptized a Presbyterian. My mother and stepfather became Christian Scientists which disgusted me very much.

MH: *The name Schuyler goes back to colonial history.*

JS: Yes, it does. A big New York State family. I am related to General Phillip Schuyler and to the travel writer and translator Eugene Schuyler. He was the first person to translate Turgenev into English. General Schuyler served in the Continental Army. I believe he fucked up the battle of Saratoga. Instead of being court-martialed, he was allowed to resign because of his high family background. He was Alexander Hamilton's father-in-law. The family came here from Holland very early in the seventeenth century. There are two branches, one up near Albany and the other in New Jersey. There's even a Schuylerville in Upstate New York. Mine is the New York family.

MH: *What was your mother's family name?*

JS: Connor. She was born on a farm in Minnesota. She's half English, half-Irish, that's why I have this Irish mug (laughing).

MH: *Where did you go to college?*

JS: I got a scholarship and went to a college called Bethany in West Virginia which is associated with the Disciples of Christ with which I had nothing to do. It was a Protestant denomination. After two years I left to go into the Navy during the war. I served on a destroyer in the North Atlantic doing convoy duty. I guess I was nineteen when I went in.

MH: *You got out when the war ended?*

JS: No, but I'd rather not talk about it (laughing).

MH: *Any teachers or professors you can remember?*

JS: Yes. I was very influenced by my English professor, Dr. Florence Hoaglund, who was a grand woman.

MH: *English was your major?*

JS: Yes, but in high school my major was History. What I did mostly in college was to play bridge which I learned to play when I joined a fraternity. And that was how I liked to spend my time. In high school there was one English teacher who also directed the school paper for which I wrote. He introduced me to James Joyce's *Ulysses*, though he said that I was too young to read it. I went ahead and read it anyway.

MH: *What were you planning on becoming?*

JS: I very much wanted to be an architect. My stepfather, who was in construction and who wanted to be an architect himself, convinced me that I couldn't draw, ergo I couldn't become an architect. While I was in high school, I switched my ambition to writing.

MH: *What did your mother do? Did she have any ambitions?*

JS: My mother used to write poetry, though it wasn't very good. It was religious poetry.

MH: *Did she show it to you?*

JS: Yes. But my stepfather used to punish me by not letting me have a library card though I went ahead and had a library card anyway. I used to have to smuggle books into the house under my coat.

MH: *That's a very strange punishment.*

JS: He was a sort of hunting and fishing man and that's what he wanted me to be. Which is what my brother became when he grew up. When he was mad at me, he'd say, "That's what comes of grandmother taking you to museums." Which is what she used to do (chuckling) when we lived in Washington.

MH: *Maybe you got your love of nature from your stepfather.*

JS: I think I got more from my grandmother Connor who was a real nature lover. She used to take me out and tell me all the names of wild flowers.

MH: *You constantly mention different flowers in your poems.*

JS: Well, I like them and I miss them. At home I was a gardening slave. I had to weed my ass off.

MH: *You mentioned Joyce's* Ulysses. *I was wondering if you read any other books that turned you on as a youngster?*

JS: What decided me to become a writer was one day in my tent in the yard in the back of the house, I was reading Logan Pearsall Smith's *Unforgotten Years*, his autobiography. He described how Whitman used to come to his family's house in Camden and what a wonderful person he was, and the idea came to Smith that he might become a writer when he grew up, and I looked up and the whole yard started to shimmer, and I thought, "I'm going to be a writer," which I never really thought of before.

MH: *How old were you?*

JS: I was somewhere in my teens in high school.

MH: *Were you reading any poets back then?*

JS: Yes. I used to read whatever anthologies were available in a small town like East Aurora—Louis Untermeyer, Sheldon Robbins, etc. We had a very good Mark Van Doren, *World Poetry in Translation*.

MH: *Who were the poets you were aware of then?*

JS: Oh, Edna St. Vincent Millay (laughing), Sara Teasedale, Frost, etc.

MH: *Did you enjoy Frost?*

JS: I think I liked Frost more then than I do now, although he is perfectly all right.

MH: *Who were the first major poets you came into contact with when you were young?*

JS: When I was quite young and living in New York City in the forties I met W. H. Auden of whom I became a very close friend. I typed up a lot of his poems for manuscripts. I used to think if this is what poetry is like I'll never be able to write it.

MH: *Did you show him your own poems, or were you not writing poetry at that time?*

JS: I didn't start writing poetry until I was twenty-five or twenty-six. My ambition before that had been to write short stories for The New Yorker. I have had poems in The New Yorker but no short stories. It used to be good when John Cheever and John O'Hara were writing stories for them.

MH: *So, you started writing poems later than usual?*

JS: Well, I came to New York after the Navy and worked for the Voice of America. Then in 1947 I went to Italy for two years, and then I came back and lived in New York again, then I went to Italy a second time in the mid-fifties.

MH: *For the Voice of America?*

JS: No, no, by my own hook. I inherited a farm in Arkansas from my paternal grandmother which I sold and I went to live in Italy on that. I just wanted to goof off. And be somewhere beautiful. I had a lovely apartment in Florence.

MH: *How did you meet Auden?*

JS: Well, his muse was a young man named Chester Kallman, who's dead now, and I met Chester and had become a very close friend of his. Meanwhile, Auden had been teaching in Michigan and came back to New York, and that's when I met him. I typed the manuscript for his book Nones and I also typed his translation of Jean Cocteau's Les Chevaliers de la Table ronde.

MH: *What did you do in Italy?*

JS: I really hadn't started writing yet. I used to try but nothing came of it. I just travelled. I was then a great opera buff. I lived in the house that Auden had rented on the Isle of Ischia.

MH: *How did you come into contact with Frank O'Hara?*

JS: Through the art dealer John Meyers. He had worked in Otto Ulbrich's, the best bookstore in Buffalo. I used to hang out there when I went to Buffalo as a teenager in high school. I got a nodding acquaintance with him. When I came to New York he was working for Peggy Guggenheim. Back then the first thing I had ever published were three very short stories in a magazine called *Accent* which Howard Moss published, and Meyers called me up to congratulate me. Meyers said, "You're a poet!" And I said, "There's a poem in that magazine that I like very much titled 'Three Penny Opera' by Frank O'Hara." And John Meyers said, "Why, Frank is in the room with me." So, a little while later I met him at a party after a Larry Rivers opening. And John Ashbery was there too.

MH: *What year was this?*

JS: 1951. Later on, Frank and I shared an apartment on 49th Street, where, still later, John, who had gone to France, came back and stayed there with me for a year.

MH: *And Kenneth Koch and Barbara Guest?*

JS: I had met Barbara then, too, but I hadn't really become a close friend of hers until quite a bit later. Kenneth Koch was rather a pain in the ass (laughs). He later became a friend of mine. He was in California when I first got to know John and Frank, and when he came back and found out that I had joined the group he rather resented it. He tended to put me down, which I didn't care for. I was very fond of his wife, Janice, who's dead now. She was a very close friend of mine. I'm also very fond of their daughter, Katherine, who got married recently. Frank and John treated me like one of the boys, one of the group, even though I hadn't been at Harvard with them. Alex Katz once said something to me at a party that implied I went to Harvard, and I said, "Alex, I didn't go to Harvard, I went to a hick school in West Virginia." And Alex said, "Nah, you're Harvard ..." (both laughing).

MH: Was Alex Katz at Harvard?

JS: Scarcely (chuckling), he's Cooper Union. Fairfield Porter went to Harvard.

MH: What were you doing at this time?

JS: I was working in a bookshop run by a man named Bob Vanderbilt, "The Holiday Horoscope," which specialized in imported English books. It was located on 54th Street. Bob, who was very well off, later married and moved to Switzerland to play golf (laughing).

MH: And after the bookstore?

JS: Then I was writing a good deal, poetry mostly. Frank and John encouraged me very much with my poetry writing. They seemed to like my poems, which made me feel great, because they were obviously very talented themselves. They turned me on to Pasternak, whose poetry influenced me very much.

MH: Which poems? Do you remember any that inspired you?

JS: One, beginning "Waving a Bough Full of Fragrance." The only poems of his that were available in English were in the back of a little anthology of Pasternak's writing which included Pasternack's autobiography *Safe Conduct* that New Directions published. Have you ever read *Safe Conduct*? It's marvelous. It's the story of his early years.

MH: No, I haven't read it.
When did you get on board the staff of the Museum of Modern Art?

JS: After I stopped working at the bookstore. For several years a friend financed me so I could write a novel, which was *Alfred and Guinevere*, my first novel. Then in 1957, I went to work for MoMA. I had begun reviewing before then for "Art News" in 1955, which I did for quite a while. I did it so much that I can hardly bear to go into an art gallery now.

MH: *Who were the first painters you met when you arrived in New York?*

JS: I had a friend named Charles Heilman, who was a decorative painter, whose work I liked very much. He was more of a designer than a real painter. Then I got to know Jane Freilicher, whose talent I admire very much. Then Fairfield Porter, who is my favorite painter. I lived with the Porters for twelve years in Southampton, Long Island.

MH: *What years were those?*

JS: 1961 to 1973. Fairfield is indeed my favorite painter (pointing to the wall above his bed). There's a portrait of me by him when I was younger.

MH: *Have you ever tried to paint?*

JS: No.

MH: *Did Fairfield Porter like your poetry?*

JS: I think John Ashbery was the one he liked best, but he did like mine. He once said that I was much more visual than he was (laughing).

MH: *Did you ever write poems about his painting?*

JS: No, but I tried to write poems that were like his painting. I used to read to him a lot while he was painting; things like *Anna Karenina*. Then, every summer, we would go to an island that Fairfield's father had bought in Maine, which was very beautiful—Great Spruce Head Island—it really turned me on.

MH: *Of the painters, who do you see any more?*

JS: Jane Freilicher, Alex Katz, George Schneeman (pointing to wall above bed), who painted that nude of Bill Berkson, and Joe Brainard and my friend Darragh Park (pointing to a small painting between windows). That's a Darragh Park, the little one of a street in front of a brownstone in the snow.

MH: Who are some of the other painters you admire?

JS: I'm very fond of the painters of the "Venetian School": Bellini, Titian, Veronese, Tiepolo, Guardi. I'm very fond of Longhi. There are some beautiful ones in the Met. I like all the Impressionists, and I like Delacroix very much. I greatly admired him as a man. Have you ever read *The Journal of Eugene Delacroix*—? Oh, it is so great. I like painting in general. Fairfield thought Velasquez was the greatest painter.

MH: Alex Katz (trouble hearing)?

JS: No, no, Velasquez (laughing). Fairfield liked Alex's paintings but I don't think he went that far.

MH: You said you wanted to be an architect.

JS: I was very turned on by an issue of the magazine *Architectural Forum* that was devoted to the work of Frank Lloyd Wright. I'm not very much into the immediate work of architecture today. I don't care for Phillip Johnson. I like Mies van der Rohe very much, and all of the "Chicago School"—Sullivan's iron grille work.

MH: What do you like about New York City?

JS: Not much (laughing). I'm fed up with it. I used to love it. When I first lived here, I used to walk and walk and walk. My favorite part of the city was the part downtown that's now torn down where all the old cast iron buildings used to be below City Hall. I have a very nice book called *Brick & Brownstone* about the row houses in New York.

MH: You mention that book in "The Morning of the Poem."

JS: Right.

MH: What was it like being in New York City in the fifties?

JS: Well, it was very upbeat. There was a very strong concerted action among the painters, the "Abstract Expressionists." The old Artists Club used to exist and we used to go to the Cedar Bar where all the artists hung out, when we didn't go to the San Remo, which was gay (laughing). And for me the big thrill was getting to be friends with Frank and John—particularly with John. He and I were inseparable at that time.

MH: What was O'Hara like?

JS: Oh, he was exceedingly charming, he was very witty; he talked a blue streak.

MH: And Ashbery, what was he like back then?

JS: Ah, witty (laughing), like Frank. And I don't know, he was very-off-the-wall (laughs). Frank got mixed up with the artists much more deeply than I did. That was really his bag.

MH: Did you ever get the feeling that you were all in competition with the so-called academic poetry of the time, or even amongst yourselves?

JS: I don't think it occurred to any of us. We were just doing our own thing. We really weren't in competition with the "academics." And among ourselves, well, no, we all enjoyed each other's work. Once, I was walking through the slush in Washington Square Park with Frank going to a bar, and we were talking about our own poetry, when suddenly, Frank said, in his very bitter tone, "Let's face it, John's the poet!" which rather pissed me off because I thought I was a poet, too (laughs). That burst of modesty was not very characteristic of Frank (laughs).

MH: Who do you read now, who do you keep up with?

JS: Well, a lot of little magazines come floating in and I read them. I like Eileen Myles very much; I like Helena Hughes (sitting in the room with us during the interview), I like Ron Padgett's poetry very much, and Michael Brownstein, Anne Waldman. I also like Gary Snyder. I have a pen-pal whom I've never met, whose poetry I like—Geoff Young. He published my little book of poems—*Early in '71*.

MH: *Howard Moss?*

JS: I like his poetry. Howard was the first person to publish my poetry, my poem "Salute." He published it in a little pocket-sized book that came out for a while in the fifties.

MH: *What were your five favorite books last year?*

JS: Two books by Barbara Pym, Paul Violi's *Splurge*, Eileen Myles's *Sappho's Boat*, and *A Nest of Ninnies* (laughing) by me and John Ashbery.

MH: *Do you write with music in mind?*

JS: I write with music playing. I don't think necessarily in mind. I usually have the radio turned on to WNCN, the classical music station. I take what they give me (laughs). When I was first in New York, I used to go to jazz clubs. I remember hearing Pearl Bailey when she first made an appearance at the old Blue Angel in the forties. I heard Billie Holiday at the Apollo in Harlem. I was very fond of Teddy Wilson.

MH: *Any "popular" music?*

JS: I like some, like The Beatles, but my interest is really in serious music—classical. My favorite composers are Mozart, Verdi, Chopin, Scriabin, and Prokofiev.

MH: *How long did it take you to write "The Morning of the Poem"?*

JS: I wrote it during the summer of seventy-six when I was visiting my mother in East Aurora. I guess it took me a little less than two months. When I left East Aurora, I tended to go on with it when I got back to New York City, but the vibes weren't right, so I just wrote a brief ending. When I started writing it, I intended it to be about one hundred pages.

MH: *How did you control it?*

JS: Control it? I don't control my poetry! Ernest Hemingway said you should always keep going if it's going bad, and only stop if it's going good.

MH: *Was it written in the morning?*

JS: Yes, sometimes very early. I spent most of the morning at the typewriter. I pretty much write on the typewriter. Only if I'm going to the country for a few days will I take a notebook along and write in that.

MH: *What started the poem?*

JS: I think I woke up one day with a title in my mind, and as I say in the beginning of the poem, I just dreamt of Baudelaire's skull for some reason.

MH: *You seem to have a morning consciousness in a lot of your work.*

JS: That's when I usually write. I never liked writing at night the way some people do, Ted Berrigan, for instance. Well, Ted lives at night.

MH: Freely Espousing *came out in 1969?*

JS: Yes, but it was ready two years before that (laughs). I think that when I thought up the title, I thought of it as Whitmanesque. *The Crystal Lithium*, or rather the poem by that title, was directly influenced by Whitman's "Song of Myself."

MH: *You begin the title poem "Freely Espousing" with the line, "A commingling sky," which seems to be a very Wallace Stevensesque word— "commingling."*

JS: Oh, I wouldn't be surprised since I read Stevens very intensely at one time. He influenced me tremendously. I had read him in anthologies when I was in high school, and when I was in the Navy aboard a ship, I kept his book *Harmonium* with me. A friend and I once went to Hartford, Connecticut, just so we could walk past his house (laughing).

MH: *You have more of a stated subject matter, let's say, than John Ashbery does.*

JS: My poems as they develop are very different from my early poems which were inclined to be Dada or surreal. John Ashbery once told me that a poem didn't have to make sense. But then I went on to write poems that do make sense (laughs).

MH: *Edmund White writes, "You're the closest of any American to rendering, in English, the Chinese response to nature."*

JS: I was heavily influenced by Arthur Waley's translations from the Chinese, and also the translations I read of Tu Fu in particular.

MH: *You seem fond of writing elegies for seasons in* Freely Espousing. *Your poem "February" is a good example.*

JS: Yes, it's a poem about February. I don't really think of it as being elegiac. Sometimes they are. I think my poem "December" is. That's one of my favorites among my own poems.

MH: *A few of your poems have that Olson-Creeley look in the way they're broken up and stretched out across the page.*

JS: That came through John Wieners who suggested that I look at Olson and try using that field that he used. But to tell you the truth I was never very much interested in Olson's poetry.

MH: *Creeley?*

JS: Not really. I think they're both very good poets, but they don't turn me on the way other poets do.

MH: *They tend to move chronologically from left to right forward in time by going down and across the page.*

JS: Right. Yes, there's a poem in *Freely Espousing* called "Flashes" that's written in that style.

MH: *Also, "Rachmaninoff's Third" and "March Here."*

JS: At the time I wrote those I was carrying on a very intense correspondence with John Wieners. I like his *Hotel Wently Poems* very much and I like John.

MH: *What is the relationship of your titles to your poems?*

JS: I think they are fairly intrinsic. I like giving a poem a name rather than a number. I very rarely call a poem "Poem." I never have any trouble finding titles. I usually do have the title at the same time I'm writing the poem. Once in a while I think it up later. John Ashbery has told me that he thinks of his titles first. Although, the other day, I thought of a title that I can't seem to make a poem for, which is "White Night Black Easter"—maybe that's the poem (both laughing).

MH: *Howard Moss says, "There is no one quite like Schuyler because his writing is very straight and yet it so transcends itself all the time. No one else quite has that peculiar talent of sounding like a diary and yet not losing the effect of lyric poetry."*

JS: Good old Howard.

MH: *Do you ever write parodies?*

JS: No.

MH: *I found a type of parody. It was in your book* The Crystal Lithium, *"The Cenotaph." It's subtitled "Three Idylls for Kenneth Koch." It reads very much like Koch.*

JS: I don't think so. I mean I don't agree.

MH: *It's reminiscent of the style he employed in his* The Art of Love.

JS: (interrupting) That was written before *The Art of Love*. When I wrote a poem called "Money Musks" which I dedicated to Kenneth's now dead wife, Janice, I showed it to Fairfield Porter, and he said, "I see you've been reading Kenneth Koch." This infuriated me. I didn't think it was remotely like Kenneth Koch.

MH: *Marjorie Perloff has said about Frank O'Hara, "His poetry is a series of painterly arrangements." You, too, seem to write this way; you can conjure up a painting in words. Your poem "After Joe Was at the Island" from* The Crystal Lithium *is a good example.*

JS: Well, that was a poem about a painter. Joe being Joe Brainard, of course. It was written after he had gone. It wasn't about a painting.

MH: *I notice that you arrange your poems seasonally according to time as in* The Crystal Lithium *and* Freely Espousing.

JS: I tend to arrange them, not in *Freely Espousing*, but in my other books, in the order in which they were written as best I can just because there is a sequence of time. I also usually divide them up into the various places where they were written.

MH: *You've got a poem in* The Crystal Lithium, *"The Dog Wants His Dinner" for Clark Coolidge, almost a parody.*

JS: Well, perhaps. I didn't just dedicate it to him, I wrote it with him in mind. I like Clark's poetry very much, although writing in that style is not for me, like playing with words or making hieroglyphics out of words. I think Clark is very talented.

MH: *Do you ever get the feeling while writing that you've written the same poem over and over?*

JS: If I do, I stop. Luckily, it doesn't happen very often.

MH: *I would say that many of your poems have Baudelaire's synesthetic quality.*

JS: That's very flattering. I really don't read French very well so he can't be a direct influence, but of course, I've read Baudelaire in translation. I liked him very much when I was young. For some reason there was a copy of *The Flowers of Evil* or "Selected Baudelaire" in the house when I was growing up. I can't imagine why, nobody else ever read him.

MH: *Well, that image of Baudelaire's skull keeps popping up in "The Morning of the Poem." Also, in that poem, you shift from that long couplet style of yours into skinny stanzas that run along the margin about four or five times.*

JS: It's really just one long line.

MH: *One long line?*

JS: When I wrote it, I set the typewriter as wide as I could and that determined the length of the line.

MH: *That's curious. You didn't enjamb by dropping down to a shorter line which gives it that couplet appearance?*

JS: No, that had to be done for printing—it was changed for typesetting. I think I would have preferred it the other way, but it worked out, so I really didn't care.

MH: *Who is the painter in "The Morning of the Poem" who lives on 22nd Street?*

JS: Darragh Park, to whom the book is dedicated.

MH: *When did you feel that you made a breakthrough in writing?*

JS: When I wrote the poem "Salute." I was in the hospital in White Plains, New York corresponding with Howard Moss. As I said, it was the first poem I had published.

MH: *When did that come out?*

JS: 1952, I guess. The book *Salute* came out in 1961, but all the poems that were in *Salute* are in *Freely Espousing*.

MH: *You write with bigger emotions than Ashbery does.*

JS: I think John draws on his dream-life quite a bit, or he used to. He doesn't write much about his personal feelings. It's very difficult to write creatively and not have your emotions somewhere or other.

MH: Edmund White says, "You're the most musical poet we have."

JS: I'm very conscious of sound, that is, when I read other poets. I like the sound value in Elizabeth Bishop very much. She is one of my all-time favorite poets.

MH: *You frequently resonate off a single sound in your poems.*

JS: Well, I do it consciously, but I don't know how I got into it.

MH: *Do you do it silently or do you voice your poems?*

JS: I speak sometimes. I test them with my voice.

MH: *Edmund White also says, "There's a certain lack of punctuation in your poetry which promotes a delicious ambiguity which is slow to resolve itself."*

JS: At times I try to do without what seems superfluous punctuation. At other times I'm more conventional.

MH: *Edmund White goes on to say that you are "an aesthete of the particular, gourmet of the real, and it is this outlook, along with some of his jokey, gee-whizzy mannerisms, that he shares with other members of the New York School, notably, Frank O'Hara ..."*

JS: (laughing) What "Gee-Whizzy Mannerisms!"

HH: (Helena Hughes sitting near us breaks in) You know Jimmy, when you read the papers in the morning (laughing)!

JS: I think we're all part of nature willy-nilly!

MH: *He goes on to say that the best short poems are in the present tense.*

JS: I don't think about what tense I'm using. It's whatever is appropriate to whatever I'm going to say in a particular poem. And I don't have any scheme. At one time I was rather religious, though I'm not now.

MH: *What did you make of O'Hara's essay called "Personism"?*

JS: It didn't interest me. It's not one of the things of Frank's that I liked.

MH: *Why do you think he wrote it?*

JS: He wrote it because he could never shut up (laughs).

MH: *You wrote a statement for Donald Allen's anthology for your own poetry where you mentioned the poets and painters in New York as a group more or less in the same boat, but it was the painters who were steering the boat!*

JS: I guess I believed that at the time. It doesn't seem so true to me now.

MH: *As you were writing the title poem "The Crystal Lithium," did you feel that it was another breakthrough—the long poem?*

JS: Yes, it seemed to break through into what I wanted. It was also a breakthrough because it was turning out to be one of my best poems. I was very aware of that.

MH: *Did you feel a need to write a long poem?*

JS: I don't know about feeling a need. As I said, it was triggered from having read "Song of Myself" by Whitman. The length of that suggested a length to me. I couldn't end it. Then I met somebody and fell in love and I ended it.

MH: *Again, Edmund White says that, "Only through the long poem can Schuyler recreate the experience of time living through us."*

JS: That may be true, but I don't think about things like that. I think I just want to keep the story going.

MH: *You write well with other people in collaboration.*

JS: I enjoy it.

MH: A Nest of Ninnies, *with John Ashbery.*

JS: John and I had a ball writing *A Nest of Ninnies.*

MH: *How did it come about?*

JS: John and I were being driven back to New York by somebody we didn't like, so in the back seat of the car we started writing it, primarily, I think, to bug the driver.

MH: *It must have been a long ride?*

JS: Well, we didn't write the whole novel that day. It took sixteen years!

MH: *How did you write it?*

JS: On and off. We started out by writing it line by line, but then we allowed ourselves more freedom to write whole paragraphs as we went along.

MH: *You never quarreled over a line, or edited each other?*

JS: No. I've never really quarreled with John about anything.

MH: *And now you're writing another collaborative novel with Helena Hughes?*

JS: And another novel with Tom Carey called *Small Crimes.*

MH: *How does it work out?*

JS: Well, Helena gets to do the typing … (laughing)

HH: I sit here and Jimmy sits there.

MH: *Who gives each other the lines, or do you just do your own work?*

JS: We say out loud the lines we thought of.

HELENA HUGHES

MH: *Do you outline a plot together?*

HH: No.

JS: I wanted to call it "In County Wexford" but Helena won't let me because her parents live in County Wexford, Ireland.

MH: *Getting back, how did you know when or where to stop* A Nest of Ninnies?

JS: At the penultimate chapter I was willing to stop but John said, no, we needed more. So, we went on and wrote the last chapter that takes place at the ristorante.

MH: *Do you feel the same about writing prose as compared to writing poetry?*

JS: In a way, although writing prose is a more relaxed affair.

MH: *More relaxed?*

JS: Yes, it's less intense.

MH: *Do you feel freer when writing prose?*

JS: I feel free when I write, but poetry and prose are like two different states of mind.

MH: *So, you do separate them?*

JS: Yes.

MH: *When and where was* What's For Dinner *written and how did it start?*

JS: I wrote the first page one day in Maine in the sixties and I put it in a drawer and didn't think about it for years. Then I got it out, I think it was the summer of 1972, and worked on it quite hard, but I couldn't seem to finish it. When I moved back to New York City in 1973 I did finish it. Then it was turned down by every publisher in New York until it was finally published by Black Sparrow in California.

MH: *How did you get such an easy conversational tone into the dialogue? It seems almost overheard.*

JS: That's just the way I write dialogue.

MH: *But it sounds authentic.*

JS: The characters are not based on real people. It's entirely invented, except for the hospital where the leading character goes to take a cure for alcoholism. That was based on a hospital where I had been, though not for alcoholism.

MH: *So, you do have a familiarity with convalescent wards and group therapy sessions?*

JS: Yes. They weren't wards. They were all in private rooms.

MH: *Taken as a whole, the book appears to be a discourse on the suburban mentality.*

JS: I spent a lot of my youth in the suburbs, so I know about that. I rather like the lifestyle.

MH: *In your novels, as well as in your poetry, I get the impression that most of your work deals entirely in the concrete of daily life.*

JS: Yes, well, I don't think I have a philosophical cast of mind. I'm more of an observer.

MH: *Do you read philosophy at all?*

JS: No, never.

MH: *Not even in a vicarious way from other people's reading of it?*

JS: Perhaps, slightly, I don't think very much. The only philosophy I've read is Catholic, at the time when I was thinking of becoming a Catholic.

MH: *Thomas Aquinas?*

JS: Yes, but more Pascal. Pascal, I liked very much, so I guess I have read some philosophy.

MH: *It's more evident when reading* The Home Book. *There's a few sections in "The Infant Jesus of Prague" and in other sections where it becomes theological.*

JS: Yes, well, "The Infant Jesus of Prague" is really rather a cryptic description of a nervous breakdown.

MH: *That's very interesting, because the way it's written seems like a prose poem.*

JS: It is. At the time I was very much under the influence of Rimbaud. I think I was trying to imitate "A Season in Hell." Whereas the title poem "The Home Book" was an attempt to write in the style of Boris Pasternak's early stories. They're both very early efforts.

MH: *The separate sections in those poems remain autonomous, yet in a certain way connect by making metaphorical leaps.*

JS: Yes, that's correct.

MH: *Were you writing it while undergoing a nervous breakdown?*

JS: Oh no, only in retrospect.

MH: *When was "The Home Book" written?*

JS: "The Home Book" and "The Infant Jesus of Prague" were both written in 1952.

MH: *How did it come into print, because the date of publication is 1977.*

JS: It was printed in *C Magazine* in the sixties, and in *Art and Literature*. The book of those separate pieces was put together by Trevor Winkfield, an English friend of mine, who used to put out a very good magazine in England.

MH: *The Home Book ends off where "The Morning of the Poem" begins. The last line is about Darwin and in the beginning of "Empathy and New Year" from your collection,* The Morning of the Poem, *you mention Darwin.*

JS: Yes, I was keeping a little diary at the time I wrote those poems. I love Darwin, he had a very open and loving, generous character. I felt this about him from having read his autobiography.

MH: *There's a poem, on page 34 in* The Home Book, *which I believe to be truly representative of a brand of "New York School" writing—it's called "Things to Do."*

JS: It wasn't invented by the "New York School"; it was invented by me! Ted Berrigan has stylized a version of it in his "Things to Do in Providence."

MH: *When did you meet Ted Berrigan?*

JS: While I was living out in the Hamptons during the sixties, Ted called up and said Edwin Denby had shown him some poems of mine and that he would like to publish them in *C Magazine*. Later on, Kenward Elmslie had a little get-together at his place where I met Ted Berrigan and Tony Towle and Joe Brainard, the painter. Joe, in particular, became a very close friend of mine. Ron Padgett was maybe at that meeting, too. I remember going to Ron's house for dinner one night, and Ted and his first wife, Sandy, were there. After that I saw quite a bit of Ron Padgett. At one time, Fairfield Porter used to give him his house when he and his wife were away. Ron would house-sit.

MH: *You've written a funny sketch of Ron Padgett in* The Home Book, *called "At Home with Ron Padgett."*

JS: Yes, that was a reply to a sketch he did of me. It's really entirely a collage.

MH: *What did you think of those, then, younger poets? Did you think of them as a second generation to you and Ashbery and O'Hara?*

JS: I think they're fine. Yes, I think of them as a continuance. You've seen Ron Padgett's and David Shapiro's *New York Poets Anthology* by Random House?

MH: *Yes, I have a copy. They should reprint it.*

JS: Maybe Full Court Press would. I think it was a publishing disaster. It didn't sell at all. The only mistake in it was that they left out Barbara Guest. At that time, Ron Padgett didn't like her work, though I'm told he later apologized to her for it. Kenneth Koch went to see him and practically went down on his knees and said, "You can't do it without Barbara!"

MH: *Do you like Barbara Guest's poetry?*

JS: Yes, I do, very much. I loved her novel *Seeking Air*.

MH: *Do you write sonnets?*

JS: Not any more. A friend of mine, Arthur Gold, a man I once lived with, encouraged me to try writing in the formal styles, so I did for a little while—this irritated John Ashbery very much, who once said, "Have you written anything lately that would interest me?"

MH: *But Ashbery's written formal verse?*

JS: I don't know. I know that he was very mad at Frank O'Hara for writing the sonnet "A City Winter" and using the conventional form of the sonnet.

MH: *Were you taken with Denby's sonnets?*

JS: I think they're great but I wasn't influenced by them.

MH: *Or John Wheelwright?*

JS: I like his poetry.

MH: *What do you like about it?*

JS: (quoting lines of a Wheelwright sonnet) "What was that sound I heard fall in the snow? It was a frozen bird, why must you know?" I think that's a great way to write.

MH: *He's very difficult.*

JS: In some poems, not in all. He was a good friend of Fairfield Porter. He has a poem dedicated to him.

MH: *I believe that Wheelwright, Fairfield Porter, and James Laughlin were all at Harvard together.*

JS: And Lincoln Kirstein. Lincoln had big eyes for Fairfield which scared the shit out of Fairfield (laughs)—this great huge towering brute positively luring over him.

MH: *Did you ever meet Dylan Thomas in New York in the early fifties?*

JS: I once went with Howard Moss to hear him read. I told Frank O'Hara I was going and Frank said, "I can't stand all that Welsh spit!" I thought he was too theatrical as a reader. At one time I liked his poetry more than I do now.

MH: *When did you meet Edwin Denby?*

JS: I first met him in Italy when he and I were both living there, then I got to know him in New York City in 1952. We had sort of a relationship and that ended very badly. I used to go to the ballet with him and to the concerts. He was a very elegant man, very aristocratic, Harvard background; his father was an admiral. There used to be a senator, Edwin Denby, and there was this Edwin Denby cigar which was quite his style. He's about twenty years older than I am. He appeared older.

MH: *Was he at all influenced by you and O'Hara?*

JS: No, he'd already published a book of poems. Frank admired him very much.

MH: *Do you think writing formally is easier?*

JS: Oh, it's sort of fun titillating round with a form. There's a translation of a Dante sestina in Freely Espousing which I enjoyed doing very much.

MH: *Do you internalize the poetic forms?*

JS: No, I don't write that way at all. I write as I go along, even in the strict forms of a sestina or a villanelle. Those technical aspects of poetry are something I simply never think about.

TOMPKINS SQUARE PARK

Interview with Gerald Stern

In 1979, I was shelving books in the Brentano's Bookstore where I worked, and in my hands, I held a copy of Gerald Stern's *Lucky Life* that I couldn't put down.

When I met him for the first time to interview him, I was just starting out on my series of interviews with New York poets, and I learned a lot from his poetry and from what he said to me about poetry and from that first interview, our friendship grew and we became close.

In October, 2023, along with other poets, I spoke at Stern's memorial in Manhattan. And what he said to me about poets when I first interviewed him forty years before resonated so strongly with me after his death at age ninety-seven, that I decided to read his last words from that interview because of what he meant to me as a poet and as a friend:

> ... Poets are witnesses, living proofs of the uniqueness of the individual soul, of the unforgivable sadness of its perishing ...

Stern's poetry has been a touchstone for me and whenever I read his work, I hear his strong voice.

When I first knew him, he kept an apartment in Tribeca, a fifth-floor walk-up on Vandam Street. "Jerry," as he liked to be called, was at home in his New York apartment, and he made it his city. Many of his poems, although not "New York School," are poems rooted in his life and memory of his adopted city.

When Ted Berrigan died, Jerry came at my invitation for the funeral service at Saint Mark's Church and I walked with him in the subsequent parade down Second Avenue with all the East Village poets, over fifty of us, walking together. I introduced Jerry to many of the poets that July day in 1983 who were part of the "second generation" New York School.

The poem I read at Jerry's memorial was a poem from *Lucky*

Life titled "At Bickford's," a very "New York" poem, and one in which his speaker recounts moments of his past with rancor and who is now ready to begin a new life filled with forgiveness for his troubled past.

Stern comes from a generation that I miss as I get older, a generation that knew what the world was like before WWII. The stories of his growing up are what I miss, the stories that Jerry would tell me about his life. He was like a poetry father to me and I will miss him.

GERALD STERN AT HOME IN MANHATTAN

MH: *In the poem "In These Shadows," from* The Red Coal, *I get a feeling of communion with nature. You seem to be in two worlds—the country and the city, and write about their differences. You understand both; this seems unusual.*

GS: These are two separate issues you're raising. One, the dialogue between city and country; the other, the issue of communion with nature. As far as the first issue is concerned, clearly, I have a dialogue with whatever's going on; as far as the second issue, I am particularly, and passionately, concerned with the connection between city and country. New York is my city now, though it is not my original city, and there are memories of other cities—Pittsburgh, Philadelphia, Paris. On the other hand, there's where we are now, Raubsville, Pennsylvania, two hours west of New York and two hours north of Philadelphia, yet ironically so close. That answer's a little vague.

MH: *But you live in both worlds.*

GS: I live in both worlds, yes, but if it were just that it would be boring. It's what those things stand for. I think it is probably the most ancient dialogue in literature. Aesop writes about it—the country mouse and the city mouse. In America, it's a particular issue—Hawthorne, Cooper, a thousand other writers have addressed it: "Evil" city, "innocent" nature, etc. It is reflected in the great myth Freud is touching on when he talks about the conscious and the unconscious. As far as I'm concerned it goes back as far as Gilgamesh, the rural bumpkin, the stranger coming into the center of things, civilization, or as Joyce called it, "Syphilization," with its strange order, with its 100,000 books. It's a religious center, an economic center, a cultural center. The other place, the "country," is revealed in the unconscious, the past, the interior, the resource place from which, through which, we provide—against which, we work to provide—the logic and the rules of order, of civilization. I mean this metaphorically, not literally—mythically.

Before I moved here to Raubsville, I was obsessed with these two places although they were for me imaginary or, as I say, mythic locations. What I did was discover my own myth here in my front yard. In *The Pineys*, a long epic poem which I spent seven years writing, and which I finally published in the early 1960s, I deal with the two poles. It's a poem about the presidency, a comic political poem. The two poles are the White House and the "Black House." The White House is a perfect example of what I'm talking about since not only the physical building but the idea behind it comes out of the eighteenth century, the age of reason, the age of order. And just behind and under all that order is chaos and destruction and disorganization and timelessness and simplicity and primitivism and childishness. The "country." That's what the poem is about, the

GERALD STERN IN FRONT OF HIS CANAL HOUSE IN RAUBSVILLE

connection between those two things. I think of the "Pineys," the so-called inhabitants of the Pine Barrens of southern New Jersey, (so-called because there really are no Pineys), as the symbol of the one order and the White House, or its inhabitants, as the symbol of the other. Philadelphia, where I was living then when I was writing *The Pineys*, is the city of reason and logic and order, dramatized by the streets being laid out in a grid, organized, so to speak, from the mind. It becomes the seat of "civilization." Ironical, of course, considering Mayor Rizzo, and the self-destruction. About one-half hour away, just outside Camden, New Jersey, begins the chaos, the invisible world of the Pine Barrens, the million-and-a-half acres of darkness stretching into the dim past, and to the Atlantic Ocean. I view this ironically, as I say. When someone goes from Philadelphia in that mad drive of an hour-and-a-half to Atlantic City, he passes right through the "unconscious"—and he doesn't even see it! And of course, being a Philadelphian, being orderly and logical and hell-bent for fun, he's not even interested, so he doesn't slow down. Dozens of poets have touched on this idea in different ways. It turns out that when I discovered this house by the river, I said, "My

God, there's my metaphor!" I'm practically in New York City. I can get there in an hour and a half on a good day. But yet, I'm in the past here. This house was built in 1820; there's a canal right outside my door.

MH: *Then there's the mysterious force of the Delaware River.*

GS: Exactly. An example of what I'm doing can be seen in "The Roar," which appears in *The Red Coal*. It's a seduction poem, which takes place in New York City, in my apartment on Vandam Street. The poem describes taking a woman upstairs; it describes the Empire State Building, which I refer to as the "red and blue beacon of Empire," which I can see from my window, but I always return to the memory of this place. Let me just read it:

> That was the last time I would walk up those five
> flights with a woman in tow, standing
> in the hall patiently trying my keys,
> listening to my heart pounding from the climb.
>
> And the last time I would sit in front of the
> refrigerator, drinking white wine and asking
> questions, and lecturing—like a spider—
> and rubbing my hand through my hair—like a priest.
>
> Look at me touch the burning candle
> with my bare palm and press a rusty knife
> against my left eyelid while she undresses.
>
> Look at me rise through the cool airshaft
> and snore at the foot of the bed with one hand
> on her knee and one hand touching the white floor,
>
> the red and blue beacon of Empire
> just beyond those little houses
> as familiar now as my crippled birch
>
> and the endless roar out there
> as sweet as my own roar
> in my other dream, on the cold and empty river.

There's the birch tree right out there [points out the window]. We're looking at it! It's a sort of bastard, a cripple, a pathetic orphan. I had to lop off a limb twelve years ago. These are the two worlds I'm living in; it's very personal. It's not an idea I'm dealing with, it's passionate, it's my world. In *Lucky Life*, I have a poem called "One Foot in the River." Again, there are two worlds, New York's "river" (Seventy-Second Street in the poem) and this river, the Delaware. But it's the two. I don't prefer one to the other.

MH: *Is the relationship I-Thou?*

GS: I think the I-Thou relationship exists for me in both places. Although "I-Thou" is a little pretentious, perhaps inaccurate. It's not that I have peace in the country and conflict and tension in the city. Ironically, in fact, I go to my apartment in New York for isolation and peace. I don't get my mail there; I get it here. That's my little cave, my little pocket of secrecy and anonymity, on the fifth floor. It's pockets of secrecy that I have always been searching for. Things that no one else wanted. I have a poem that ends, "the one thing in life no one else wanted." Things that are ignored or overlooked; weeds. It is amazing what is passed by.

MH: *Do you think the reader needs a poet who understands both the city and the country?*

GS: Yes, because they exist in a new way now. I think the poems I write, the language I use, even the tone of them, are absolutely identical in either city or rural poems. The subject matter is different, and when I write a poem about a country experience, I write about natural objects, of course, flowers, animals, the river. But it's dealt with symbolically. It's my journey through the world, and this happens to be where I am. I'm not a nature poet. I don't glorify nature or find God in nature. I find the urban experience just as mysterious; equally, not more so. They interpenetrate.

MH: *So many city poets omit nature from their writing.*

GS: That's right, and it's interesting. I am always in a blurred state. That is, I am living in two places at once, literally, always. That's my joy, that's my secrecy, that's my survival. That's why

I don't get my heart attack. That's my peace. I have my secret in my hip pocket. In one of my poems, I mention that I am carrying the secret of life in my hip pocket. I walk through the Village and I'm somewhere else. I think it's quite possible that urban people have lost memory. It might be that country people have, too, except that I think they are in a better state in terms of their mental health through contact with nature, though I don't know what the statistics are. Poets and artists who live only in the city, if such can be the case, are to be pitied; they're cripples. I mean who live "psychically" only in the city. I know a writer from New York—he's an essayist in his early sixties—who's been out of New York twice in his life, once to New Orleans when he was in the Army, and once to London. One night after a concert, we were walking down a street and he started to question me about soil, about earth. We were talking about that garden out there [points out the window], and it occurred to me that he didn't know, literally, that there was dirt, soil, under the streets of New York. He didn't know where the soil came from. He was literally out of touch. He was like Antaeus, weak from not touching the ground. One other example: there was a woman also from New York, who came out here to visit a number of years ago. She had a child with her, a little girl, who looked up at the sky after supper and saw the stars for the first time and started to scream with terror.

MH: *In absolute fear?*

GS: The anonymity of the city provides a kind of security. There's an endless hum practically everywhere. Even though there is the myth of isolation and the terror that nobody will notice you dying next door, you still know that there are people all around you, and that gives you a sort of comfort. Whereas in the country you are alone, or can be alone. You and nature, you and mystery, you and yourself. I love being alone, I love it! I have to be alone. I guess a lot of people are never alone. It's kind of crazy but it's true. Of course, being alone may not be a natural state either, or a sane one.

MH: *For a poet, it's important.*

GS: For a poet, it's critical ... I'm interested in how the city poets feel.

MH: *They give you the city.*

GS: Well, that's not enough. They're creating a surrogate natural world. That's interesting, but they're probably out of touch with nature. They probably have a certain amount of contempt for it.

MH: *You have the other extreme, like Gary Snyder.*

GS: Yes.

MH: *He preaches death to cities.*

GS: I suspect that he has some mainstream western prejudices. He presents the city as if it were not natural, not sound, that is not the way humans should live, that cities are corrupt and destructive. But when I hear someone talk that way about cities, I'm always a little suspicious because of how he benefited from them. One used to have to literally go to the city for stimulus, for art and information and education. Now the city, because of technology, can be spread out. There are university campuses which have the aspect of the city. We have radio and TV and movies, which provide an extended and symbolic city. But we are still dependent on the actual city. And I suspect that what Gary Snyder is living off of still comes from the city. The very ideas. Maybe technology has made cities obsolete, or even impossible to live in, or unnecessary. Maybe we can live in groups of twelve with all the advantages of the big city. An idea from the fifties. But I don't think so. The city, as city, is still very important. There are things you can get there that you can't get anywhere else. Accessibility to information, stimulation. I'm a little uneasy, a little bored, by the "know nothing" attack on cities. It's fundamentalist and reactionary and fake bucolic and sentimental; and ridiculous. It comes out of the eighteenth-century court, and the nineteenth century mud farm. It comes partly from our inability to pursue or stick to an idea, or be loyal to it. It comes from our failure, and our devotion to the ugly, and our habits of dumping. From our very hatred and fear of life and people and their things. And it's mostly a privileged position. I haven't seen Chinese or Black or Puerto Rican writers espousing it. Poor people in the cities don't know where Big Sur is, or how to get there. And I'm sure poor people in New York, and Philadelphia, don't know how to get to Raubsville. There are poor people in the country, but that's not what we're talking about. Anyhow, I love cities. I love Venice and Glasgow and Cleveland and St. Louis. I love walking through them. And I love only the old parts. And I love New York most of all. It's our one great city.

MH: It's our Europe.

GS: It's our Europe, it's our past, and of course it's the one place in the East where non-whites live in great numbers, and naturally.

MH: *Your poetry has a strong Yiddish element, being that you are Jewish and from a big city.*

GS: My mother was born in a city in what is now Poland and was then Polish Russia, but which the Jews identify with ancient Lithuania, in their crazy archaic way, the city of Bialystok. My grandfather was a holy man and killed chickens and taught boys, and wrote essays on Tolstoy and Goethe; and his family lived in a ghetto, both in Bialystok and Pittsburgh. My father was born on a farm in the Ukraine, eighty miles from Kiev. He remembers, as a child, sleeping, in the Ukrainian style, on top of the stove. He remembers them having a cow, one cow, that provided all the sustenance for the family. He remembers riding on a horse and wagon with his older brother through the woods, and wolves snapping at the legs of the horses. His father was a stogie manufacturer in Pittsburgh. My father's oldest American brother and my grandmother's second husband had farms near Pittsburgh. There's a strong element of the farmer in the Jewish tradition, at least in ancient times, a longing for the land. The city was foreign, and mysterious, and a little evil. Jews didn't have their own city until relatively late in history, and then it was more a religious center than anything else. It wasn't until much later that they became city people—when they left their own land. And if they became stunned and baffled in the country, it was because it was alien to them. Jews are now city rats, of course, but I think that somewhere in the Jewish unconscious—that's a Jungian term—is the vision and the experience of the country. That explains early Zionism. I myself grew up in a very crowded dense city, but which, because of the hills, has little silent pockets—hillsides and valleys—and little woods. That landscape was very important to me. And the tree I identify with those little pockets is that dear weed, the black locust. Those little woods were redemptive. My own synagogue.

MH: *There is an element of Jewish sadness in your poetry— "Four Sad Poems on the Delaware."*

GS: Right, you remember that because of the mention of the black locust tree, "growing more and more Jewish as its limbs weaken." And notice I call it the "black" locust. I identify it by its bark.

MH: *"regretting its life on the stupid river,"*

GS: That tree is also called the "yellow" locust, a reference to the wood, or the "white" locust, a reference to the blossoms. My identity with that tree has something to do with Judaism, and with persecution. The tree is short-lived—forty years maybe—it's asymmetrical, considered ugly, worthless. Farmers value it only as a source of fence posts. People, when they buy land, chop them down to replace them with shade trees—I love that tree, I identify with it; it's my poverty tree. I sometimes see the concentration camp number on the forearm, or forelimb. I write about it constantly. I don't identify a lot with the oak or the smooth maple—*Ah zeh geht es*, as we say in Yiddish—so it goes! I'm reaching an age now where I'm going to make my choices and say, "That's what I like, fuck it." Some people like their eggs dry, some wet; well, I'm not going to apologize anymore. I'm realizing that life is short and I'm going to say, "That's what I want."

MH: *There's also a sense of loss. The poems "At Bickford's" and "Straus Park" are two good examples. They're completely void of humor.*

GS: There's more humor in the later poems, but there is a lot in those, too, in the language and the juxtaposition. I began to realize, at a certain point, what loss meant to me personally [reaching for his briefcase]. I've just recently written a long essay for a book that's coming out called *In Praise of What Persists*. I address your question in my essay and I try to explain what my loss was. The name of the essay is "Some Secrets" [pulling out papers]. Without explaining everything, let me just say that in talking about my development as a poet and the influences on me, I refer to a "crisis" that occurred on my fortieth birthday, *a crise de quarante*, right on target. "I think when I look back now"—I'm quoting from my essay—"that it was my own loss and my own failure that were my subject matter. As if I could only start building in the ruins. Or, that loss and failure were a critical first issue in my finding a new subject matter, that they showed me the way. Or, that my subject was the victory over loss and failure, or coming to grips with them. But I certainly started with loss and failure. Moreover, in a certain sense, I always did start with these two and I was merely, finally, coming into my own, doing the thing more purely now that I had always done, more perfectly. It was as if I had been preparing for this all my life—certainly since my sister's death and my mother's sadness—and now I was ready. At any rate, after a little agony, the poems started to come easily and simply. The first group were written in the winter and spring of 1966, at the time of my forty-first birthday. These poems are collected in *Rejoicings*, (the name of the tractate on mourning in the Talmud), and there's been no letup in the writing from that day to this."

My "sister's death and my mother's sadness" became a critical factor in my loss, and I think that generated or triggered a larger sense of loss. (I had no other brothers or sisters.) It wasn't just my sister's death, but my parents' response to the death in relationship to me, and my reaction to their response. It's not just an issue of nostalgia, it's hopeless loss, irretrievable loss. The American notion is that everything can be overcome or rebuilt—Bullshit! Some things are gone forever, not only passenger pigeons.

MH: *Peter Mathiesson said that whenever a creature becomes extinct it's like punching a hole in creation.*

GS: I like that. The American notion is that we can destroy nature but make it up later. There are irretrievable losses and everyone of us dies. It's hard to face in a country which will not truly acknowledge death, if I may add my plaint to the others. I talk about it in "The Shirt Poem." I write about the old Jews and the radicals who are lost forever. They will never come back. Somebody has to record it. Sometimes it may become sentimental or indulgent. I love old buildings. I spent some time in a burned out barrack in Camp Kilmer, New Jersey, and I wrote a short poem about it called "On the Far Edge of Kilmer." It's in *Rejoicings*. Here, I'll read it:

> I am sitting again on the steps of the burned out barrack.
> I come here, like Proust or Adam Kadmon, every night to
>   watch the sun leave.
> I like the broken cinder blocks and the bicycle tires.
> I like the exposed fuse system.
> I like the color the char takes in the clear light.
> I climb over everything and stop before every grotesque relic.
> I walk through the tar paper and glass.
> I lean against the lilacs.
> In my left hand is a bottle of Tango.
> In my right hand are the old weeds and power lines.
> I am watching the glory go down.
> I am taking the thing seriously.
> I am standing between the wall and the white sky.
> I am holding open the burnt door.

So, I love the ruin. What is it I'm writing about? It's very much the elegy, remembering and keeping the holiness for a while and saying, "Forgive me, brother building." But the wrecker never says that. I have, in *Lucky Life*, a poem about an old building in New Brunswick, New Jersey that was eventually torn down. I spent a lot of time there grieving over that building, walking through the ruins. Was that sentimental? Was it idle? Was it stupid? It may be that, but also, I was in a kind of religious state, or at least ecstatic. When you think of the elegy you think of somebody going down, of something ending, and you try to save something of him or her—in this case "it"—by writing about it. I have a series of poems in *Rejoicings* about an old friend of mine, Robert Summers, from Philadelphia, a magnificent playwright, who died about ten years ago. In the first poem in the book titled "Rejoicings," I bury Bob in a crazy imaginary ritual in the sand in Atlantic City in front of the Marlborough Blenheim (now destroyed). I call him Nietzsche in that poem, and throughout the book. The Nietzsche of will, the anti-tender Nietzsche. But I am treating Bob in a non-Nietzschean, even anti-Nietzschean way at the end of the poem. I say, in my own ritual [reads a few stanzas of his poem "Rejoicings"]:

.....

I make a good circle before digging
so I can close the whole world in my grip
and draw my poor crumbling man
so that his tears fall within the line.
.....

I pour a little mud on my head
for the purification
and rub the dirty sand into my shirt
to mix everything with crystal.

I put a piece of shell for killing birds
in the open hand
and all the paraphernalia of the just,
bottle and paper and pencil,

for the work to come.
I wait one hour. That is the time it takes
to free the soul, the time it takes
for reverence.

Once or twice I have to alter the grave
so the water can come in quietly.
I am burying our Nietzsche;
I am touching his small body for the last time.

MH: *You bury yourself in "Rotten Angel."*

GS: Right, and the angel of death, the Malacamovitz, comes swimming across the river to an unfamiliar island where it's dirty and the water is covered in green slime, and he's angry that he has to come to that distant place when he's really more accustomed to coming to Baltimore or Boston or New York; and why did he have to come so far—where I've assigned myself a grave—and have to go through his ritual, his duty? It's a series of redemptions. You have to start over and over again. That's why spring is so important to me. And others. I have poem after poem about birth and rebirth. I have a poem I just finished titled "Leaving another Kingdom" which describes a walk to my graveyard with Phil Levine. The island graveyard. It's a spring poem. I'll read the first few lines:

> I think this year I'll wait for the white lilacs
> before I get too sad.
> I'll let the daffodils go, flower by flower,
> and the blue squill, and the primroses,
> Levine will be here by then,
> Waving fountain pens, carrying rolled-up posters
> of Ike Williams and King Levinsky.
> He will be reaching into his breast pocket
> for maps of grim Toledo
> showing the downtown grilles and the bus stations.
> He and I together
> will get down on our hands and knees

.....

Spring is a sad time because it is a time of rebirth. That means death. That's why Easter and Passover are so sad, and joyful at the same time. The two are connected. That is why a mother weeps when her child is born. I hope this doesn't sound too awful, or too mushy. She sees death! And the hard life ahead. The unbelievable miracle is going to end in a "second." A second may be a lifetime of sixty, seventy, or eighty years, but it's a second. And the mother knows that. Then she fortunately forgets and goes on with living. That's why the sadness in spring, the sadness in adolescence; that's why suicide.

MH: *That's why T. S. Eliot could write those old-man poems in his twenties and thirties.*

GS: That's right. As you get older you get younger. I'm getting younger every year. I'm actually almost happy now. Sometimes I have an hour or two of actual happiness. It's not that I'm seeing new colors or hearing new sounds, it's just that I'm enjoying life. Of course, friends think I'm a creature who, because of his excessive response to things, loves everything. I love to eat and talk and sing, but happiness is something else.

MH: *How do you deal with the stereotype image of being "the poet" living in the country?*

GS: I don't know if you're putting me in some category or if that's a literary question. This is a river town and a working-class neighborhood, democratic and tolerant, and not too far from Easton and Scranton, which are urban. My neighbors see me as an ally since I've helped them fight the bastards that want to destroy everything, be it through rezoning or fake recreation or nuclear power plants. In fact, my plumber, who is a township supervisor, never charges me because of some things I've done to save the life on the river. My place is open; my kids went to the public school. I'm part of the community. The people here are a hell of a lot more tolerant than they are in the suburbs. And wiser. When *Lucky Life* came out, a local general store sold fifty or sixty copies off their little book rack. Sometimes people here even ask me about individual poems. I've never had a problem with my neighbors. I've had problems with neighbors in Philadelphia and Pittsburgh and New York, but not here. And their problems are the same as mine; they are not bucolic, and quaint.

MH: *You seem to mention certain famous literary names in your poems, like Nietzsche and John Ruskin and Spinoza.*

GS: Part of it is the love of the name. And the very love of their existence. Great minds in themselves are like cities. They are concentrations of energy and memory, and they are constantly being praised or reclaimed and rekindled. I just love contemplating the idea of an Einstein or Ruskin as he goes through his time. It's also a love of my elders, and a reverence for the past.

MH: *You mention van Gogh; how do you identify with him as an artist?*

GS: I identify with his devotion as an artist, not with his insanity. I've written a number of poems which honor the artist trying to survive in an unkind world. I'll eventually get over that self-pity. My last poem in *The Red Coal*, "Here I Am Walking," or "Self-Portrait," from *Lucky Life*, deals with the artist in this way.

The life of an artist is almost the only holy life I can imagine. There are other people I honor, political radicals such as Emma Goldman and Eugene Debs, and also losers or "victims" like Bob Summers, a victim but a great playwright. It's difficult, it's almost impossible, to honor, or write in a positive way about anyone who has benefited, or is identified with the master culture. Anyone with power. So, our poets write about the weak and the old and the lost. And the poor animals. All the best poets—Roethke, Wright, Levine, Berryman, C. K. Williams, and William Carlos Williams. And, of course, bad poems are produced about dying grandmothers, and helpless fathers and sick children.

MH: *At the* Paris Review *reading in New York City a few nights ago, you mentioned that your poem "Here I Am Walking" is really a celebration of the poet's life.*

GS: With tongue in cheek. I talk about how I'm trying to make up my mind for the great time to come, when I will become a pure poet again and relieve myself of all other duties, and where I will settle [reads the end of the poem]:

>   —I am still making my mind up
>   between one of those art deco hotels
>   in Miami Beach, a little back room on a court
>   where you could almost be in Cuba or
>   Costa Rica of the sweet flesh, and
>   a wooden shack in one of the mosquito marshes
>   in Manahawkin or the Outer Banks.
>   I am planning my cup of tea
>   and my sweet biscuit,
>   or my macaroni soup
>   and my can of sardines ...

I get into the daily life of the artist. The dream life.

MH: *Wallowing in your own ritual.*

GS: Right, my own ritual. And I end the poem:

>   I will be just where I was

307

>   twenty-five years ago,
>   breathing in salt,
>   snorting like a prophet,
>   turning over the charred wood;
>   just where I was then,
>   getting rid of baggage,
>   living in dreams,
>   finding a way to change, or sweeten, my clumsy life.

That's what art is about, finding a way to change or sweeten your life.

MH: *There's a great similarity with the poem you just read and your first poem from* Lucky Life, *"At Bickford's."*

GS: That's a memory from my youth. Yes, it's similar in tone. It was a madness, living on four dollars a day. Pure dream.

MH: *In those poems, and in much of your other poetry, you're writing about a life that is constantly re-examining itself.*

GS: It's what I do. And I must do it over and over. I'm never satisfied. It's my nymphomania, my satyriasis.

MH: *There's doom in it.*

GS: There's doom in it. You've got to start over every time. I have now two hundred, three hundred, decent poems. Why shouldn't I just sit back and retire and say, "Bring me my cup of tea." But if I go a couple of weeks without writing I get anxious, unlocated. Each time I write it's like starting over. I give myself no credit for anything I've ever done. It's not that I don't like my work, I admire my work. I hope that doesn't sound egotistical, but I like what I'm doing, what I've done. But I've got to constantly start over. Maybe it's guilt, that says I have to earn my keep in the world. William Merwin is my house guest now during the Roethke festival up at Lafayette College, and I think he's the same way. He has seventeen books and is included in every anthology; he showed me new poems last night and he too is starting over. Beautiful poems.

MH: *Roethke writes in his poem "What Shall I Tell My Bones"—"Beginner, perpetual beginner ..."*

GS: Exactly, I love it! I don't know what it would be like not being an artist. Maybe I'd be unhappy, or dead. This work gives me joy. I love the community of artists.

MH: *When you're among poets you don't have to explain yourself.*

GERALD STERN AND JACK GILBERT

GS: Right. I find myself talking to Merwin and trying to explain things and he'll say, "Jerry, I see, you know." It's just because I'm so used to being with younger people who don't yet understand, or non-artists. I find myself more and more writing poems about other poets, too. I have a poem called "Steve Dunn's Spider" that's coming out in *Poetry* this summer—along with some poems by Steve Dunn himself. It'll be fun to have them side by side. I love that community, but not in the political sense of who got a grant, or who got published, or who got laid. You talk about that to some degree, but I find myself talking more about it to younger poets who are desperate for recognition and identity. I don't know if Merwin even knows that I recently won an award for my last book from the Poetry Society of America. It would be really silly of me to mention it to him. It never occurred to me, or for him to mention that he just got a grant. If he did. That's not what our friendship is about, to my relief. Jack Gilbert is at this festival and he and I practically grew up together, you know. His new book is just out and it's getting a lot of praise and I'm utterly delighted. Although, I hate the jacket flap. Linda Gregg, who is also here, just won a Guggenheim. I wrote her a glorious letter; I feel a little responsible, but a community of artists in not a community of bankers. At least, that's how I feel today. Some days I wish we would behave with the socially acceptable indecency of bankers. Instead of hiding our greed and terror. Maybe I have two subjects going.

MH: You write about poetry entering your life as a burning coal. When did you realize that you had this feeling for poetry?

GS: Ah, the burning coal. I discovered after I wrote the poem, "The Red Coal" that Shelley had mentioned the coal and Isaiah. But I may have been thinking of Moses' tongue. It's a hard question to answer. I had a late start. Not exactly a late start, but late recognition. I started to write as a freshman in college. I carried a little notebook around with me. But I didn't think of myself as a poet. And I wasn't an aesthete. There were no workshops in those days; I didn't hang out with poets. I was straight. I wore wing-tip shoes, white shirts, double-breasted suits, neckties. I played pool; I was on the football team. A walk-on. I was a pre-law student, and I also wrote poems, and I didn't know that that was a strange thing to do. I did that for years, and it was only after I went into the Army and was isolated and had a couple of traumatic experiences, a court-martial, a short stint in the guard house, that I began to write with more seriousness and to think of myself in a vague way as a poet. Although back then I thought that my main job was to read books, to arm myself, to learn, to change. Being a poet was something that would happen twenty years later. So I started off by renting a room, and I just read books for a couple of years. And I didn't become a dentist or a judge.

MH: *Did you feel that you had to catch up?*

GS: Yes. I was desperate. Part of that feeling, being an outsider, a peasant, is still with me. I'm always surprised when people see me as if I'm at the center of things. It embarrasses me and encumbers me. My God, I haven't fully studied *The Song of Roland*. I don't know Arabic literature ... But I was writing when I was twenty-two, and taking myself seriously. I ran into a couple of other poets at that time, Jack Gilbert and Dick Hazley, probably the only others in Pittsburgh. And we became friends. We read each other's poems and we talked about writing. Our prevailing myth was the poet in a hostile world. The world we were beginning to treat with scorn. We were learning that posture. A year or two later we went to New York, then to Europe. I was reading Pound and Auden, Rimbaud and Ben Jonson, Yeats and Crane; and studying languages, and studying Keats and Marlowe and Chaucer and Shelley, and Donne and Eliot, whatever I could get my hands on. But I kept starting over. I was publishing poems in my early twenties, good poems, poems that I'm not ashamed of even now, in good magazines. I would accumulate a group of thirty, thirty-five poems, and instead of publishing them as I should have done in a little book, I'd bury them or throw them away. It's as if I have two or three books locked away in my attic. Then finally I started when I was in my early thirties on *The Pineys*, and suddenly I was forty years old and I had been a practicing poet for twenty years and I was nowhere and had no recognition and people ten years younger than me were winning prizes and getting recognition and I went through a few crises and suddenly I didn't care and then the new poems happened.

MH: *You felt like giving it all up?*

GS: No, no, I never stopped being a poet. But it was as if I didn't care about the competition, even the recognition, and suddenly something happened. I think what happened was a recognition of aging and death in the most literal way. The end of protracted adolescence, I'm a little ashamed to say, that lasted until I was forty. Metaphysical adolescence. I was an eternally young teacher, an eternally old student. Putting obscure dictionaries in the baby carriage, that kind of stuff. Having a moustache, smoking cigars, driving old cars. The happy time. Then suddenly I was alone. I didn't have the props; or they didn't count. Suddenly I didn't want to do that anymore. It may be that the poems I was writing, the language say, changed the life, as well as the life changing the language. But the poems that eventually appeared in *Rejoicings* all of a sudden came pouring out of me when I was forty, forty-one years old, and there's been no letup since. The "red coal" entered my life when I was twenty, maybe. In the poem, of course, it's Jack Gilbert and I walking around Paris, New York, Pittsburgh, as young men, imagining what it was like when Williams and Pound walked around their cities.

MH: *With the whole world in front of you.*

GS: Yes.

MH: *You refer to those mentors a lot in* The Red Coal.

GS: Yes, my mentors ... I guess Ezra Pound, Wallace Stevens, Hart Crane, Auden ... but most of all Ted Roethke, and Whitman, and the Bible, the rhythms of the Bible. I mean the rhythms of ancient Hebrew.

I've always loved Roethke. In a way, Roethke has not gotten recognition yet. I think he's an extraordinary poet, maybe a great poet. His recognition will come in the future. The poems of his I like best are in *The Far Field*: "The Geranium," "Meadow Mouse," "The Thing," "The Storm," "Journey to The Interior," "Otto." His influences are Whitman and D. H. Lawrence and Robinson Jeffers and maybe the Bible and Rilke—my influences, too. He belonged to an interesting generation. I have more and more affection for them—Berryman, Rukeyser, Schwartz, Bishop, Lowell, Goodman. Most of them died like that [snaps his fingers]! By suicide, heart attack. So that Bill Merwin and I and Galway Kinnell and Phil Levine and Jack Gilbert and others are left without masters. We're orphans. Koch, Ashbery, Bly, Creeley, Ginsberg, belong in the same group. Isn't that interesting! We're orphans! We're a group of orphans [throwing up his hands]! It's amazing! Isn't that marvelous!

Who do we have to look to? We all look to Yeats of course, or Lawrence, or whoever the god is—Stevens, Pound. But the point is we don't have anybody alive now. If Schwartz were alive, he'd be a healthy sixty-eight. Olson would be seventy-four. Shapiro's alive, yes. And I like his poetry. But he's not an influence. Ciardi stopped writing many years ago. We don't have anybody in their late sixties who is either an authority or an influence, except Ignatow, of course a great poet! And Stafford. Stanley Kunitz is in his seventies. He was never part of that generation. He stands alone. He would say he was part of Roethke's generation. I think that's true. He developed late. Or received recognition late. But aside from Kunitz—and I don't think his influence as a poet is that extensive, although his poems are marvelous—there's nobody.

I forgot Warren, who's written his best poetry in the last ten years. There are a number of poets now, including myself, who have certain authority and influence over the younger generation, but we are still young poets in a way, even though we are in our fifties. Maybe we're not so young. Anyhow, maybe the others feel old; I shouldn't speak for them. There's no central authority, like Eliot. So, we have a series of things going on simultaneously. We have the world of Merwin, the world of Kinnell, the world of Levine. Ginsberg's probably the most popular. He's a fine poet in spite of his violin. Ashbery is the most popular among the professors. But he's also a fine poet. Ashbery on the one hand, Ginsberg on the other; they're very different.

MH: There's the "language-centered" poets vs. the "experience-centered."

GS: Except that I would describe it in a different way because I think of myself just as much language-oriented as experience-oriented. At any rate, it's nice to be living in a world where literary forces are diffused, where you can have the freedom to choose. Of course, freedom is terrifying. There's no one to lean on. And there's a younger generation of poets, some of whom aren't all that interested in reading or discovering the past. The question about the relationship of language to experience is something one could talk about endlessly. My own prejudice is that when you address yourself to language in poetry it should not be an obvious factor. That is, as far as the reader is concerned. I like the reader to read my poems, like the one on Levine, and think that what I'm writing about is Phil and I walking down to the island. Just that. I want him to be fooled, taken in. And I like the fact that when Jack Gilbert reads that poem, or Stan Plumly, or Steve Berg, they'll understand that what I'm also writing about are certain words in relationship to each other. I don't care who does what, but I'm inventing the experience, I can invent senselessness or I can invent sense. Of course, I believe in that walk, and it did happen, and it changed my life.

And what I'm suggesting is that a reference to what is called the real world is only a nominal reference, that it is not the real world as such, although on a certain personal level it is, because one gets caught in his own hallucinations and delusions. It might be more complicated if possible. Levine is involved in something equally difficult. Your tricks don't have to be spelled out. There are ways that poets have of acting and reacting which are unique, as far as language is concerned, and they are not to be taken at face value, and they're to be studied carefully, particularly the ones that are apparently very simple. Now this may sound anti-Ashbery but I don't mean it to be; in fact, I think he illustrates what I'm talking about sometimes. I think in some instances he's quite simple and loves the real world and understands that it is a dream. I share that with him and understand that we're talking about a dream place, that we're inventing this birch tree. But another part of me knows that the tree is real. Maybe it's really not that complicated. The important thing to realize is that we're talking about something critical, not an idle academic problem. I guess I believe poets can save the world if they get it right. At least their own lives.

MH: *What do you make of Robert Bly's notion of the "deep image"?*

GS: I think the poems in *Rejoicings* are more connected with the deep image than the later poems. I'm very much attracted to the deep image; I've always been there. I don't altogether understand it—every poet is involved with the deep image. Whatever it is, but giving oneself credit because of a vague allusion is not enough for me. I want the poem to have resonance in several different places at once. I want it to be arduous, yet simple. I want a person, after reading one of my poems three or four times, to say, "I didn't notice that before." I don't want to say the "gray gray" and let go at that. I want it to live in a number of worlds.

MH: *You would do what Baraka says to do, and that is to give the reader the real world.*

GS: Does he say that? The reader must have the real world. He must have it for survival, he must have it because it's there, no matter what the obscurantists say. And the mystic's world is the same as the agitator's world. It must be!

MH: *There's a very strong political element in a lot of your poems, "The Shirt Poem," for example, or "Joseph Pockets."*

GS: In neither case did I set out to consciously write a political poem. In one case, I was writing about shirts with souls; in the other case, I was writing about the sweet place. I think in both cases, I was being forced back into this world. That's the political act. It means eventually paying attention to the things of this world. And it means loving them, and grieving over their loss, or destruction. Although elegy can be an act of political avoidance. When you talk about political poetry you are talking about a kind of poetry, not a kind of politics. Of course, political poetry has to be plain and direct. But maybe not. Maybe the poem can be as difficult as Mallarmé or Hart Crane and be political. Maybe it can be political, but not a vehicle for political action. Pound approached that. Why is political activity less complex than other activity? Every twenty years we get onto this boring subject.

MH: *What about your own politics?*

GS: As far as conventional politics go, I identify with the Left, and I once loved Humphrey, and I loved Debs more, and I can't stand giving Bobby Kennedy credit for his belated leaps, and I'm kind of an anarchist, and I'm kind of a nihilist, the way all poets are. But I can't be a good political poet because I'm too nervous and I can't stick too long to a god.

I sometimes write poems that can be identified as political poems; but I sometimes write them thirty years after the issue. I suspect that political poetry has to do essentially not with the subject, as such, but with the state of mind of the poet when he's writing. The kind of political poetry I write can be seen in *The Pineys* and *Father Guzman*. I would obviously stop writing poetry for five years, if that could stop a war; I'd even write bad poetry, if I could. I hate posturing and pontificating and sighing no matter if the cause is good. Most of all, I hate profiteering. Sometimes, it turns out, my poetry is political in the best, that is the worst sense of the word. Which is fine with me. I detest Reagan. I detest the lethargy and complacency and stupidity of those who share in the power. I can't believe how dumb, and selfish, my brother Americans are. I ask Whitman to forgive us.

MH: *Your poetry sometimes sounds rabbinical.*

GS: Why not? I'm a rabbi! I was raised Orthodox and quit when I was thirteen years and one day old. I never had a negative feeling toward my religion, though I was sometimes bored. I am maybe a little hard on Reform Jews. I think it is because I hate organ music. My parents, who were born in Europe, fell in love with America, with cleanliness, canned food, and suburbs—the new. They had a hatred for the past. Unless they were listening to a record; or reminiscing. It was my generation that returned. Or started to. I am my mother's and father's "parent," even though true access was denied me. I don't blame the older Jews for being agents in the destruction of the Jewish culture, along with the rest of the past. There was no choice for them. They were becoming Americans. I have a certain pity, and I love that culture, though I know its weaknesses and its boredom, and I know that to live in 1880 in a ghetto was not so "Aye yi yi!" I love its crazy combinations, I admire its joy and optimism, its love of the mind, its hatred of violence, its acceptance of life, its sensuousness, its music. I can't accept the loss. Every year it becomes more overwhelming. One of my daydreams is that there is no slaughter, and there is a great Yiddish-speaking city in the east, and theatres and universities, and restaurants. And I walk among the tables. I say "the east" and I am thinking of New York, not the Levant.

MH: *Some of your lines seems to be out of Proverbs or Psalms. "The Blue Tie" for example. "More and more I go into the dark / sighing for what I leave behind me / instead of caring for what lies ahead."*

GS: I think my own use of the biblical has a lot to do with rhythm. I gave a reading with Grace Paley at the YMHA in Philadelphia a few years ago, during Jewish Week (it's just before Greek Week).

We went out to dinner and talked about what we were going to do that night. I said, "What are you going to do Jewish?" She asked me the same. Well, I gave the reading and a couple of people objected that it wasn't Jewish enough, then later a woman came over to me and pointed out how one of my poems, "The Rose Warehouse," starts off with language right out of the morning service. Listen to this [reads the beginning of "The Rose Warehouse" from *The Red Coal*]:

> Ah tunnel cows,
> watching over my goings out
> and my comings in,
> you preside, like me, over your own butchery.

Then she recited the lines from the morning service, in English, including the words "my goings out and my comings in." The very same words, and of course the rhythm, would influence the whole poem; so would the choice of words. The memory is strong.

MH: *You use anaphora in several poems to create rhyme at the beginning of lines.*

GS: My use of anaphora comes partly from Whitman, partly from the Bible. It's an ancient system. Like rhyme, and English stress, and free verse, it lends itself to misuse. It's something that just took me over—I didn't adopt it. I don't know why. It is chanting. You see it in Egyptian poetry, in American Indian poetry.

MH: *You have a new book coming out?*

GS: I may have half a book done. "Father Guzman," which is book-length, has just been published in the *Paris Review*. I'm productive.

MH: *Do you sit down to write every day?*

GS: I don't have a regular method. I only did once in my life, when I was twenty-four and living in Paris. I seem to be always carrying two or three poems around with me, and I turn to them in odd places. I don't have the leisure to be meditative, even to be organized. My dream is to have no responsibility; to have time. Maybe in the next life it will be like that.

MH: *Do you revise?*

GS: I was reading something recently that Hayden Carruth said about revising; he said that the whole poem is a revision. I work very hard.

MH: *You're more spontaneous?*

GS: The poem for me comes in two stages. The first stage is the germ, the inspiration. The poem may come like that [snaps his fingers], and I'll write it on an envelope or a piece of paper, and I'll probably write it in a kind of prose, and that's eighty percent of the poem. It happens in about ten seconds. If I'm lucky, I can get back to it in time to save it. I'll be in the same state of mind. My second stage is the labor, more and more of a pleasure for me, seeing if it's really a poem and what form it's going to take—short lines, long lines, stanzas, what length it will be. I don't think of it as a revision but as a second stage of the art. There is a final stage, which I suppose is truly a kind of revising or polishing. It is the least pleasurable because I agonize, I fight, over the words. Not to get them perfect. I used to believe in perfection, but now I try to get them efficient, to make them work. I used to believe in the perfect line. Marlowe and Keats. No more.

MH: *Do endings give you trouble, last lines, the summation, or is there too much of the grand statement making in poetry?*

GS: Several commentators say they like my endings and I guess I'm good at them, but I don't think that the ending is necessarily the critical part of the poem. The poem has to prepare the way to the ending. I've been working on a certain poem for about six or seven months now and I can't find the right last line for it, so the poem, in a sense, does not exist. The thought, the feeling, isn't realized yet. The grand statement might not be grandiose, it might not be melodramatic. It may not even be beautiful; it may even be a letdown. It has to be aesthetically—that is, verbally and morally—right, but not necessarily "better" than the rest of the poem. Everything depends on your signature, your breath, your person. Maybe your rhythm. Your peculiarity, your uniqueness. Your crankiness. That thumb print of yours. Poets are witnesses, living proofs of the uniqueness of the individual soul, of the unforgivable sadness of its perishing, or its immortality. Their poems cry out against all imprisonment. The more living the poet, the more unbearable the death; the greater the poem, the more it ransoms.

Interview with Tony Towle

The last time I saw Tony Towle was at the memorial reading for Paul Violi at The New School that was hosted by David Lehman in December 2011. I was one of the readers, and we all read our favorite Violi poem. Towle was a good friend of Violi's going back to the early 1970s when Towle was already teaching poetry workshops at The New School and Paul was one of the participants. Towle himself had taken poetry workshops from Kenneth Koch and Frank O'Hara at The New School in the early 1960s.

I first heard of Tony Towle from John Ashbery who mentioned his name as a poet I might be interested in reading. Afterwards, I went to the Saint Mark's Bookshop and found three of his books. He lived downtown in a loft in Tribeca and that was where my interview began and where I asked him questions about his early beginnings and how he got started writing poetry.

Towle once roomed for a while with the poet Frank Lima in an apartment that Frank O'Hara had once rented on East 9th Street, and when Lima moved out, Ted Berrigan's friend from Tulsa, Joe Brainard, moved in, and from watching Brainard work on collages, Towle incorporated collage in his poetry.

By just looking at the covers of Towle's books, you learn a lot about how close-knit the New York poetry world was, and how they published each other in their small presses, and how close they all were to the New York Abstract Expressionist painters.

Towle's first major collection published by Columbia University Press, titled *North*, won the 1970 Frank O'Hara Book Award, a Jasper Johns design graces its cover. Towle's next book, *Autobiography* published by Bill Zavatsky's *SUN*, has a Robert Motherwell drawing on its cover. Towle's *Works on Paper* published by Paul Violi's Swollen Magpie Press, has a Larry Rivers cover.

Not only did Towle write art reviews for *Art in America*, he worked for fifteen years at Tatyana Grosman's Universal Art Editions in West Islip, Long Island, where he met many of the New York School painters such as Johns, Rauschenberg, Motherwell, Newman, and Rivers, the place where they all printed their lithographs.

When I go back to read Towle's poetry, I enter that New York world of literary and artistic references to painters and poets, and to references to the city itself, its streets and places and architecture and to the very notion that Towle explores of how we all explore the city within ourselves in our own worlds.

MH: *Where were you born?*

TT: I was born in Manhattan in 1939 and my parents, who were middle class and came to New York from the Midwest, lived in Inwood on the northern tip of Manhattan. My father was from Omaha, Nebraska, and my mother was from Decatur, Illinois. They were both WASPS and came to NYC in 1935. Then we moved to Queens in 1941 to 1953. So, I really grew up in Queens, in what turned into an almost 100 percent Jewish neighborhood. I was the token goy. All my friends were Jewish. I could see the Manhattan skyline in the distance and I always knew that I wanted to be there. Then we moved to Westchester in 1953 and I went to high school in Westchester, two years in Dobbs Ferry and two years in East Chester. My father was an architect and did interior design but never made that much money.

MH: *Towle is what kind of name?*

TT: English. It is a Middle English variant of toll, either a trade name ot someone who took the toll. There were lots of toll roads and highways in Medieval England. It must have been a hideous job. I'm half German. My mother's name was Rigg, it's English, too, but my grandmother was List—German.

MH: *Any relation to the composer?*

TT: We used to think so. But my cousin, Garrett List, who's a musician, told me that's BS. I always liked history even before I got into literature on my own. I found history a more imaginative escape than stories until my twenties. It was just the fact that you're in one place and time is passing, and being in Queens, the whole range of time in sci-fi speculation, you don't know what the future is.

I've always had a sense of time passing. I always knew that at

TONY TOWLE

some point I was going to be older sitting back looking back, and no matter how old I got and regardless of my age, be it eight or nine, or thirty, or ninety, that all the previous time would have flown in that one instant. I felt that way in grammar school.

MH: *You hadn't read Proust yet either?*

TT: (laughs) No. Those thoughts made me feel peculiar since I liked history. Well, there was something on the radio about "Sons of the American Revolution" and my mother said, "Oh, that sounds interesting; we could belong to that." And, I said, "Why don't we?" And, she said, "They don't let Jews or Negroes belong!" My mom was a Midwestern liberal.

MH: *Church?*

TT: We usually went to Presbyterian Church. I went until fifteen or sixteen. I was always basically an agnostic. Church was social. I was skeptical, and still am.

MH: *Anybody in your family write poetry?*

TT: No. Mom read a lot. Dad never had the patience. He was very much of the moment.

MH: *Did they want you to be an artist?*

TT: No. It was always unclear what I was supposed to do. I was good in language. I knew a lot of history—Useless.

MH: *Knowing languages is useful.*

TT: Yes, but you didn't think so in the '50s. In the '50s, if you weren't going into science or math, anything else was considered useless. Then, you'd be a teacher! That was the attitude and I always felt resentful and obstinately stubborn about it that these were the things that I liked—tough shit! I hated science and math!

MH: *You didn't write poetry yet?*

TT: I never thought about literature. I didn't write a poem until I was twenty-one, and that sort of came out of the clear blue sky.

MH: *College?*

TT: I left college. In my senior year in high school, I knew that I was going to Georgetown Foreign Service School. That was the only college I applied to that didn't have a science or math requirement. They required languages, history, and geography. They did put me in third year French. In the meantime, unfortunately, I had knocked up my high school girlfriend on a high school class trip to Bear Mountain. She kept getting more and more pregnant. She was a year behind me. I was now in my freshman year at Georgetown Foreign Service School, so she came down to D.C. and we got married and I dropped out—1957.

This leads up to how I started writing poetry. Our daughter had a brain disease and was institutionalized and then she died. Our marriage was not good. But the next year, in a moment of reconciliation, I got her pregnant again. Long story short, I have a son who's twenty-four.

By the spring of 1960 things were really unbearable. I was working at this furniture store (I had about twenty stupid jobs) and was the college type, but who hadn't graduated—and I was too naïve to lie about it. These were very penurious times. I had a job of thirty-five dollars a week as a mail clerk. I was alone, no money from family, and having to support a pregnant wife. Raw times, late 1950s recession in D.C., to be a college dropout. Anyway, I got this job in a furniture store as a salesman and by spring our marriage was getting very bad. By July 1960 I called in sick to work and I went out into this park and wrote two neo-Elizabethan poems.

MH: *What prompted that?*

TT: I don't know. It came out of the blue, from left field.

MH: *How were they Elizabethan?*

TT: They were sort of phony Elizabethan. They rhymed in a sort of sonnet form. I didn't know how to write a sonnet. Anyway, when I came back home, we had one of our usual fights and I said, "That's it!" and left. The poetry was actually a catalyst for changing my life.

MH: *Do you still have those poems?*

TT: Yes, but they're bad.

MH: *And you never shared them?*

TT: No, never. They're unpublishable.

MH: *But historical.*

TT: (laughs) There was actually one before that, a couple of months before. I guess it was building up. So, I moved out, quit my job, and started going with this girl who introduced me to some of the Beat Poets and their work. I remember Ferlinghetti. She was a sort of hip chick from White Plains. Then she left me; she got tired of me real quick. So, in August, about a month later, I came back to New York City—in 1960. I was twenty-one. I was sort of looking for this girl, she had mentioned the Cedar Bar (Tavern)—my parents lived in Rye, New York, so I was living with my parents. I came back home with thirty dollars in my pocket—well, I had to get a job! I couldn't freeload off my dad. He really didn't want me there. I arrived home on Saturday. On Sunday, I looked at *The New York Times* "Want Ads" and took the train to Grand Central Terminal, and started walking to this employment agency on 42nd Street, and started to go in, but I turned around and said, "Fuck it! I don't really want a job." I threw the *Times* in the trash and walked down 5th Avenue to the Village. I started to hang around and spend a lot of time at Village coffee houses such as the Figaro on Bleeker Street. In 1960 it was different then. The "Beat" thing was still new, and little did I know that later in life I would meet Ginsberg and Corso. In the meantime, I kept writing poetry. I had one friend that I showed them to.

MH: *Who was this friend?*

TT: He's not around anymore. I went to school with him. I don't know him anymore.

MH: *Was there a teacher who introduced you to poetry?*

TT: No, we didn't get beyond Longfellow in high school in West Chester in the 1950s. We didn't even get to Wallace Stevens—absolutely no modern lit whatsoever! In 1961, I stopped writing for a while. I didn't know any poets. I had only been writing for a year and a half.

MH: *And your poems, you didn't know what to do with them?*

TT: Yes, I didn't know what to do with them. I was hanging around coffee houses, but not the right ones. I didn't have the right attitude for those coffee houses anyway because everybody liked to sit around and talk, and I always liked to sit around and talk and get drunk (laughs). In 1961, I did buy Donald Allen's anthology. That was a revelation. I knew some of the names, but I didn't understand what any of these poets were saying: John Ashbery, Kenneth Koch, Frank O'Hara, and James Schuyler, etc. Then there were all these West Coast poets, The Beats, and it was inspiring, but I still didn't know what to do with poetry. In 1962, I was living over in the East Village on Avenue B and 3rd Street with these two South American roommates. Well, I started going with this woman who turned me on to Wallace Stevens. Also, I was working in the NYU library, where the Grey Art Gallery is now. NYU allowed me to take courses, and I began hunting down books, the great Moderns, Eliot, Pound. Eliot was my first love out of that group. I didn't know any of the history about him. I just liked the lyricism of it. I didn't worry about the footnotes in the "Wasteland." So, I began to get into serious Modern poetic literature. I was beginning to understand and I didn't have any teachers.

In the summer of '62, there were a series of readings at The New School, and the woman I was seeing, well, her parents sent her to Paris to get her away from me. She was Jewish and I was a no good *shayguts*. She lived in the Riverdale section of the Bronx, and I ended up living with one of her roommates on Sullivan Street in the Village. Every week, I recognized these names from the Donald Allen anthology that appeared on fliers for poetry readings at The New School. And every week, I thought about going. It was two dollars, which then was a lot of money, and I could get beer and cigarettes for that. So, I finally went on the fifth week of readings and it was Kenneth Koch, who was teaching at The New School. I learned later that Ted Berrigan and Ron Padgett were in the audience. I remember Ted as this thin guy with a beard. I didn't know who they were then. But anyway, a lot of people were laughing, and I knew some of Koch's work from Don Allen's anthology, not much, since I didn't quite get why everyone was laughing. I presumed it was funny, so I went back the next week to the last reading and it was Frank O'Hara, and I didn't understand what I was reading either, but nobody laughed. So, I actually felt sorry for him; he was reading this heavy stuff.

MH: *Do you remember which poems he read?*

TT: Probably his "Odes" I believe that were fairly new at the time. So, Koch and O'Hara were the first two poets I went to hear read and it gave me something to think about. A few weeks later, I was in the Cedar Tavern [located at 24 University Place near 8th Street, famous as a hang-out of New York School painters and poets] of which I had become an "habitué" and saw Frank O'Hara standing at the bar talking to this elderly, almost cadaverous-looking gentleman who I later realized was Edwin Denby.

MH: *Even back then (1960s) he looked that old?*

TT: He was a good sixty then but he still looked the same at eighty. So, as I walked into the bar, I said to myself, "Should I say anything to O'Hara?" I had just heard him read a couple of weeks before, so I went up to him and said, "Oh, excuse me, Mr. O'Hara." And he said, "Yes." I said, "I just want to tell you that I enjoyed your reading at The New School." And he said, "Oh, thank you very much!" And that was it. But there was room at the bar, so I stood there and got a beer. Eventually, Edwin Denby left and O'Hara turned around to me and said, "You know, you made my evening." He talked slightly like John Ashbery.

MH: *Did you know he was gay?*

TT: You could tell right away. I didn't know before. It put me off a little bit, but this guy was a poet, a real poet. So, we just started chatting, and as luck would have it, I didn't tell him I wrote poetry. Finally, he asked me at some point, he had tried to cash a ten-dollar check, and it was a new bartender who didn't know O'Hara, and as it turned out, I had some extra cash in my pocket and I lent him five dollars so he could have a couple more drinks.

MH: You lending O'Hara money!

TT: I know, on our first meeting and I was basically penniless. But I thought it was the least I could do, how could I not? So, he stayed for a few more drinks and made some arrangement that we would meet back at the Cedar Tavern to pay me back. He gave me Mike Goldberg's [Michael Goldberg (1924-2007) was famously mentioned in O'Hara's poem "Why I Am Not a Painter"was one of the New York Abstract Expressionist painters] number out in East Hampton, and there was no way I was going out there. It was a curious set of circumstances. I don't know if he ever gave me the five dollars back. I didn't see him for a while. I left the city for three months and bummed around California and Los Angeles. It was a strange time and I wanted to go to Paris.

MH: Where were you working?

TT: Still at NYU Law Library. So, I quit. I ended up in Hollywood. I had about ten dollars to my name. I wanted to go to Mexico and never got it together, had a couple of jobs, one selling transistor radios.

MH: Your folks weren't on your back?

TT: No, they never pushed me into becoming anything, but they thought poetry was pretty peculiar, especially if it didn't rhyme. They never encouraged or discouraged. I was one of three children. So anyway, in Hollywood I went into a bookstore and I found Koch's *Thank You and Other Poems* and O'Hara's *Second Avenue* which was the only thing in print by him at the time. So, I bought those. Then, I started writing out there. The people I hung out with went to a twist club every night and I went along with them. If you knew the doorman, he wouldn't charge you the dollar to get in. Maybe Sal Mineo came in once, and Kirk Douglas came in there once. I saw Broderick Crawford on the street once. Those were the only "stars" I saw the whole time I was there.

I remember that Koch was giving a poetry workshop at The New School and it was forty dollars for the semester. I thought it would be constructive and serious and adult. I didn't know where I was going to get the forty dollars. Also, I didn't know how I was going to get back to New York City. Finally, my grandmother sent me one hundred dollars. I had ten dollars. The Greyhound bus had a ninety-nine-dollar cross country fare, so there went my one hundred dollars.

MH: *Sounds obliquely like Kerouac.*

TT: Yeah! As much as I don't empathize with the "On the Road" mentality—I was sort of doing it in a half-assed, semi-bourgeois way (laughs). I was running out of food money and it was over Christmas, too—1962. Well, I made it back. It was slushing in cold New York City and seventy-five degrees back in Los Angeles. I never liked Los Angeles: Santa Clauses on Hollywood Boulevard; Christmas lights on palm trees! I was glad to be back.

MH: *What was the mood like—Kennedy was president?*

TT: I voted for Kennedy, but I wasn't thinking about politics, I was too wrapped up in my own problems. I was in L.A. during the Cuban Missile Crisis, and all the assholes I was with had no idea that this could have been real serious. Los Angeles is as big a target as New York City. That solidified the California mentality for me.

I went back to the Cedar Tavern, this was in January, and there was O'Hara talking to a young poet who turned out to be Frank Lima, who I later roomed with. My grandmother gave me an additional forty dollars to take Koch's poetry workshop. O'Hara said, "Oh, I'm giving one, too." I ended up taking them both. As I'm standing there talking to O'Hara, at the mention of taking Koch's poetry workshop, O'Hara said, "Oh, really, Kenneth is right here!" And this guy turned around, it was Koch, and I just went completely tongue-tied. I didn't know what to say and Koch was standing there with his drink waiting for me to say something and I was nonplussed so I finally said, "Oh, Mr. Koch, I've been reading your work. I really like it a lot. It's so snotty." I had meant to say "sophisticated." Well, Kenneth Koch just turned away and went back to the bar.

MH: *Probably made O'Hara laugh.*

TT: Oh, it did! Later, when I got to know O'Hara better, he told me how hilarious it was. He said, "I went back to Kenneth at the bar and Kenneth said, 'He said my poems were snotty!'" (Towle laughing). I think I brought it up to Koch years later, and he isn't an easy person to get to know. I didn't really know Kenneth Koch at all, until after O'Hara died. He was unapproachable in his poetry class.

With O'Hara it was the opposite. Anyone in his class who wanted to could go out with him for a drink at the Cedar Tavern afterwards, and that's where you learned.

Interview with Paul Violi

It was James Schuyler, who when I asked what his favorite book of poetry was, said to me, "*Splurge,* by Paul Violi." The next day I bought a copy and I was hooked after reading the first poem, "One for the Monk of Montaudon," a poem inspired by Violi's love of the Provençale troubadour poets of the Middle Ages.

We became friends, and I saw Paul on many occasions, and at many poetry readings and I got to know his wife, Ann. I even sat in on one of his poetry classes that he taught at Bloomfield College, an adjunct teaching job he held for many years. And I would meet him for dinner after his poetry class at Columbia. Paul had taken over Kenneth Koch's classes after Koch passed away in 2002.

Paul was good friends with Bill Zavatsky, a fellow poet, and publisher of SUN, a literary press that published many of the "Second Generation" New York School poets. Zavatsky was one of the poets who would come out of Kenneth Koch's poetry classes at Columbia, along with David Lehman and Bob Holman. It was Zavatsky who published Violi's *Splurge* and *Harmatan*, Violi's book of poems about his time in the Peace Corps in Nigeria.

In talking to Paul about poetry, I realized how erudite and knowledgeable he was. And the best part was that Paul never came across as pedantic or academic. When I sat in to watch him teach a class in British Romantic Poetry at Bloomfield College, he impressed me by how passionate he was about teaching, and with how much he was able to get out of his students. Paul was able to recite whole passages of poems by Wordsworth and Coleridge from memory.

In getting to know him, he would casually reveal things like the time he ran down a thief who had ripped a handbag off a woman in Washington Square Park. Without hesitation, Paul took off

BILL ZAVATSKY

and tackled the thief, and retrieved the woman's handbag. This was after teaching a class in poetry at NYU—all in a day's work!

Paul was the Interim Director of the Poetry Project at Saint Mark's Church in 1977, and he also helped organize the poetry readings at the Museum of Modern Art during the 1970s.

Paul loved the city and loved walking its precincts, and in so doing would encounter things that would set off meditations that would end up in poems, like the way that he could take something like soda bottle caps that get pressed into the baking summer asphalt around hot dog vendors at city intersections, and turn that

PAUL VIOLI SHOOTING POOL

into an image of stellar constellations the way he did in the poem "Tycho, Tyche," a poem in which the speaker meditates on space and time while trying to locate himself in a meaningful way.

And it was in that same way that Violi could capture a city moment in a few lines, and turn a personal experience into a comic poem with wit and irony, like his conversational poem "Counterman" about a sandwich order at a deli as the poem's counterman-customer dialog rises to an esthetic discourse on applying the mayonnaise just right so as to resemble Beaux Arts architectural details from famous cathedrals.

MH: *When did you start writing poetry?*

PV: I remember writing short stories and poems when I was twelve. The first story I wrote dealt with trapping. I grew up on Long Island, in Greenlawn, and I used to trap along the North Shore and sell the pelts. Of course, the story had a moral: The greedy trapper's heavy load made him crash through the ice and drown. What I do remember is becoming very dissatisfied with prose. Once the ending came into view, I'd lose interest in the story, whereas with poems, the possibilities multiplied with every line. So, I wrote many dense, obscure, turgid poems (laughs). I thought they sounded sonorous, but they didn't make sense.

MH: *Were your parents literary?*

PV: They always encouraged me. I remember the anthologies they bought me, the Louis Untermeyer and Oscar Williams mausoleums. I was also very interested in history. And I enjoyed drawing and painting more than writing.

MH: *What did your father do?*

PV: He was in the drugstore business. I was working in his stores when I was twelve. You know, dropping malteds, spilling milkshakes. Long Island was an idyllic place to grow up—farmland, woods, the Sound. I was very conscious of the rapid changes and I was writing these sentimental, sanctimonious poems about the encroachment of developments in the postwar boom, the rows of neat houses replacing potato fields.

MH: *Did you make treks into the city?*

PV: Oh, yes. I was working in New York City for *Cook's Tours* when I was sixteen. And I was writing very short, imagistic, very hard-edged poems. In college, and later, the big influence was Pound. I went to Boston University and there I encountered poets like Williams and Pound through a few professors, even though the academic poets were dominant. Much of what Pound said as a critic made sense to me. He did for Modern Poetry what Frank Lloyd Wright and Mies van der Rohe did for modern architecture: He cleaned house.

MH: You weren't pursuing a literary career in poetry?

PV: Poetry was just something I did. I was writing as I was travelling when I was in the Peace Corps after I graduated from Boston U. When I got home, I found myself with a great deal of poetry which was all pretty terrible. I set myself up in my parents' house and wrote for three or four months, supporting myself as a clam digger. Later, I published a few things in pamphlets. Looks like juvenilia to me now, profoundly embarrassing. I also had a job on a cruise ship going back and forth to Bermuda. After that, I settled in the city and worked for magazines and newspapers.

MH: You had no sense of a poetic career?

PV: I was doing what I wanted to do. I wasn't considering alternatives. I also worked for a TV station. It interfered with my writing. It was a hell of a conflict, but sometimes, when I was working for *Architectural Forum*, it was terrific. Now, it's teaching, which I love, even though that takes much time.

MH: Who published your pamphlets?

PV: At first, I did, in Swollen Magpie Press, a "vanity" press. The name was taken from a line from one of Pound's Cantos: "Thou are a beaten dog beneath the hail, a swollen magpie in a fitful sun ... pull down thy vanity ..." (laughs). I also co-edited a magazine titled, *New York Times*. Then Allen Kornblum's Toothpaste Press published *Waterworks* (a chapbook of Violi's first poetry published in 1972) and I still feel very good about that collection.

MH: What years?

PV: 1969 to 1970. I was looking around New York for places where there were readings and workshops. Saint Mark's was the most appealing. Tony Towle was teaching a workshop. I took it and met Charles North; we became good friends. I also met Ron Padgett, Bill Zavatsky, Larry Fagin. I liked the sense of freedom toward poetry they had. The Poetry Project at Saint Mark's Church-in-the-Bowery seemed to attract poets who were quite experimental and open-minded, who took poetry seriously, but who didn't feel it had to be so solemn. There was much energy, much experimentation, and a great affinity with what the painters were up to.

MH: *Did you feel that you were part of the "New York School"?*

PV: That's such an amorphous moniker. I really don't know.

MH: *You have trouble with the term?*

PV: Yes, because it is a term that's best applied in a limited way to five or six extremely influential poets whose work I admire, and those John Bernard Meyers included in his *Poets of the New York School* published by U. of Pennsylvania Press, 1969, which included: John Ashbery, Barbara Guest, Kenneth Koch, Frank O'Hara and James Schulyer, along with Joe Ceravolo, Kenward Elmslie, Frank Lima, and Tony Towle. But their connection eludes me. One of the things that attracted me to the "New York School" poets was that even though they all knew and inspired each other, they maintained distinct voices. You share influences and friendship, a sensibility, an attitude toward life, but your work has to be your own. At the same time, if poetry is your life, it's important, it's natural to have friends who think that way. You're lucky if you do.

MH: *What other poets were you interested in at the time?*

PV: I was—I still am—a rather indiscriminate reader. That's when I came across many modern French poets, especially Apollinaire. Also, I was going back to translations, namely Paul Blackburn's, of the Provencal poets, the troubadours, as well as Villon and Rabelais, whom I had first read in college. The troubadours—there was something fresh and casual about their writing. I had been using mock forms and I liked the way they wrote in mock forms. What also opened my eyes at the time were painters like Larry Rivers and Claes Oldenburg and Jim Dine. Influence is such a peculiar thing.

MH: *You see poets who've mannerized others to great effect.*

PV: I see poets who write like Frank O'Hara all over the place, but God! I don't think they're paying O'Hara a compliment. A good poet will make new things possible, give you something to grow on, not copy.

MH: *But there's a likelihood that good poetry can continue to be written in the style of a mentor.*

PV: In a way, but I feel a territoriality in terms of style and form—the idea that a person's style is his own, what he has made of himself.

MH: *Did you ever find yourself not writing because of influence?*

PV: No, I don't have the time (laughs). I get into periods when I can't get anything finished. This happened when I first came across all the translations of the troubadours. I felt as if I had made a great discovery. It's inspiring. Guillaume IX of Aquitaine has lines that go: "I think I'll write a poem, take a nap, then go stand in the sun." What a great beginning for a poem. I've tried innumerable times to begin a poem with those lines.

MH: *How do you come up with a poem, or a line?*

PV: Usually, I'll get an idea for an entire poem, not just a line. The "idea" involves the way the poem will move—a formal impulse. I keep notebooks and work from them: phrases, words, observations of people, things that occur. Sometimes just an ordinary word that strikes me in a new way. I look at paintings, sculpture—Tony Smith's work, Paula North's, Jean Holabird's watercolors—they've meant a great deal to me.

MH: *Do you find yourself jotting things down when travelling or just walking around?*

PV: Constantly. It gets a little risky when I'm driving.

MH: *You're a poet of very grand physical gestures—earth, sky, horizons, seasons. What makes you want to write about these absolutes?*

PV: Connections, some unusual or wild extreme of location or weather, I suppose. The weather does a pretty good imitation of the absolute (laughs). It doesn't have to be a grand gesture. It could be the way a wet oak leaf imprints itself on a new concrete sidewalk. There are instances in nature which are just magical, and if common objects are part of it, fine. The image of a frozen mop that's been left outside all night during winter can surprise you, a symbol of your own stupidity. I remember a beach in Agadir, Morocco, a gold beach with wide black stripes running across it, making it look like a tiger's back. The fact that the stripes were the result of an oil spill is something you have to deal with (laughs).

MH: *Is place important to you?*

PV: Not in the sense of regional poetry, backyard poetry. You mean people getting tangled in their roots?

MH: *I meant place in the sense with which Charles Olson used Gloucester in his* Maximus Poems.

PV: I have a very difficult time with his poetry, though I admire much. His tone is elusive. And what I do get from him sounds a great deal like Pound. I have to read him again.

MH: *How old were you when* In Baltic Circles *was written?*

PV: Most of them were written in '69, '70, and '72, '73 when I was in my late twenties. I think it was a very uneven book, but what the hell, it was a big one (laughs). I had room to play. But in terms of a first book, I think one of the nice things about *Kulchur Press* was that it gave me 128 pages. I remember putting it together. I enjoyed the expanse.

MH: *"To Cisco in the Swamps" from* In Baltic Circles *is an early poem of yours but it reads with a great deal of your later style. It seems to define the way you'd be writing in* Splurge.

PV: I can see that in retrospect. It's a mock translation but it's also completely serious. I wanted to deal with a sense of loss about some friends I'd had. I needed a poem that had more than one side to it to deal with my different feelings. Mixing up the chronology, the modern and the medieval imagery, helped resolve things. The persona I used gave me the leeway.

MH: *What has changed for you in how you write or what you write about?*

PV: I still feel that I can contradict myself with a poem tomorrow. But generally, I think *Splurge* built on things that were in *In Baltic Circles*. I don't think it was that conscious a development. I just bulled my own way into a particular style. There were certain things that I was doing that I just went with. I remember that I used to hear expressions like "That's a Violi poem." This wasn't necessarily derogatory. I wasn't sure how conscious of that I wanted to become because I thought it would narrow things down too much. I still wanted to keep the game open.

MH: *You didn't want to be labeled?*

PV: Yes, particularly for the constraints it might put upon me. I believe in something like a voice, but I also believe that it's something that's going to develop in an unconscious way. That's you; that's the way you are, and eventually that comes out. Then again, that's a question I shy away from for self-protective reasons. But it's one I mull over.

   I like to think I was able to incorporate that imagistic hard edge, or keep the images but put them in a language that was conversational and natural, instead of imagistic poems that are too rigid and crammed, at least for me, which also enabled me to get into certain thoughts and themes.

MH: *Do you write every day?*

PV: Yes, sometimes I don't get all that much done. But I like to write every day.

MH: *Is there a particular time or place?*

PV: There's a certain mood I like to catch—or that catches me. It usually strikes when I'm in the damn car or in front of class. I usually write in the afternoon. It takes about four or five hours of putzing around, doodling, smoking too many cigarettes, drinking coffee, going for a swim, that enables me to concentrate very intensely. Or, I'll just sit down and write wherever I happen to be. I'll be walking in New York City and go into a café and sit down and write. When I'm home, I'm more sedentary. It's more of a discipline. I'll go in my study and stay there and think. I'll play tapes—Django Reinhardt, Mozart—and then fade away from them.

MH: *What makes you sit down in a café to begin writing?*

PV: I like to walk around. That's one of the things I like about New York City. I have a freedom of mind when I'm walking in the rhythm of perception and the rhythm of thought.

MH: *You're an ambulatory thinker.*

PV: I remember when I was writing *Harmatan* a great deal of the visual stimuli came from walking down Canal Street and Fourteenth Street.

MH: *Not Africa?*

PV: What would send me back would be the market place. In New York City, those two streets are like the vast African markets I remembered.

MH: *Was it a sense of being overwhelmed?*

PV: Abundance. New York City is very stimulating for me because it gets me to write about things other than itself. I wrote a poem titled "Abundance," a sort of homage to William Carlos Williams, his poem titled "The Dance" which begins: "In Breughel's great picture, The Kermess." And as long as I knew that poem, I had always misread it. I had always thought it was one long sentence. And the fact that it begins and ends with the same line made me think of it in a Futurist sense, a Marinetti sense—as a round poem. It wasn't until I had written "Abundance" and had gone back to the Williams poem that I realized it was written in two sentences. But I liked the idea that the form followed the content, that Williams was describing a reel danced in a circle. Anyway, I had this idea of roundness, fullness, crazy abundance—a poem that began and ended in the same place. It starts off: "In Breughel's great picture Canal Street." It would have been a perfect subject for Breughel if he were painting today. Canal Street can get pretty weird, the juxtaposition and contrast of all the objects and the whole idea of "too much"—the junk, the necessities, the contradictions.

MH: What has each of your books meant to you?

PV: There sometimes is such a delay between the time a poem is written and then published that you're already onto something else and you've been building a bridge since then and you're not sure where the bridge is going to end but you're sort of beyond one book and into another. This is aside from the feeling of having just cleared the deck because every single book I have ever had has been a long time coming. In that time, you're already looking forward not backward.

MH: Harmatan *was written how long after your stay in Africa?*

PV: Five years.

MH: *Did you need all that time to become objective?*

PV: No, the location of the poem wasn't a problem. It could have been about any time I'd spent anywhere. I wasn't interested in writing about an exotic place. I don't consider it a poem about Nigeria, but about the way memory works, about perspective. It's about the way memory isolates an object, an experience, and how an object takes on a vividness when you see it in a desert or a savannah. I was trying to imitate that; I was hoping to. Many sections of *Harmatan* begin by naming a place. You think of a place, name it, and it begins to recreate itself, so to speak, attracting other memories, details, like filings around a magnet.

I'd been reading about Giordano Bruno. There's a quotation of Augustine's at the end of the book, a distinction he made between what is natural memory and what is "artificial" memory. So, each of those sections is a sort of cluster of images. There's movement, but a mnemonic movement, not linear, but cumulative, imagistic, place to place. I was hoping the entire poem would hold together like that by transposing images, "rhyming" them in a Poundian sense.

MH: *How would you characterize* In Baltic Circles, *what that book means as a group of poems?*

PV: I was trying to stake out a few different claims there. I don't think it's that defined in terms of style. It might be interesting to see it as a variable mix of poems that was actually followed by *Harmatan* and *Splurge*, and *Harmatan* went one way, and *Splurge* went another way, but the problem was that I was writing all those poems at the same time. I like to be in a position where I am free to change in any direction or distance, long or short. And *Harmatan* is a long poem about fifty pages. I like long poems.

MH: *That's evident in the more recent book* Likewise. *It contains two very long poems.*

PV: But there are poets out there writing poems hundreds of pages long. For me, a long poem is anything ten pages and over.
 Getting back to what you were asking, I was writing some of *Harmatan* before *In Baltic Circles* was published. It all overlapped. There's a poem in the current book *Likewise* that I began ten years ago. I thought it worked well in this new collection and I was still interested in what the poem was about. I thought the poem held up.

MH: *What do you throw out or discard?*

PV: A lot of poems (laughs). But do you mean while I'm writing the poems?

MH: *Yes, what do you sacrifice?*

PV: I don't cut much out; I add. The poem grows as I revise. Or, if an image has more possibilities, I'll use it in more than one poem. I like the Renaissance idea of a *"rifacimento"* where you basically use the same image in different versions, the way painters do.

MH: *How long did it take you to write "One for the Monk of Montaudon"?*

PV: Just a couple of days. And that's quick for me. Many poems I've literally worked years on.

MH: *You mentioned that "One for the Monk of Montaudon" was a favorite poem. You celebrate your feelings in your poetry to a great extent: personal triumphs, defeats, blessings mixed with disaster. "One for the Monk of Montaudon" is a kind of self-benediction. I want to know why you thought it was more successful.*

PV: It was the way the form of the poem and the subject came together. I love the word benediction. I like to think it's a celebratory poem. It's the first poem in *Splurge*. Even though it is based on a poem by the Monk—a 12th century Provençale Benedictine monk and troubadour from Auvergne—I think it's all mine, an homage to myself (laughs). It's based on his "enugs" and "plassirs." "Plassirs" were songs about things the Monk liked, "enugs" about things he didn't like. He composed them in short lyrical lists. I thought I could combine those and go with it and write a longer poem, sort of autobiographical, a summation of how I got to a particular moment.

MH: *When you wrote this poem, did you feel that you were onto something that was new, exciting, and different?*

PV: Yes, in fact, I did, even though I had written in that kind of stanza in a couple of shorter poems. I hadn't realized that I could move in a more inclusive way. A stanza should have some generative power. I work on the way lines fit in stanzas, but I'm almost looking at stanzas as shaped lines. I'm looking at how I can keep stanzas closed, in a configuration, or how I can have one move into another.

MH: *Was the stanzaic pattern new for you?*

PV: It enabled me to keep the imagery sharp but at the same time keep the tone informal, loose. I tend to favor haiku but the trouble is there's a static quality to them, whereas this type of stanza allowed me to go with a momentum that's more like a narrative. The poem clicked for me when I tried writing about something I disliked as if I liked it very much. This is what got me started; it wasn't the entire poem. I took some rather drab situations—a diner, a menu, a table mat with hideous flowers on it. If you're in a good frame of mind philosophically, you can even celebrate the ordinary and the offensively vulgar as if they weren't wasted or completely intrusive parts of life. I wrote the poem very quickly once that happened.

MH: *How were you able to pull the details together?*

PV: They'd been in my mind. Many of them occurred as I was writing. I was drawing on some autobiographical details and experiences. Some from my memory of Istanbul, from deserts, hitchhiking through Africa. There's a great deal of water imagery, the way we seem to float along, or sink (laughs).

As I moved into "Little Testament" in *Likewise*, I was using the same form. And in the new book, the title poem uses the same alleostrophic pattern. Sometimes I'll shorten a line just to accentuate an image or sound, or a certain phrasing, but generally, they're roughly the same size in terms of the time it takes to read.

MH: *You're not counting syllables or metrical feet?*

PV: Sometimes. And then I know I'm in trouble. And it's a little bit of both. I still find myself challenged by a sonnet form that's strictly iambic. I find that I'll toy around with these poems, then incorporate them or destroy them. There's something in there that wants to get out and then it will develop into a longer poem. It's just my temperament. When I work in such a closed form, things get congested. By trying to squeeze something into a sonnet, I find myself working within these boxes, then one day I see how I can use it in a different way.

MH: *But in terms of your overall stanzaic pattern, is it determined aurally or visually?*

PV: I like to think it is both.

MH: Do you experiment running lines together instead of breaking them up into stanzas?

PV: I'm thinking of the title poem in my next book *The Curious Builder* where it starts off like an oneirocriticon, like all these old silly dream works where they are pretty much two-line analyses for what you can expect the next day if the night before you dreamt of this.

MH: Before the poem is written you have a plan?

PV: Well, I knew I was going to move out of the dream-work couplets and move into the stanza form and close with these salutations and these beginnings of letters. The whole poem is based on interruption. I was looking for a way to have some kind of continuous interruption.

MH: Which is the nature of life.

PV: Well, yes, but I wasn't sure whether it was some interrupted continuity, or a continuous interruption. I just know that a maze is not necessarily a place to get lost in. It seemed like the way the mind branches out. The dream-work section blends into a very common dream where people find themselves in familiar surroundings that suddenly expand into unfamiliar ones. They dream of their own home but there's a door they've never opened or something like that. It's so blatantly symbolic, but there are days like this in a person's life where wonderful new things happen in a familiar context and things happen in a haphazard and irresistible way.

MH: Some people might say shit happens.

PV: (laughing) There are those days, too, for sure. But I was hoping to see if a pattern like that would develop in a poem.

MH: And you found it successful?

PV: Yes, but it took a while.

MH: How long?

PV: Years.

MH: *Was this the poem that you worked on for ten years?*

PV: No. That was pretty much a straight narrative poem called "Narrative Drift."

MH: *In this new book?*

PV: Yes, they're both in the new book. But "Narrative Drift" is the one that I started ten years ago.

MH: *I like the title. What's the title of the new book?*

PV: *The Curious Builder.* The title's from a poem by the Elizabethan poet Samuel Daniel in which he talks about his poetry as a building he could renovate, add onto when he wanted. There's a sort of freedom of construction and an insistence on having that freedom and a delight in revision, renovation.

MH: *So this idea of Daniel's struck a sympathetic chord?*

PV: Well, the way he described building a poem, comparing it to building a structure, is the same procedure of this maze where you're free to build an ever-expanding maze or mansion. I like the idea because that's how I perceive the imagination proceeds. Curiosity just keeps you on that edge. If a poem could catch that edge, I could capture its transformative pattern of growth.

But what hung me up in the poem was that I didn't know how to get from this particular restaurant, which had become its symbol. It's based on an experience I had. Every time I went to this restaurant in Manhattan, this amazing building, a bank that had been converted into a restaurant in this massive dinosaur of a building, they had broken through a wall and had gone into another room. This restaurant just kept expanding upstairs, downstairs, sideways.

MH: *What was its name?*

PV: Blue Willow.

MH: *Still there? (The Blue Willow opened in 1983 and closed in 1990. It was on the northeast corner of the intersection of Broadway and Bleeker Street.)*

PV: It's still there (at the time of this interview) but it's shrinking now because business hasn't been too good.

MH: *They had to put the walls back?*

PV: Yes. Then I found out it been the bank that my father used to go to when he was a young man.

MH: *What a coincidence.*

PV: Yes, it was a wonderful coincidence and I knew I was going to write about this place, and because it had tied into what I was thinking about in terms of the imagination and how it moves. And the poem, through a series of interruptions, finally moves into a restaurant that's being interrupted because it's being renovated, and I couldn't get from that part to the letter. I knew I had to close the poem on a series of interrupted letters.

MH: *Are these actual letters?*

PV: No, no. I made them all up. And the letters interrupt each other. I really had a musical construction. I like to think of it that way. But how was I going to get from the restaurant to the letters, and this is what took me so long, one or two lousy lines really. I needed just the right bit of confusion to clear everything up, pull the poem together, a resolution. I had a waitress finally deliver my order and she apologizes for the confusion and delivers my mail instead (laughs). This is the way things work in a dream when perfectly weird things happen very normally. But at least that got me into the letters and the hell out of the poem (laughs).

MH: *Sounds difficult.*

PV: This enabled me to incorporate the Samuel Daniel lines. So, the conclusion is really a beginning of a poem by Daniel and I'm paying him an homage. I feel he's underrated. I'm not too interested in his historical poems, but I really think he's a poet readers should look at, and he's overshadowed.

MH: Who wasn't overshadowed by Shakespeare?

PV: Buried (laughs).

MH: *You raise an interesting issue, how the poem started, its psychogenesis, the inspiration which was this restaurant and Daniel, those two things combining to form the poem. The other issue is how you got out of the poem, how you ended it.*

PV: I find it interesting, but I often wonder if anybody else would. Take Byron for example, he is amazing for writing faux narratives. The narrative line was an element he could play off at will. I always thought that was Byron's great natural invention. I knew he'd been influenced by the Italians, but I thought that was just formal. I thought the mood and the voice were all his, but it seems he got it from an anti-Jacobin, John Hookham Frere, in England, another English poet. After reading Frere, he wrote *Beppo* then he wrote *Don Juan*. He found that voice, that freedom.

MH: *It doesn't hurt to have genius.*

PV: Exactly.

MH: *So how long is "Narrative Drift"?*

PV: Three pages. The title poem, "The Curious Builder" is about fourteen pages or so.

MH: *"King Nasty" from your last book,* Likewise, *is over 500 lines and "Little Testament" is over 500. Those are long poems by today's standards.*

PV: I guess.

MH: *Milton's* Paradise Lost *is roughly 10,000 lines of blank verse. So, combining "King Nasty" and "Little Testament" you'd have one tenth of* Paradise Lost.

PV: Yes (both laughing)! I guess we've got to shut down the theaters again and maybe people will write long poems.

MH: *It seems like an intimidating length but it does keep going. It reads in short segments or sections.*

PV: That's what I like to think, that the short stanza does, opens it. I don't know if I'll ever write anything like "King Nasty" again. I'm not sure I'm done with "Testament." I think it's as durable a form as it was during Villon's time. It's something you can go back to any time and pick it up again.

MH: *"En l'an trentieme de mon age ..."*

PV: Right (laughs).

MH: *Villon was only thirty at the time. Today, that would make him sixty. So, you had turned forty in the opening line. Tell me about that poem, how it started. Were you reading Villon?*

PV: Yes, I always loved his poems.

MH: *Was it his sense of humor?*

PV: What appealed to me was a poem that could incorporate seriousness and satire at the same time and switch back and forth within a unifying vision.

MH: *Bill Zavatsky (Zavatsky, a close friend of Paul's, published two of Violi's first books) feels that your humor is sometimes overdone. He singles out "Fable," the poem about the goat, "Kid Blanco." He can't stand the play on the color white and the animal clichés (Violi burst into laughter at the mention of this), but he feels that "Index," the last poem in* Splurge, *is a triumph.*

PV: Maybe he's heard "Fable" once too often. I thought I was writing a tragedy! Kid Blanco is blind to his own faults—the whiteness with which he's obsessed. But in terms of humor being generally received, I think things have changed for the better. Ten years ago, humor had come along with some defense, that if you used humor in a poem, you ultimately weren't a serious poet. The sensibility has changed and its expected now for a serious poet to be able to incorporate different moods in his work. Humor can be just as complicated, just as illuminating as anything else. The same light of recognition clicks on. You're not avoiding truth, you're using truth. Kafka, Aristophanes, Rabelais, Moliere, they're all inspiring.

MH: *Single out a poet who has no humor.*

PV: Poets who write out of a sense of dread. Would you trust someone who never laughs, trust their perceptions or ideas? Some poets are so solemn that I find them funny. They confuse an egocentric, defeatist point of view with a realistic one. Poetry should ultimately delight. I don't think I've written that many humorous poems, though I perhaps tend to rely on them at readings, if I'm in the mood. Some things are unavoidably ironic. If there's more than one side to something, and you see that, the serious and the comic coexisting, it results in a tension that I think poetry can exploit very effectively.

Getting back to Villon and "Little Testament," I think—if I took a quick look at it (Violi pages through his poem) ... it started as a poem having to do with my fortieth birthday.

MH: *That was eight years ago?*

PV: Yes. And it started off originally titled as "Epithalamium for Absurdity and Squalor," which eventually appears as a line in the poem, and it grew out of that. I remember I was reading Lord Rochester's work, too, which is utterly delightful.

MH: *You read some very obscure poets (John Wilmot, 2nd Earl of Rochester 1647–80).*

PV: You know what angers me is that he shouldn't be obscure. I don't know how he could have been squeezed out of anthologies. He was a surrealist, amazing, what a sense of humor, outrageous.

MH: *Violi's anthology wouldn't be an academic's anthology.*

PV: I don't know. Rochester used to be in many academic anthologies. Politics squeezed him out. It's a shame. In a way, he's like Byron in that there's a romantic side to him, a satiric side, and a surreal side. (Johnny Depp played Lord Rochester in the 2004 film *The Libertine*.)

MH: *Have you felt that you have squandered your own magic as you mention in "Little Testament"?*

PV: No, no. I felt that at times. I think the poem moves out of that feeling. I think everybody has those times when they doubt what they've accomplished or they doubt their own efforts.

MH: *How were you able to keep it all going?*

PV: I guess I was just enjoying myself.

MH: *Were you conscious of making segues as you were writing, as you wrote from one day to the next, or did you work on it sporadically?*

PV: I worked on it over a couple of years and I'd go back to try to cover up some of the seams. I remember I had a beginning; I had an end. This happens to me occasionally. Then I had to go back to fit things into the middle. I remember doubting the inclusion of that part about the cathedral. It's the low part of the poem, the center where images take over.

MH: *You use the semicolon well at the end.*

PV: (laughing) I just love them, they're little fulcrums. I remember having qualms about putting things into the poem that weren't mine, the borrowing. I wanted to acknowledge them but work them into the poem in a graceful way. I don't believe in stealing outright.

MH: *What would that be? How do you see the difference?*

PV: I don't know about the difference between them, but the way I got around it is that reading to me is as important an experience as life itself. If I incorporate a borrowing into a poem, that if I can work that into a poem to acknowledge that here's this great image say from Malaparte, these faces under the ice that he saw, that the reader will understand my infatuation with that image. It's one of the most horrific images that came out of World War II that I've come across. And also, the sentimental value that translation of Pound had for me for many years. I first remember I read that back in '66. That poem is always a beacon for me in terms of the naturalness of it and the great spirit that's in there—the life of Arnaut Daniel had—not Samuel Daniel! These two poems both end on "Daniel" (laughs)—but Pound's ability to catch that, to catch that music, catch that spirit, too, is truly remarkable.

MH: *But he did something more with it. It's a big issue, a writer's issue.*

PV: What has to happen if you've expropriated something from another poem ... first, you should acknowledge it in some way in the poem even if you have to work it in informally. I mention their names. I'll work it in somehow or I'll leave a hell of a big clue in there.

MH: *You wouldn't place quotation marks around it?*

PV: Usually, I'll try to find a way to put quotation marks around it. But even so, there has to be some justification for taking something from another poet, either a tribute or some formal justification. There has to be some meaning to it.

MH: *Homage.*

PV: Exactly, it's a form of homage. It's not that imitation is a form of flattery, stealing sure as hell is. I don't want to call it stealing since I acknowledge it. I question a poet's motives when he does, even if there's a poetic license to do so. I don't understand what pleasure they derive from it. Usually, it is just so blatant which lines aren't theirs (laughs). Does it enable them to play Milton for ten minutes? A joke is a joke, but if it's a mode of procedure, then I have strong suspicions. It's almost voyeuristic, vicarious. I admit, I've picked up phrases over the years.

MH: Eliot justified it.

PV: He's a collagist. That's okay. He got it from Pound. And if Pound is writing history as poetry and he considers literature part of history, then of course he has to lift and put things together. It's an ongoing tradition, cross-cultural fertilization.

MH: *But borrowing from dead poets is different than borrowing from living contemporaries.*

PV: Oh, yes, but maybe the same reasons apply except that the audience may not recognize a contemporary theft.

MH: *"In Praise of Idleness" in* Likewise *seemed to take off from Coleridge. Your poem was similar to some of his in that it seemed to deal with the loss of imagination. Coleridge was obsessed with that artistic dilemma in poems such as "Dejection, an Ode."*

PV: He's losing Sara at that time, too. There was much going on. I think he had just been slammed by Wordsworth's "Intimations" ode and probably thought he would never match it and realized his hopeless addiction to opium and losing his health, his power. I think the ironic part of both those Romantic poets was that they wrote great poems about not being able to write. That's the irony. But in terms of idleness, what I love about the Romantics is they're in the Industrial Revolution. This is especially true of later Whitman. He has a suspicious fondness for verbs like "to loaf" and "to lounge." The joys of doing nothing! They're the poets of this truly energetic age and yet Whitman is a very lazy man. He loved to walk around and watch people work. He loved to see the hustle and bustle of New York. He really had this luxuriating power to do nothing. He luxuriates in laziness the way a true bum does.

MH: *It's a Romantic ideal.*

PV: Exactly, idleness at a time when something is growing but you're not sure what. It's a seed time.

MH: *Wordsworth's "emotions recollected in tranquility" as a way to get a poem.*

PV: In a way, you have to let the emotions subside. In a way, that counters the Romantic idea of writing in some kind of swoon. You wait for it to die down, then recollect it when things have evened out.

MH: *There's a Romantic strain in your work, to use that term, "in media res," getting away from the Neo-Classicism of the eighteenth century, to start anywhere, in the middle of things. I felt that in your poem "In Praise of Idleness" you were building the same world Coleridge was building in his odes, writing about surroundings in the middle of his feelings of being unable to write, the way you describe the spider web in the corner.*

PV: What amazes me about Coleridge are his images of suffering—"Viper thoughts coiled around my mind." There's an image from someone who knows he's horribly addicted—the agony of that sort of thing. Such an intense poem prefaced by such a beautiful image— "The old moon with the new moon in her arms"—a 'Pieta' image.

MH: *Your eye is good, your details are accurate and well placed throughout the poem. What for you is a typical Violi poem? What is it that keeps you alive and coming back to the poem? Describe your sense of metaphor.*

PV: The pleasure of recognition, making new connections. It's the way a thought grows by describing one thing in terms of another. It should be a discovery, an expansion of perception, imaginative, transformative. I don't think poems have to be jammed full of them, though. There's something very refreshing about clarity and factuality in a poem. And if you can maintain that distinct visual sense, and also get it to express something wild, but at the same time keep it anchored in fine details, you've got a better poem. Again, that's Pound's influence.

I like to think if a poem captures many different sides of simultaneous events, the multiple aspects of any given moment, that a poem is sort of ironic. Then I think I'm writing something that's true. I think that's it. First of all, I like to think a poem is true to myself and true to the way I see things. I get very annoyed by a narrow perspective on things. I don't think people should tolerate that in poetry any more than they should in an essay or a novel. Poetry shows an awareness for how complicated things can get and yet at the same time cohere. What I'm getting at is there are poems that provide me with this framework or this space in which I can bring in multiple aspects of a given subject.

Recently, I've written a poem ("From Provender Books") based on those brochure catalogues from companies that collect out-of-print poetry books, and you get to see that one of your books that was published twenty years ago is actually worth a few cents more. It's a stock market for poets (laughs). These brochures incorporate little descriptions of the book, of how it's damaged or whether it's inscribed or not. I tied that into some thoughts on posterity. Then you look at one of these brochures and it blows it all to hell. The Romans had this saying that you could no more control posterity than you could the past. These catalogs are a reminder. It's also an opportunity to have some fun at my own expense. I list myself. I place a poem in the future and give some outrageous prices. I put in some poets and make up some books for them.

MH: *Signed or unsigned?*

PV: That's what I work with in the poem because I put my own name in there and misspell it, of course, because that's my luck. If you look in *In Baltic Circles,* my name is misspelled in the goddamned book! There I was, a young poet, I open my first book, and the first thing I see is my name misspelled. The printer was blind, a little professional drawback; a sad but true story. But anyway, I managed to throw in some painting I'd seen at the Fitzwilliam Museum in Cambridge, these big, iconographic paintings by artists like Cesare Ripa with titles like *Warnings against Mutability* and *The Transitoriness of Life.* Despite the overstatement and melodrama of painting like that, I think I manage to work them into the poem in a way that you'll say, "Yeah, this is true." Literally, the book is being eaten away.

MH: *Acid paper?*

PV: I don't mention acid paper directly. I leave the reader suspicious of what's eating away the paper, but it's Saturn, it's Chronos, it's time. It's based on one of the images I used in *Harmatan*. When I was in Nigeria, I stayed at this bush house where I found an old book that was literally round because the mice had eaten all the corners. I mentioned this to Tony Towle one day and he said that Jean Holabird had come across a book that was so gnawed by mice, it was *Hunger* by Knut Hamsun (laughs). So, I thought here was a chance to take that metaphor literally.

MH: *You can't make this stuff up.*

PV: No. Literally, it's the idea of time eating away whatever we manage to accomplish. So, in a way, it's a funny poem, but, it's on a serious theme. So, if that's a signature poem, or typical poem, yes.

MH: *Maybe signature is a poor choice of word, maybe characteristic is better, characteristic of the way your mind works.*

PV: Okay, it's a personal poem even though I'm using this prose format. But it's personal in the sense that I've had these feelings about time's "winged chariot" running right over me (laughs). I put it in a more contemporary format than a Ripa, (Cesare Ripa 1555–1622) painting.

MH: *Sounds like a funny thing to play with, the absurdity of posterity.*

PV: Yes, the joke's at my expense.

MH: *You do that frequently. It's one of your strengths. I wish more poets did. They generally take themselves too seriously.*

PV: I take myself just as seriously as the next poet, but I think I've always been a naturally clumsy person and this has helped me to develop a sense of humor about it, to amuse myself, at least.

MH: *I wrote in my notes: Violi combines ecstatic celebrations of life with mystical defeats.*

PV: Hey, can I use that on the back cover of a book (both laughing).

MH: *There's your sense of the absurd that emerges in your poetry, as in the poems "Captain Bravo" or "Splurge."*

PV: It strikes me as one aspect of life and I like poetry that covers all the bases. I'm not sure, though, whether absurdity is the pitcher's mound or home plate (laughs). I remember the first romance-adventure novel I ever read by Rafael Sabatini, when I was thirteen, the very first sentence: "Born with the gift of laughter and the sense that the world was mad ..."

MH: *In your poetry, there are many funny moments—this sense of the absurd flowing through this sense of the absolute.*

PV: (laughs) I couldn't put it any better. It's how I perceive things.

MH: *What bothers you about your own poetry and what would you like to change?*

PV: It's a good question. It's something I confront each time I decide to write a poem. I'm always looking for a new way. I like to think that I'll always write lyrical poems or that I should be writing more of them.

MH: *Lyrical poems?*

PV: Yes.

MH: *Why lyricism when everything seems so anti-lyrical?*

PV: The beauty of it. Incorporate it in a prose form—the invidious lyric.

MH: *I just finished an interview with a poet (Barbara Guest) who's tried all her life to be anti-lyrical.*

PV: Sounds like nonsense to me, like a quarterback saying, "I try to throw the ball so it wobbles" (laughs). But a lot of us have incorporated anti-poetic diction deliberately—it's a tradition by now.

MH: *It's hard working against the lyricism of the language.*

PV: It seems to define Modernism. I like to think there are lyrical passages, that some of the shorter poems are purely lyrical.

MH: *Are you thinking in sounds? There's also lyrical imagery.*

PV: I just stick to the meaning of it as personal and musical. But I want to write more narrative. I feel what I should be doing is more of what I'm already doing. I want to write more lyrically and narratively. I want to write poems that have more to do with history, also certain experiences I've had that I'm afraid will get too far away from me.

MH: *What do you like least about your own work?*

PV: I'm trying to think about particular poems I've changed my mind about and what it was I disliked about them, the poems I wouldn't include in a selected or collected volume of my poetry. I'm not sure I could generalize about them except that they're poems that haven't held up for me. I think there are some poems that I've published I knew were slight. I think they provided a good interlude in a book. For instance, I have one poem which is simply a list of Haitian names because Haitians tend to have these beautiful names due to their history. I tried to see if I could make something musical by arranging them in rhymed quatrains.

MH: *Yes, they have extraordinary-sounding names like Toussaint L'Ouverture.*

PV: Yes. I manage to include a few names of assassins from Haitian history. To me that seemed like it was worth a poem. But whether I'd include it in a selected works, no. I don't think so.

MH: *Minor work.*

PV: Yes. There's another poem based on watching boxcars go by and trying to read them. I think it works in a swivel-neck way. It's another list poem. Let me put it this way. I just hope readers tolerate things like that. I myself will never write another list poem.

MH: *Do you think about your readers?*

PV: I don't think it is a healthy thing to do. I'm not writing for them directly.

MH: *Whom are you writing for?*

PV: Myself.

MH: *One of the dangers in poetry is the narrowness of always writing from the same place.*

PV: I think this gets back to something you were saying before. There's this short egocentric poem out there that workshops have encouraged—my God, enough! You know what I mean, the half-pager, the poem that's all-immediate perceptions of self. Poets should start retrieving things that they've seemingly forfeited to novelists and playwrights.

MH: *They don't know how to do it anymore.*

PV: No, because they're not encouraged to write anything but these gratuitous half-pagers. If a good poem came out of the academic tradition over the last twenty or thirty years, it's that detailed, concentrated galvanizing moment. Unfortunately, the damn thing imploded. It's time to push things back a bit, to open things.

MH: *What have you learned about who you are from what you write?*

PV: You mean poetry as a form of self-discovery?

MH: *Is that possible?*

PV: I don't know if I'll ever get too comfortable with myself, but if a poem, as Yeats said, is an argument with yourself, where a novel is an argument with the world, then a poem enables you to carry on that argument, engage different sides of yourself, it might lead to some resolution, or maybe you get to enjoy yourself more. I don't know. Being a poet you have to give readings and that's told me more about myself.

MH: *What does that tell you?*

PV: That I'm forever going to be a shy extrovert. I'll always be this oxymoron.

MH: *But you hate it at the same time?*

PV: I wouldn't say I hate it.

MH: *It's a conflict.*

PV: It is. It was a tremendous change for me to read before people. It took years for me to enjoy it.

MH: *When did you become comfortable?*

PV: In March of 1979 I gave a reading at Saint Mark's. It wasn't the first time I read there, but it was just an enjoyable occasion for me because I read with enough nervousness to get an edge and just keep that edge going through the work. I really had a good time that night.

MH: *Which poems do you like to read?*

PV: I like to read parts of long poems. I've read the end of "Little Testament" because there's a place where I can just pick it up, and the same with "The Curious Builder." "King Nasty" I can't read anymore.

MH: *You lose the narrative.*

PV: You're not going to get a good poem by just hearing it once. I like to think there's something in the poem that will carry it along for the listener. I like to think there are things hidden in the poems, too, that unfold as they are being read.

MH: *It's never fixed.*

PV: When I read poems that I love, I realize years later that I'm finding out things about them, or seeing things. And these are poems that I really know.

MH: *For instance?*

PV: Say, Wordsworth's "Surprised by Joy," where there's nothing in it to indicate that he wrote this after a period of personal grief, which makes it a completely different poem. That's a discovery. There are just some poems that I love where there seem to be some blind spots, or some lines I never realized the extent of their importance. I'm thinking of Keats' "On First Looking into Chapman's Homer," or Shakespeare's sonnet "That time of year thou mayest in me behold"—Sonnet 73.

When I realized that Shakespeare is sort of describing a walk through the fall woods, but that the trees overhead are like the rafters of an old, burned-out church, and where there's a choir up there, the birds, a wonderful series of spondees like gongs in that poem, and how the poem is based on the phoenix image at the end, bursting forth from the ashes. But if you take the archeological image of the trees overhead being the rafters of a church, you get into Vitruvius's idea that the pre-Gothic churches were formed by people tying the tops of trees together to form an apex, a rood, so you're going back to the beginnings of an architectural style. I'm not saying that Shakespeare ever read Vitruvius. But at least I get these resonances from that poem. Then there's how the poem starts off in years and works its way down to a moment in such neat quatrains progressively from a year to a season to a day to a moment.

I think it would be wonderful to write something that is so rich that it will keep surprising you all your life.

MH: *How would you characterize the current state of poetry?*

PV: In this country there's a double-edged sword swinging back and forth. Poets identify, even against their own instincts, with particular groups racially or politically. The good news is that there's new content, "new" in quotations. The bad news is that "multicultural" risks being another term for ethnocentric, which was another term for provincial, which was another term for being narrow-minded (laughing). So there's a great risk there about becoming very predictable and self-stereotyping that is counter to what art has always been.

MH: *How would you respond to an offer to publish in an Italian-American anthology?*

PV: Very warily. I've rejected some invitations. I've accepted one, which was in a magazine. The reason I accepted was because I thought the editor knew and liked the poem. This editor had the same feeling I did that it's almost meaningless since Italians are such a broad spectrum of people. Let me put it this way. I'm very suspicious of professional ethnics. I don't think that a good cause necessarily means a good poem. I'd rather be in an anthology because the poems in it make me feel that I'm in good company, where the anthology is defined by a sensibility rather than a name.

I hope this is short-lived. I think it delays important work. It still avoids the tough question: What makes a poem good? These anthologies include poets for sociopolitical reasons. They're avoiding the critical question. Ultimately, even if you get poems by poets with identical backgrounds, you still have to deal with why one poem is better than another. Racial and ethnic boosterism is tedious.

MH: *It has opened publishing to new voices.*

PV: Good things are happening at the same time.

MH: *Did any poem of yours surprise you after having written it?*

PV: Surprise in a good sense (laughing)? Yes, sometimes I lucked out in that more connections were made than I realized and maybe there was a little more there than I was aware of and I'm grateful.

MH: *In the earlier interview I did with you, you mentioned your envy of Desnos, his lyricism. When I compared the two of you, you said you loved distorting the image for the sake of a finer expression. You love Desnos's ability to do so?*

PV: Something that will carry, that will express feeling and stretch reality along with it, but always knowing when to not stretch it too far and end up with the ridiculous instead of the sublime.

Desnos had that. That's the best of surrealism. Desnos wasn't just a charter member of the movement, he represents the best in it. Whereas Breton, despite his beautiful love poems, seems mechanical, too cranky with his over-reliance on anaphora. Automatic writing has never interested me in the least. But the biggest contribution of the surrealists was their serious use of hyperbole in a lyrical dimension, and that godless mysticism of theirs, the wildness in their sense of beauty, and how they would carry humor as far as anything else. Supervielle is amazing. There's a sincerity in Supervielle that reminds me of Joe Ceravolo's poetry.

MH: *Who are the prose writers you most enjoy?*

PV: Sean O'Faolain. Like everyone else, I'm waiting for Garcia Marquez to write another book as marvelous as *One Hundred Years of Solitude*. I'm trying to track down more of Curzio Malaparte's novels. Jim Harrison's *Legends of the Fall*, that's a great story. I'd like to read Rabelais again, and more of Gibbon, and Toynbee's *History of the West*. Recently, I've been reading Lytton Strachey, a brilliant essay he wrote on Pope's use of the heroic couplet.

MH: *If you could live as a poet in any other period, when and where would that be?*

PV: The Quattrocento. Sienna or Urbino. I wouldn't have to think long about that one. I'd trade for Elizabethan England or Revolutionary America.

MH: *You wouldn't want to be in Paris near the turn of the century?*

PV: Yes—with Stanford White's crowd—and no. It's not far enough away. Too much excitement over technology that I don't think I would have shared.

MH: *The London of Johnson and Boswell?*

PV: I think I would have been lost in some compound-complex sentence and I would still be trying to find my way out. When I consider groups like that, I think of Pietro Aretino, Giulio Romano.

They knew how to enjoy themselves (laughs).

MH: *If you could visit any poet who would that be?*

PV: Eleanor of Aquitaine. We could talk real estate, or start a dynasty. I'd like to have raced cars with Marinetti. I would have liked to have spoken to Coleridge—or rather listened to him. I wish I had known the painters Delacroix, Raphael, and Giulio Romano. I'd ask Romano about his tossing a joke into a masterpiece, deliberately screwing up the symmetry of a building in a defiant way.

MH: *If you could have written any poetry published in this century, which would it be?*

PV: Elizabeth Bishop's poem "Shampoo." Robert Fitzgerald's translations and particular poems by Stevens, a great deal of Yeats, so much of Yeats. What a question! Apollinaire's "The Pretty Redhead," Eliot's "Preludes." There's much I read with a mix of envy and love, but to have written them means I would have to be that person, and that's usually no bargain.

MH: *How about books from any period?*

PV: *The Book of Job* (laughs). No, *The Rubaiyat of Omar Khayyam.*

MH: *Seriously?*

PV: I'd trade it all in for *The Rubaiyat*. I'd trade everything in for "To His Coy Mistress." That's the perfect poem. Shakespeare, of course, Sonnet 130. John Crowe Ransom was blind to that one. One thing I'm extremely envious of is Boccaccio's introduction to *The Decameron*. The way he begins with a straight piece of reportage on the effects of the plague and then works into the tales. What great piece of journalism that is, and a neat trick.

MH: *You recently gave a reading tour in England. What was that like?*

PV: The nice revelation was that at each place the audience was different. Some reminded me of a Saint Mark's audience in that they were young or there was a mixture of old and young and that these reading series had been going a long time.

MH: *Were they used to your brand of American poetry?*

PV: In some places I had the impression that no, that wasn't the case, but in other places, yes.

MH: *You felt well-received?*

PV: Oh yes, that was the nicest thing about it.

MH: *How was the audience different?*

PV: You might get the same thing over here in five days reading at five different places. You know, a reading at the 92nd Street Y, and a reading at Saint Mark's. You're still in Manhattan (laughs). So there were uptown and downtown readings over there. However, I thought that some poems wouldn't travel. I was surprised because "Police Blotter" really worked and I was astonished because what the hell is a police blotter in England? I don't even think they print such things in their newspapers let alone see a poem in the form of something like that. I remember on one occasion I read "King Nasty" thinking that it would be appropriate for the particular audience and boy was that a mistake (laughs). It was late at night.

They have this wonderful tradition of poetry and they glory in it. This makes for poetry rich in allusion. At the same time, there's a great weight on contemporary poets in England that American poets don't necessarily have. American poets should have more of it in some respects, to have a certain obligation to know what's already been done so that the poetry will gain. A radically different poem only makes sense in a traditional framework or else its best elements are lost. I think the English are in a good position to do that. It's unfair of me to sum it up because I try to read a lot of contemporary work from over there but there's still a great deal I haven't read.

Interview with Anne Waldman

I saw Anne Waldman for the first time at a reading she gave at the Saint Mark's Poetry Project where she read her new poem "Skin Meat Bones." I was transfixed in watching her move as she read and enunciated the three separate words in their tonal scale from high soprano to middle tenor, to deep bass. I wrote a poem afterwards titled "Watching Anne Waldman's Feet" that tried to capture her balletic moves on stage.

Along with Ted Berrigan and Ron Padgett, Anne Waldman was one of the major forces in the Saint Mark's poetry world, that "Second Generation" New York School, that grew out of the Poetry Project, and of which she was one of the founders.

When I interviewed her at her Greenwich Village apartment, she was raising her two-year old son with her husband, the poet Reed Bye. She was enjoying motherhood, and at the same time, going off to Boulder, Colorado to help with developing the writing program at Naropa University, an experimental school for creative arts and meditation called "The Jack Kerouac School of Disembodied Poetics," a program she began with Allen Ginsberg and Diane di Prima.

What impressed me was that she would attend all the events at the Poetry Project and she would be there for all the first meetings of the workshops that I attended, such as John Godfrey's poetry workshop, and Ron Padgett's French translation workshop, or Simon Schuchat's Chinese poetry workshop.

After Berrigan's death, she enlisted my help in putting together all the photographs for the memorial book for Ted Berrigan titled *Nice To See You*, and she was using some of my published poetry interviews in her classes at Naropa.

Anne Waldman

MH: *What inspired you to write poetry?*

AW: I always loved reading poetry and had grown up in an environment conducive to reading. My mother had a lot of poetry books in our home. Also, several of my teachers in high school were wonderful in that they made us read poetry aloud and generated a continuing interest in literature by their excitement. I was writing as a youngster.

Going to the Berkeley Poetry Conference in the early sixties triggered a lot of writing. I met Lewis Warsh there, who had been a student of Jack Spicer's, and we began *Angel Hair Magazine*. This opened up a lot of correspondence with older established poets. We were also looking at poems from poets our own age as well and started *Angel Hair Books* shortly thereafter. I began to work with the magazine while still in college at Bennington. I also edited *SILO* from Bennington and I helped produce a poetry series for WRVR in New York.

In terms of my own career, I think I was probably lucky that Bobbs-Merrill and Corinth published my first books of poems, *Baby Breakdown* and *Giant Night*. Perhaps Bobbs-Merrill was looking for a "token woman" poet, that sort of thing, who was also an "embodiment" of the Lower East Side energy at that time. But Bob Amussen, the editor there, was extremely supportive. He also published Sam Shepard's first plays and the first *World Anthology*.

MH: *You really believe that?*

AW: Well, young women poets weren't published profusely then. My first books, in turn, led to other writing. It's your friends support and encouragement that keeps you going, although you develop a bull-headed confidence that you're going to write no matter what. But it helps enormously to have some recognition as well.

MH: *Your parents were literary. Your mother wrote, your father wrote; your mother translated Greek, I understand.*

AW: Yes, she did translations from the Greek poet Anghelos Sikelianos, and from the French of César Moro, a surrealist who was actually South American, and she wrote some poetry herself.

Community is very important to me and I've always enjoyed working with people. I had a vision about "changing the world." Poetry seemed to be a way one could realize that. Poetry heightened my senses and awareness. It would be wonderful to think that you could touch people's lives through mysterious combinations of words.

MH: *What is the Buddhist term ... "Sanga"?*

AW: Well, Sanga is the community. The Boddhisattva ideal is that you're working constantly to liberate others.

MH: *Do you think that this has shaped the idea of the community?*

AW: Definitely. There's always some kind of community, I think. This particular (East Village) New York City neighborhood is conducive to the notion of "community." The Poetry Project is still very much a focus for the poets in the neighborhood, but poets should go off by themselves occasionally.

MH: *So that they can open themselves up to new experiences? But you've been like a poetry mother to a lot of younger poets.*

AW: I like that word "mother." I appreciate it more now that I am one.

MH: *A nurturing influence?*

AW: I've always been interested in other people's work as much as my own. It works both ways.

MH: *Who helped you? You mention the poet-dance critic Edwin Denby, as your root guru. That's curious. I wonder what you mean by that?*

AW: It's not only his writing, which of course I admire, his poetry and his dance writing have been a tremendous inspiration to me. It's his manner, his panoramic way of seeing things. He simply sees

Sept 23.84

Dear Mark,

Thank you for your letter! I'll send along corrections when I get a minute. Very busy tonight preparing for classes tomorrow which inspires me to write this. Can you send me a copy of your interviews with Kenneth, Edwin & Jimmy? They'd be most useful in the class I'm teaching (MAKING IT NEW: Contemporary Poetry & Poetics.) There are so few good "poetics" sources, and I like getting the word from the mouths of the poets. I would greatly appreciate having these soon. Best address is c/o Naropa, 2130 Arapahoe Ave., Boulder 80302. I even tried calling you today, but your #'s unlisted. Had a good time in NYC last. Allen G. & I & Holman launched the first poets' MTV style vidoes at the Public Theatre. Seemed like a success. Wonderful to see Alice & the boys looking so well, & other friends.

Yes, I like "Independence Day 1983"; it's just that there are too many poems at this point with a similar feeling, all strong, but...I've had to reject quite a few . But I also think there will be further outlets for any work inspired by Ted's presence & teaching. It's all just beginning.

Reed & I will be coming to NYC together the first or second week of May - he for a reading at the church, & I'll be doing a "lecture" for Chas. Bernstein's Series. Perhaps he and I could do something together at the Williams Center? We might be staying with Reed's parents in New Jersey. Little Ambrose is coming off a bout of asthma now. He was fine all summer, but the weather change can often bring things on. Not as bad as attacks in the past & we do feel the situation is much more workable out here. If we were in NY he'd probably be having a harder time, and in Bellevue. We're moving again next week and hoping that "being settled" finally will make a difference. I'm almost finished with the book I'm collaborating with XXXX artist Susan Hall on (for Lita Hornick). I still have to write an Intro for the Homage book. (Your help and support has been tremendous on this project.) Looks like United Artists wikk publish my travel book! So things are busy, tho this town feels slow.

Looking forward to the interviews. I'll try to get some $ from Kornblum towards those photo reproduction bills; I haven't forgotten.

Let us know about possible reading.

ALL the best

ANNE WALDMAN TO MARK HILLRINGHOUSE

things as they are. He has mirrorlike wisdom. Neutrality might be a good word here. I see him as a truly enlightened being. He rarely complains. His mind and his eyes are, for the most, focused on something else entirely. When you're with him, you get a glimmer of the way he sees things. You can learn so much from him. In that sense, he's a wonderful teacher and a wonderful presence. He transforms the world for you constantly.

MH: *When did you first meet him?*

AW: It must have been in 1966 or 1967. The poet Bill Berkson introduced us.

MH: *In a way, that's when you began writing poetry.*

AW: Well, that's when the St. Mark's Poetry Project was officially beginning under the auspices of the Office of Economic Opportunity. I was taking myself seriously as a writer.

MH: *Did you know Frank O'Hara at all?*

AW: I met O'Hara at a party at Bill Berkson's in the summer of 1966; the early part of the summer before he died. It was a party perhaps honoring him. Bill was living up on Fifty-seventh Street at the time, and at one point Frank O'Hara and Larry Rivers breezed in.

I don't know if you saw the poem "Panegyra" that appeared in the Poetry Project Newsletter. It was written for the occasion of the Larry Rivers show at the Marlborough Gallery, which was a benefit for the Poetry Project. I have a line in there about "metabolic brothers," where I recall meeting Rivers and O'Hara for the first time. Of course, I'd read his poems and heard about his magnetic and magnanimous personality. He was very friendly and warm and told me to come work at the Museum of Modern Art after I got out of college, for no salary, of course. I wanted to do it but I couldn't afford it. He was very encouraging. I was introduced as a young poet who had started *Angel Hair Magazine*. I said something about how I'd love to publish him and so on and he was interested. He was killed soon after that, but we did publish some of his poems posthumously.

I think he was probably always that generous with any young person interested in poetry. I was tremendously interested in him, too. There was definitely a spark there. He was seductive.

MH: *Ashbery and Koch, did you meet them at about the same time?*

AW: Probably, yes. I can't remember the exact occasion or who introduced who to whom. When I was working at Riverside Radio in 1965, where I hosted a poetry show. This was part of a work term from Bennington College. I led discussions with poets. I had a panel that focused on the subject of little magazines, which brought quite a few poets together. Peter Schjeldahl was a guest on it, who edited *Mother*, and Ashbery, who edited *Locus Solus* and *Art & Literature*. John Perrault, who edited *Elephant Magazine*, and Ted Berrigan, who had started *C Magazine*. That was the first time I met John Ashbery. I remember Ted Berrigan joking about it later, saying that I was "putting out" more for Ashbery than I was for him! I had met Ted at the Berkeley Poetry Conference at a party after one of his readings. He was usually surrounded by attentive females, so he wasn't paying that much attention to me.

MH: *Well, he pays attention to you now; he says that you're the most talented of all.*

AW: He's a sweetheart. I can't think of all the specific occasions for meeting everybody. The Donald Allen anthology, titled *The New American Poetry*, had just been published by Grove Press, so I was unfamiliar with all those poems. I studied with Howard Nemerov in college, and he used to play tennis with Kenneth Koch. He was curious about what I thought about all the New York School poets I had recently become interested in.

MH: *Auden was in New York at that time and was admired by both the academics and the New York School.*

AW: I used to see him jogging down St. Mark's Place often at dawn. I'd just be turning in and would gaze out the window or go out to get the paper or an egg cream at the Gem Spa newsstand, and would see him running in a University of Michigan sweatshirt with his wonderful craggy face. He was one of the first joggers!

MH: *I can't imagine Auden jogging. Did he take an interest in the younger poets at all?*

AW: At a distance. I think Ed Sanders had made some overtures and he was very friendly, but didn't plunge into the Lower East Side scene. He used to go to services at St. Mark's Church, but after they changed the litany to make it more plain spoken ...

MH: *You mean more American?*

AW: ... Well, plain spoken in the sense of this Lower East Side Manhattan neighborhood, this particular community. Sometimes the closing benediction would be "power to the people." For Auden, who had been a Church of England, Anglican follower, and who loved the language of that kind of service, this was too much. I don't know if he went to another parish or not, but he ceased coming to St Mark's. But he was around. Just having him in our midst was provocative. I think Kenward Elmslie at one point interviewed him for the *Paris Review*, but I don't think it worked out finally. I remember Kenward talking about visiting Auden. Then, there were people I knew, older poets, who had known him. Allen Ginsberg had some rapport with him.

MH: *Did you suffer any anxiety, to use Harold Bloom's term, from exposure to other writers you admired?*

AW: Anxiety? Well, it's very funny. When Ashbery came to visit my class at Stevens Institute of Technology in Hoboken, New Jersey, the students were expecting to see someone who looked and acted entirely differently, the bearded sage. This is because they are engineering students. I think if anything, that visit dispelled their previous notions. Later, I had them write their impressions. So many of them wrote that he didn't seem like a poet at all, but like "the guy next door." I thought this was wonderful. He does have an invisible quality.

But, anxiety, I don't know. Susan Sontag was asked a similar question about being intimidated in the company of great philosophers and thinkers and writers. She said that she was happy to be a foot soldier in the lower ranks. Anxiety ... ? You need time just to work on getting your own mind down. Most of the poets I admire have been a great help.

MH: *Now you're in that position of creating a certain amount of anxiety now that you are a known poet.*

AW: I hope that's not true. Poets shouldn't make people more miserable than they are. I think we have to help each other. There's no time for fighting—feuding, as Robert Creeley says. If you're interested in writing, you're either going to do it or not. Nothing is going to stand in your way. It's a command. The chances are, because we're all individuals, that something you do will be different from something someone else is writing. There's probably no new topic or theme under the sun. But there's always new writing. I don't think poets have even begun to explore the outrageous possibilities in language.

MH: *Is that where you're headed?*

AW: I'm working on all kinds of things at this point. It's hard to narrow down. "Incantation" is a very meditative long formal work. Others are collage-like. There are charts and snapshots. What I first did twenty years ago was to turn off everything I knew and go back to square one to get in touch with my own mind babble and explore that.

MH: *Is that what you've done in your most recent book?*

AW: Mind babble! My "First Baby Poems"? *Baby Breakdown*, an early book, was filled with a lot of mind babble, as are a lot of the poems from that period. I was discovering what I could do and get away with and was having a lot of excitement putting words down on paper. I was also living in a situation that gave me a lot of impetus. I think a lot of the poems in *Baby Breakdown* were phrases off the radio, overheard conversations, etcetera, things that were very much in the air just waiting to be seized upon, which is a "process" I still explore.

MH: *Like O'Hara or John Cage?*

AW: Yes, a similar sort of energy, although it was my energy and experience. But a lot of their ideas were tremendous. It was more of a Kerouacian idea of spontaneity—first thoughts, best thoughts, free associating, playing with resonances.

MH: *Do you revise?*

AW: I do, often. It depends on the piece. Some poems I don't revise at all. Some come out looking and sounding right, or else I can't look at them again. Some things I'll go back to. Some of the formal poems such as sestinas or pantoums, as in the *First Baby Poems* book, demand a different kind of attention.

MH: *It seems as if you're trying to get away from this incantorial style of yours and move into the field of language writing. I hate to employ the term.*

AW: It's useful, but then again, the more poets you talk to, I think you'll find that it's a much more open situation. Actually, there's a lot of overlapping amongst the so-called schools. I'm very interested in what the so-called language poets are doing. It is an extension of Gertrude Stein. There's an emotional passion lacking in some of the work, but there's a word headiness that is quite exhilarating. But you'd have to talk about particular poems and particular writers.

MH: *You have O'Hara's gift of free associating. The facility to pull disparate things together in a poem. Your poem "Crazy without You" is a good example.*

AW: The list of stars?

MH: *Right.*

AW: I was living in the country near a huge potato field when I wrote that poem, and stargazing. I'd look up and see constellations and try to figure out what they were in relation to everything else. It was also a love poem. It has an incantorial quality. I love the names of the stars; I love the sounds, but I always had trouble pronouncing them properly. I read that poem in Austin, Texas, and later, a fellow came up to me and said he had become an astronomy major as a result of that poem. I was tremendously flattered.

MH: *You have continued using these free associations even in the new poems in* Cabin *and in* Countries. *It's more subdued. In "Van Gogh's Room" is simply a listing of the colors in the painting: "The floor is pink, the green windows ... the blue door."*

AW: It was obvious. The poem is a little painting in itself. It creates a little room. The colors are all wrong, in a sense. That they can fit together and make a painting is wonderful. The idea was to make the room into a poem, and it was very simple. I was looking at that painting in Amsterdam in the van Gogh Museum and in a room. It was crazy trying to have all those colors work and I don't know if that comes across in the poem.

MH: *I know the painting and you can envision it with the impressions your words give. I'm wondering if you use anything like that to help you write, props—whatever?*

AW: Visual stimulus?

MH: *Yes.*

AW: Sure. I have a long poem entitled "I Digress" and it started from looking at a painting in the Cloisters in Manhattan, by the artist Robert Campin. It's quite dense and gets into a treatise on the Abhidharma, which is a particular area of study in Buddhist psychology. I think this technique is as true of me as it is true of other poets. It's true of Ashbery. So many of his titles are titles of paintings or titles inspired by paintings or music. Music, too, has inspired particular poems. Writers have to look at everything they can. There is no reason to get myopic about looking at the page or going to endless poetry readings.

MH: *That can wear you down, too.*

AW: I went to the New York City Ballet last night and saw "Apollo." It has been changed somewhat. It used to include the birth of

Apollo, where you see him bursting out of swaddling clothes. Then, instantly, the muses spring out of his head. You don't see the birth now, but he's quite young. It opened with Peter Martins strumming on his lyre much like some rock performer. Calliope is wonderful. Maria Calegari has a classic gesture where she touches her heart and her hand moves up to her lips and she throws the words out of her mouth. It's like the creation of language itself. Not language exactly, but passion spewing forth, in a sense—the need from the heart to speak. She's epic poetry. Epic: one's story, the story of a people, of a race of gods and humans. It's a powerful gesture for poetry.

MH: *I can imagine you going over to dance very easily.*

AW: Well, Edwin Denby of course, was inspiring to go to the ballet with. He would point out a dancer's particular leg movement or stretch of a neck, and you would find yourself focusing or meditating on that for a while, which seems to change your ordinary perception.

MH: *Denby can write about movement the way no one else can. I want to know if you feel that what produces a poem or makes somebody want to write one comes from some special gift or talent at birth?*

AW: Right. There seems to be a renewable source of energy that's interested in manifesting in words. It was always through poetry that I derive the most delight. But basically "I" am like an instrument on which various things play. "I is another," said Rimbaud.

MH: *Do you meditate?*

AW: Yes, Buddhist style mediation. In Shamatha/Vipassana meditation you don't meditate on anything particularly. That's the whole point. You simply use your breathing as a technique to bring your mind back because your mind is always wandering off into endless reruns of what happened yesterday, or fantastic projections of what will happen. Hopes and fears, emotions, etcetera. The idea is that by coming back to the breath you still the mind.

MH: *Other styles try to break the mind down psychologically as in*

Zen meditation. To try to snap it out of its habitual thought process.

AW: With koans, yes. It's a similar kind of thing so that your mind experiences a gap in which everything is open and there are no preconceptions and your answers aren't coming from a preconceived place. Original spontaneous mind. Uncluttered.

MH: *I've read that Jack Kerouac was very good at answering koans.*

AW: His books are full of Zen references. He would get together with Philip Whalen, who is now a Zen monk and teacher, and of course, a marvelous poet, and Gary Snyder, who is a long-time Zen student. They would record marvelous koan-like conversations. In Kerouac's novel, *The Dharma Bums*, very disparate things come together with incredible spontaneity in some of the characters' mind babble—revelations of their own thought processes.

MH: *Snyder and Whalen are very serious about their discipline and Zen training. There are so many phonies among the pop practitioners. The ones that read a few books and become enlightened cultists.*

AW: Westerners didn't know quite how to practice meditation until recently. There are now real Zen teachers and masters working in America. You're either doing it or you're not. Like writing, you either have the practice or you don't.

MH: *You're often trying to make these connections in your poems in order to open up the idea of what reality is in relation to its emptiness. Your "Skin Meat Bones" poem is a good example.*

AW: That's a meditation on three phenomena we're all walking around with all day in and day out. I think the words came to me first as sounds. I was ecstatic when I heard this poem in my head: "skin" is a high note, "meat" somewhere in the middle, and "bones" as a bass rumble.

MH: *On the page, it is hard to read or to know how to sound it with the inflected degrees of pitch you give those three words.*

AW: I had a friend trying to notate it using a tape that I had made, but my voice is inconsistent and it's very hard trying to capture my idiolect. It's not a poem to be read silently. I'm working on a recorded version of it and another version which is a pop song.

With my first vinyl single record, "Uh-Oh Plutonium," I took the text of a poem I had written for a demonstration at Rocky Flats nuclear warhead factory outside Boulder, Colorado, and put it together with the melody I had in my head. The idea was to get it released during the period of the "Nuclear Freeze" in June 1982. Some of the work I do is only presentable in that form, but I always want the words to be heard distinctly and not get lost in a musical mush or overkill.

MH: *Well, you're a great reader of your work; you move, dance, and sing.*

AW: Thank you. But those disparate things don't always work through the music.

MH: *Through a field of noise.*

AW: Right. With "Skin Meat Bones" it's an approximation of my mind and how that meditation went— (quoting a line of the poem)
   "Your body waking up so sweet to me—Skin!"
The whole poem was very clearly there to manifest. It was a visceral experience, and that doesn't happen frequently.

MH: *As in "Fast Speaking Woman"?*

AW: That's similar, but that work was built over a period of time. I feel any woman could be writing it. Over the years, I've received other people's versions in the mail.

MH: *It flows so smoothly that it seems as if you could change all the words into nonsense words—it's that musical.*

AW: You must know Gertrude Stein's great poem "Lifting Belly," where she repeats those two words ad infinitum. It's like that children's game "Telephone." After a while, you don't care what "Lifting Belly" is. It has powerful efficacy, but the phrase is shorn of meaning into becoming, finally, so many things, like breathing, like sex, like ocean waves rising. I'm not saying that there is a direct relationship between Stein's work and *Fast Speaking Woman*, but both works move in a lot of different ways so they cease to be personal or conceptual.

MH: In a lot of your long poems, "A Hundred Memories" is an example, I read where Kenneth Koch told you to "go on."

AW: Right. He liked that poem and said that he liked my vibrato, and to keep it up.

MH: *Which is the same thing O'Hara told Koch when he saw Koch's shorter version of "When The Sun Tries To Go On." And then here he was telling you ...*

AW: Well, there is a whispered oral lineage then.

MH: *Yes. But also in some of the short poems you've written. Koch has done the same. In his* Thank You and Other Poems, *there are these epigrammatic poems no more than titles that set up these bizarre connections, a sort of list. You've done likewise.*

AW: The mind works that way. We don't think in absolute, rational linear fashion. If we were to stop doing what we're doing now and just sit for five minutes, and then transcribe our mind's contents, we'd have a gigantic cut-up collage. A lot of it is simply indulgent gibberish. The point is, as you practice writing over the years, your thinking becomes refined. You instantly discard something for something else. Well, "Skin Meat Bones" came to me with no interference, no static. I think if poems could happen like that all the time, we'd all be happier poets. It seems you have to create the atmosphere in order for the magic to occur. It may take days of sitting for two hours writing nothing you'd want to keep, but at least you'd put aside a time for the work. Although, over the years I've been able to write "on the wing," so to speak.

MH: *You said that O'Hara gave "us" that freedom.*

AW: Yes, well, Allen Ginsberg, too, has that impetus where everything has a possibility for a poem and where nothing is too sacred, and where you're able to write in any situation, so you do—in airplanes, in front of TV sets. Ed Dorn has written poems while driving down Highway 101.

MH: *Do you have an example of when you wrote "on the wing," as you say?*

AW: I was travelling with Allen Ginsberg and Reed Bye, my husband, along with Peter Orlovsky and Gregory Corso, to a poetry festival in Rome. We were on the ground, being ferried from one flight connection to another. I was trying to take down what Gregory and Allen were saying because it was so amusing. It's called *The Flying Diary*. At one point, while I was writing, Gregory shouted, "What are you doing! Poetry is a private business! You shouldn't be scribbling out here in public!" I said, "What makes you think it's poetry!" And he said, "It looks like hexameters to me!"

MH: *(laughing) Do you keep journals and carry a pad around with you?*

AW: Sure. Most writers do. I carry a notebook with me.

MH: *And a dream journal of some sort?*

AW: Off and on. Of course, if you start being diligent about recording your dreams, you discover that your dreams come back to you with more frequency and detail. They cry out to be written down. But I think poets do what they can, use any device or tool, as a way of getting the poems.

I was amused by Gregory Corso's attitude concerning the "place" for writing poetry. There are infinite possibilities. I find that my time for poetry now is mostly spent in the evenings after I've put my child to bed. My child's doing all the receiving of the phenomenal world, and I'm attending to him. Yet his birth inspired a great many poems.

MH: *That's curious, because your poem "Icy Rose" is re-echoed in a later poem—"Putting Makeup on Empty Space." It is a recent poem. The former poem was written over ten years ago and has almost identical lines in it—"all day feeling space/ my face is empty space ..."*

AW: That's great you noticed. I didn't remember.

MH: *Since you've mentioned your child receiving the phenomenal world, it occurred to me that feelings of space and emptiness are something that recurs in your phenomenology.*

AW: That's what we're doing as poets, or painters, or dancers, decorating space, creating illusions out of nothing. In Buddhist psychology that's what the feminine principle does, adorn reality. That truth is powerful to me. Literally, I do find myself in front of the mirror putting on makeup, or sitting in front of a blank piece of paper, or sticking things up on the wall, or putting clothes on my naked illusory body.

MH: *Is the feminine side the dark side?*

AW: I don't know if it's dark necessarily. At times, but so is the masculine principle. It's an active side, giving birth over and over again.

MH: *Robert Bly says that poetry comes out of that dark side.*

AW: Jimmy Schuyler calls the White Goddess the Goddess of Tapioca (laughs). One side of her, of course is dark, devouring, a "Tooth Mother," a destroyer, a Kali-goddess.

MH: *Right, well, Bly writes that poem, "Teeth Mother Naked."*

AW: Yes, then there's also the lover; I want to do / be them all and then disappear. All of us are dealing with empty space. I had a lot of trouble dealing with that phrase, "empty space," it's so tedious. "Air" is a better word, but it's not accurate. In a way, it was a challenge to see if I could make the poem in spite of the word "space." "Makeup on Empty Space" came out of the experience of trying to get up a very icy canyon. It's interesting you mention "Icy Rose" because it (obviously) was written during winter. The road was one of the most dangerous roads in Colorado.

I don't know what version of the poem "Makeup on Empty Space" you've seen, because I've left out some lines.

MH: It is the version I've heard you read not too long ago at the St. Mark's Poetry Project.

AW: There's a shorter reading version. It's an open-ended piece like "Fast Speaking Woman." I can play with it. It can stretch from the middle out. I can read it without breaking lines. I can do it spontaneously—"There's a better way to say 'empty space'—and I love ending it with the admonition to myself in the last line—"That it never be mentioned again!"

I think on the page it has more of a full sense of a poem. When I read it it's more of a chant. In "Icy Rose" I was addressing winter as a female persona, a female deity whose name is Icy Rose, and who's also visiting for the weekend or something. It was written in a situation where I was living outside a city in isolation. Maybe I get more hung up on empty space in the country.

MH: *Your poem "Pressure," from* Life Notes, *is said to mark your transition from lighter to deeper themes. It's curious that it does deal with your concept of space, your "no way out," lines—"no way out of the barn / ... no way out of Africa / ... no way out of the stationary store / ... no way out of Christmas ... out of Philadelphia, Texas, Littlestown Pa. / etcetera.*

AW: Well, that too. That's what I mean about poems that come in a psychological way and have a power for me derived from the incantation of words, phrases, ideas, and images, etcetera. Basically, there's an energy involved. But the point is they have an efficacy when they work. By saying "no way out," you're challenging that concept, you're playing with that idea, you're actually getting yourself out.

MH: *Similar to a koan, in a certain way.*

AW: Right, like the poem "Musical Garden" in *Fast Speaking Woman*, where I have the repeated line—"can't give you up." I'm listing all the things I refuse to give up. In a way, I'm giving them up by writing them down. But they're also there to stay. That intrigues me when things begin to work in this double-edged way.

MH: *You've even written collaborations this way with Ted Berrigan in a long poem titled "Memorial Day."*

AW: Yes.

MH: *You follow each other's lines, listing all these place names and things that are closed—"New York is closed, Chicago is closed" and so on.*

AW: We got that from Chris Gallup, Dick Gallup's daughter, who at the time was quite young. She was riding in the back of a car looking out the rear window and saying things like "this city was closed, and that was closed," etcetera. In a way that was our final litany about death. The sensory world shuts down when you die.
   I don't know where these kinds of poems come from exactly.

MH: *Maybe it's your Buddhist inclination.*

AW: It's a natural inclination for me. Also, I am interested in what words can do to one's whole being.

MH: *Using repetition seems to break down meaning and syntax and the deep structure of language. You enter the field of semantics.*

AW: Gertrude Stein does quite a bit of that, whereby you can go really "out" in terms of the language. The words shift their functions grammatically as well.

MH: *It seems to have been moving in that direction with each successive generation of writers.*

AW: Well, contradictions interest poets as do forcing certain kinds of issues. But I think you can get too dry with the language. Too much theory does this. Energy poems arise rather spontaneously. They're really simple. Sometimes they come as a word phrase or title. This for me is a starting point, then I begin to follow my own mind.

MH: *Was Charles Olson an influence?*

AW: I was reading a lot of poetry in my late teens and early twenties and I love these poems in his first book, *The Distances*. They're magical and strange and some of them came out of dreams. They're real collages and incredibly musical. "The Kingfishers" is magical and rich and open. He seems grounded in place and history. Everything I probably read is internalized.

Basically, at the time I was in my cocoon, waiting to emerge as a "poet," everything was a message. I had begun traveling at an early age. I had been to Egypt in my teens and I fancied myself quite independent. I had an early interest in Buddhism. I had gone to visit a Tibetan lama when I was eighteen years old. My mind wasn't a tabula rasa. I had inclinations toward all the things I've always been doing from the start.

MH: *You mentioned in a recent interview that you're getting more self-conscious about reading your own work.*

AW: One is constantly self-conscious in this body that is going to decay and die and stumble along and make mistakes and wake up with hay fever and so on. I guess "self-conscious" is a sort of neurotic state to be in. I think, initially, when I first began reading poems there was a lot of self-consciousness about reading, presenting the work in public. But you have to do it in order to get out the natural music and flow and rhythm. There is a body, your own, experiencing how you exist. If I was forced to watch tapes of myself reading, I'd probably get very embarrassed, because the energy comes through you in awkward, sometimes ugly extreme ways. Just as when a musician is playing an instrument, he or she will have a certain expression that can be quite strange.

MH: *Your book* Journals & Dreams, *was it an attempt to use a stream-of-conscious technique in writing?*

AW: I was using more psychological material. It was coming out of a period of journal writing and keeping track of dreams. I was traveling. It wasn't exactly stream-of-consciousness. It was more of a collage using the dreams, using the journals and keeping them in front of me and putting them into some kind of shape of their own.

MH: *Shape is very important to you?*

AW: I love how poems can look on the page and they have to have a life of their own, not simply how they're read out loud. This is something all good poets address. One poet might choose to break a line differently from another. We're all breathing when we write or think, and we're breathing simultaneously with different mental rhythms and patterns going on all the time. How we organize for the page reflects our thinking.

Appendix: Alice in Brooklyn

It was a beautiful spring day Monday, April 22, 2013, when I drove from Englewood, NJ, to see Alice. The drive was easy over the George Washington Bridge to the FDR to the Brooklyn Bridge, then to Sterling Street, where Alice's son, Edmund, lived with his wife, a few blocks south of Crown Heights.

It was a five-flight walk-up, I pressed the buzzer. The old tile and marble steps reminded me of when I used to visit Ted and Alice in their third-floor walk-up on Saint Mark's Place in the East Village. I hadn't seen Alice since the mid 1980s. I saw her a couple of years before she married the poet Doug Oliver in 1987 four years after Ted died, and before they moved to Paris in the early 1990s.

Alice opened the door and I saw that she had let her hair grow longer than the length I remember when she was in her 30s, and her hair was almost black then, but now it was a beautiful shade of smoky-silver.

She and Ted were like a poetry team when I knew them. I remember how well they read together, and how they complemented each other as poets, and they often collaborated together on poetry. Ted of course was the bigger name, and Alice was an up-and-coming poet with a couple of books, and I was always impressed by what she wrote. She is remarkable in that, like Ted, she has lived all these years as a poet and made that her life and work.

Alice had developed a style of writing that allowed the reader to float on an open stream-of-consciousness and word play. Her poems were incredible journeys to me. And I loved how she bore down on the text when she read her work to give each word the inflection it needed to contour the sounds.

I brought all of her books with me. She had made a name for herself with her poetry and her essays on poetry. Her life now revolved around her two sons, Anselm and Edmund and their families, and around her permanent residence in Paris where she has lived since 1992, a few blocks from the Gare du Nord train station. She even started a literary journal titled the *Gare du Nord*.

I remember her book party at the Gotham Book Mart on 47th Street (store closed in 2007; original proprietor Frances Steloff died in 1989 at 101) back in 1982 for one of her early books titled *Waltzing

Matilda (with a George Schneeman cover drawing, and published by the Kulchur Foundation in 1981). Ashbery and Koch were there for Alice's book party and so were many of the East Village poets. This was something that always impressed me, that all these New York poets would come out for each other's book parties. She signed my book for someone else, and when I read what she signed, I went back to her and said, "Alice, you signed my book for someone else!" She grabbed the book back out of my hands and resigned it for me crossing out the wrong name and inserting my name. It read: "For Mark, Best wishes and all stuff, Alice, Gotham 3 Drinks," (referring to her drinking wine at the party). Ted was standing there watching all this bemused, and he said to me later, "Alice really loved that you did that." And Ted was having fun by introducing me to characters like René Ricard, who was one of Andy Warhol's people, as he stood back and smiled, watching me taking it all in as Ricard made lewd and off-putting sexual remarks about people in the room.

One time, visiting Ted and Alice, I asked her to pose for me in front of her apartment building (see photograph on page 9) along with the poet Tom Savage who was also visiting. I placed myself in the photograph and Alice has her arm sweetly resting across my shoulder as Tom Savage looks out across the street, as we all sit together on the stoop of the apartment she shared with Ted. The apartment was close to Avenue A on Saint Mark's Place, a couple of blocks from Tompkins Square Park.

My questions for Alice centered around her life with Ted. They had been married ten years when I first got to know them. I asked her about how they collaborated, and was there any conflict with both of them being poets and trying to write. She related how hard it was to live the poetry life together and raise two kids. The money that they earned was very scattershot, some of it from poetry honorariums, some from Ted's part-time teaching gigs. There was never enough money. Her short poem titled "Poem" from her book *When I Was Alive* with a cover drawing by Alex Katz, captures a kind of city moment of isolated introspection late at night:

> St. Mark's Place caught at night in hot summer,
> Lonely from the beginning of time until now.
> Tompkins Square Park would be midnight green but only hot.
> I look through the screens from my 3rd floor apartment

> As if I could see something,
> Or as if the bricks and concrete were enough themselves
> To be seen and found beautiful.
> And who will know the desolation of St. Mark's Place
> With Alice Notley's name forgotten and
> This night never having been?

Her poems in those early books are filled with East Village life as in her poem, "Dream," from her book *Waltzing Matilda*, a poem filled with images of life with Ted and other poets in a time of pills and drug-induced states. The second stanza of that poem begins:

> In the real dream, there are
> large grounds, like a collage,
> and grass, and a house with several
> stories, and rooms full of people.
> Ted has a drug which when you take it
> makes you disappear in front of
> everyone, poof, vanish into air.

Other times, going to see Ted and Alice, I'd run into Eileen Myles who was visiting, and Ted would say jokingly, "Why don't you go out with Eileen?" Eileen was just getting her poetry career going and she was always at Saint Mark's for the readings. So many of the poets who lived in the neighborhood would drop in to see Ted and Alice, and I would run into Steve Carey, John Godfrey, Elinor Nauen, Simon Pettet, Tom Savage, and Harris Schiff, and others.

I began by asking questions about her book *At Night The States* that she had dedicated to the memory of Ted. These were poems written during a grieving period after Ted had died and she told me that she wanted to write them as love poems and the poems are all dated like diary entries. I love her poem for Ted that is simply titled "Poem" from *At Night The States*, and I love the ending which goes: "You're one of the faraway map makers now / the scent of pine, then gone."

EILEEN MYLES

I had brought my camera gear and took a series of portrait shots and I had her sign her new books. We hugged and said goodbye. It was good seeing Alice again after all these years, and seeing how she has made a name for herself in the poetry world.

ALICE NOTLEY

Letters and Photographs

Cover Photograph. *101 Saint Mark's Place.* By Mark Hillringhouse. 2018.

Dedication page. *Walter Cummins.* Photograph by Mark Hillringhouse. 2018.

P 9. *Mark Hillringhouse with Alice Notley and Tom Savage 101 Saint Mark's Place.* Photograph. 1982.

P 14. *Frank O'Hara.* Photograph by Harry Redl. 1958.

P 15. *John Godfrey.* Photograph by Mark Hillringhouse. 1982.

P 17. Cover. *The World Magazine,* No. 39. 1983.

P 18. *Ron Padgett, Ted Berrigan, and Mark Hillringhouse at the Saint Mark's Church Poetry Project.* Photograph. 1983.

P 20. *Ted Berrigan Memorial Reading, November 15, 1983.* The Poetry Project Newsletter.

P 21. Harrison, Jim. (August 3, 1983). [Letter from Jim Harrison to Mark Hillringhouse].

P 22. Merwin, W. S. (July 22, 1983). [Letter from W. S. Merwin to Mark Hillringhouse].

P 23. *Gem Spa Open 24 Hours on St. Mark's Place Where Ted Berrigan Was Often Found.* Photograph by Mark Hillringhouse. 2018.

P 27. *John Ashbery with Mark Hillringhouse.* Photograph. 1981.

P 30. *John Ashbery in His 22nd Street Chelsea Apartment.* Photograph by Mark Hillringhouse. 1981.

P 47. *Amiri Baraka (left) and Allen Ginsberg (right) at The William Carlos Williams Centennial Reading.* Photograph. 1983.

P 65. *Ted Berrigan in His Apartment.* Photograph by Mark Hillringhouse. 1982.

P 66. *Ted Berrigan with His Son Edmund. 1983.* Photograph by Mark Hillringhouse. 1983.

P 68. *Anselm and Edmund Berrigan.* Photograph by Mark Hillringhouse. 1982.

P 75. Berrigan, Ted. (September 10, 1982). [poem postcard from Ted Berrigan to Mark Hillringhouse].

P 76. Berrigan, Ted. (September 10, 1982). [porm postcard of Ted Berrigan teasng Bernadette Mayer].

P 85. *Edwin Denby in His Chelsea Loft, 1982.* Photograph by Mark Hillringhouse.

P 110. *Barbara Guest in Her W. 4th Street Apartment.* Photograph by Mark Hillringhouse. 1983.

P 112. Guest, Barbara. (July 20, 1983). [Letter from Barbara Guest to Mark Hillringhouse].

P 151. *Saint Mark's Church in-the-Bowery.* Photograph by Mark Hillringhouse. 2018.

P 153. *Bob Holman and Tom Pickard.* Photograph by Mark Hillringhouse. 2018.

P 154. *Bob Holman.* Photograph by Mark Hillringhouse. 2018.

P 167. *Larry Rivers and Kenneth Koch.* Photograph by Rudy Burckhardt. 1960.

P 163. *Kenneth Koch in His Apartment.* Photograph by Mark Hillringhouse. 1982.

P 193. *Bernadette Mayer.* Photograph by Mark Hillringhouse. 2018.

P 196. *Phil Good and Bernadette Mayer.* Photograph by Mark Hillringhouse. 2018.

P 200. *Philip Whalen at St. Mark's* (Bernadette Mayer seated behind at left). Photograph by Mark Hillringhouse, 1983.

P 209. *W.S. Merwin on His Roof.* Photograph by Mark Hillringhouse. 1982.

P 210. Merwin, W.S. (October 5, 1982). [Letter from W.S. Merwin to Mark Hillringhouse].

P 222. Moss, Howard. (March 23, 1982). [Letter from Howard Moss to Mark Hillringhouse].

P 224. *Howard Moss.* Photograph by Mark Hillringhouse. 1982.

P 251. *Simon Pettet.* Photograph by Mark Hillringhouse. 2018.

P 263. *James Schuyler.* Photograph by Mark Hillringhouse. 1983.

P 264. Schuyler, James. (February 2, 1983). [Letter from James Schuyler to Mark Hillringhouse].

P 284. *Helena Hughes.* Photograph by Mark Hillringhouse. 1983

P 291. *Tompkins Square Park.* Photograph by Mark Hillringhouse. 2018.

P 293. *Gerald Stern at Home in Manhattan.* Photograph by Mark Hillringhouse. 2016.

P 295. *Gerald Stern in Front of His Canal House in Raubsville.* Photograph. Circa 1960.

P 309. *Gerald Stern and Jack Gilbert*. Photograph by Mark Hillringhouse. 1985.

P 322. *Tony Towle*. Photograph. 2011.

P 331. *Bill Zavatsky*. Photograph by Layle Silbert. Circa 1985.

P 332. *Paul Violi Shooting Pool*. Photograph by Mark Hillringhouse. 1985.

P 366. *Anne Waldman*. Photograph by Mark Hillringhouse. 1984.

P 389. Waldman, Anne. (September 23, 1984). [Letter from Anne Waldman to Mark Hillringhouse].

P 388. *Eileen Myles*. Photograph by Mark Hillringhouse. 1982.

P 390. *Alice Notley*. Photograph by Mark Hillringhouse. 1982.

Selected Bibliography

Allen, Donald. *The New American Poetry 1945-1960*. Grove Press, 1960.

Ashbery, John. *Some Trees*. Yale UP. 1956.

-----. *Rivers and Mountains*. Holt, Rinehart, and Winston. 1966.

-----. *The Tennis Court Oath*. Wesleyan UP. 1968.

-----. *Three Poems*. The Viking Press. 1972.

-----. *Self-Portrait in a Convex Mirror*. The Viking Press. 1975.

-----. *Houseboat Days*. The Viking Press. 1977.

-----. *As We Know*. The Viking Press. 1979.

-----. *Shadow Train*. The Viking Press. 1980.

-----. *A Wave*. The Viking Press. 1981.

-----. *Selected Poems*. Viking Penguin. 1985.

-----. *April Galleons*. Viking. 1985.

Baraka, Amiri (LeRoi Jones). *Black Magic* (Collected Poetry 1961–1967). Bobbs-Merrill. 1969.

-----. *Selected Poetry of Amiri Baraka/LeRoi Jones*. William Morrow. 1979.

Berrigan, Ted. *Many Happy Returns*. Corinth Books. 1969.

-----. *Train Ride*. Vehicle Editions. 1971.

-----. *Red Wagon*. The Yellow Press. 1976.

-----. *Clear the Range* (a novel). Adventures in Poetry—Coach House South. 1977.

-----. *Nothing for You*. Angel Hair Books. 1977.

-----. *So Going Around Cities: New and Selected Poems 1958–1979*. Blue Wind Press. 1980.

-----. *In a Blue River*. Little Light Books. 1981.

-----. *The Sonnets*. United Artists. 1982.

-----. *A Certain Slant of Sunlight*. (Alice Notley, ed.). O Books. 1988.

Denby, Edwin. *Looking at the Dance*. Horizon Press. 1968.

-----. *Miltie Is a Hackie (a libretto)*. Z Press. 1973.

-----. *Collected Poems*. Full Court Press. 1975.

-----. *The Complete Poems*. Knopf. 1986.

-----. *Dance Writings*. Knopf. 1986.

Godfrey, John. *Dabble*. Full Court Press. 1982.

-----. *Where The Weather Suits My Clothes*. Z Press. 1984.

Guest, Barbara. *Poems*. Doubleday. 1962.

-----. *The Blue Stairs*. Corinth Books. 1968.

-----. *Moscow Mansions*. Viking. 1973.

-----. *The Countess from Minneapolis*. Burning Deck. 1976.

-----. *Seeking Air* (a novel). Black Sparrow. 1978.

-----. *The Türler Losses*. Mansfield Book Mart Monograph Series #5. 1979.

-----. *Biography*. Burning Deck. 1980.

-----. *Musicality*. Kelsey St. Press. 1988.

-----. *Fair Realism*. Sun & Moon Press. 1989.

-----. *Quill, Solitary Apparition*. The Post-Apollo Press. 1996.

-----. *If So, Tell Me*. Reality Street Editions. 1999.

-----. *Rocks on a Platter*. Wesleyan UP. 1999.

-----. *Miniatures*. Wesleyan UP. 2002.

-----. *Forces of Imagination: Writing on Writing*. Kelsey St. Press. 2003.

-----. *The Red Gaze*. Wesleyan UP. 2005.

Holman, Bob. *Tear To Open*. Power Mad Press. 1979.

-----. *Sing This One Back to Me*. Coffee House Press. 2013.

Kernan, Nathan, ed. *The Diary of James Schuyler*. Black Sparrow. 1997.

Koch, Kenneth. *Ko; or, A Season on Earth*. Grove Press. 1959.

-----. *Thank You and Other Poems*. Grove Press. 1962.

-----. *When The Sun Tries to Go On*. Black Sparrow. 1969.

-----. *The Pleasures of Peace*. Grove Press. 1969.

-----. *The Art of Love*. Vintage. 1975.

-----. *The Red Robins*. Vintage. 1975.

-----. *The Burning Mystery of Anna in 1951*. Random House. 1977.

-----. *The Duplications*. Random House. 1977.

-----. *Days & Nights*. Random House. 1982.

Lehman, David. *The Last Avant Garde*. Doubleday, 1998.

Mattix, Micah. *Frank O'Hara and the Poetics of Saying "I"*. Fairleigh Dickinson UP. 2011.

Mayer, Bernadette. *Poetry*. Kulchur Foundation. 1976.

-----. *The Golden Book of Words*. Angel Hair Books. 1978.

Merwin, W. S. *The Moving Target*. Atheneum. 1963.

-----. *The Lice*. Atheneum. 1967

-----. *The Carrier of Ladders*. Atheneum. 1970.

-----. *The Miner's Pale Children*. Henry Holt. 1970.

-----. *The First Four Books of Poems*. Atheneum. 1975.

-----. *The Compass Flower*. Atheneum. 1977.

-----. *Unframed Originals*. Henry Holt. 1982.

-----. *Opening the Hand*. Atheneum. 1983.

Moss, Howard. *Selected Poems*. Atheneum. 1971.

-----. *Notes from the Castle*. Atheneum. 1980.

-----. *Two Plays: The Palace at 4 A.M. & The Folding Green*. Sheep Meadow Press. 1980.

-----. *Whatever is Moving, Essays*. Little Brown. 1981.

-----. *Rules of Sleep*. Atheneum. 1984.

-----. *New Selected Poems*. Atheneum. 1985.

-----. *Minor Monuments, Selected Essays*. Ecco Press. 1986.

Myles, Eileen. *Snowflake/different streets*. Wave Books. 2012.

Notley, Alice. *Alice Ordered Me to Be Made*. Yellow Press. 1976.

-----. Doctor Williams' Heiresses (A Lecture). Tuumba Press. 1980.

-----. *When I Was Alive*. Vehicle Editions. 1979.

-----. *How Spring Comes*. Toothpaste Press. 1981.

-----. *Waltzing Matilda*. The Kulchur Foundation. 1981.

-----. *At Night the States*. Yellow Press. 1987.

-----. *The Descent of Alette*. Penguin. 1992.

-----. *Mysteries of Small Houses*. Penguin. 1998.

-----. *Coming After* (Essays on Poetry) Michigan UP. 2005.

-----. *Culture of One*. Penguin. 2011.

O'Hara, Frank. *Poems Retrieved*. Grey Fox Press. 1977.

-----. *Lunch Poems*. City Lights Books. 1964.

-----. *The Selected Poems of Frank O'Hara*. Vintage Books. 1974.

Padgett, Ron, David Shapiro, eds. *An Anthology of New York Poets*. Random House, 1970.

-----. *Great Balls of Fire*. Holt, Rinehart and Winston. 1965.

-----. *Toujours l'amour*. SUN. 1976.

Pettet, Simon. *An Enigma & Other Lyrics*. 1984.

-----. *Conversations with Rudy Burckhardt about Everything*. Vehicle Editions. 1987.

-----. *Lyrical Poetry*. Archipelago Books. 1987.

-----, ed. *Selected Art Writings James Schuyler*. Black Sparrow. 1998.

-----. *Hearth*. Talisman House. 2008.

-----. *As a Bee*. Talisman House. 2014.

Ratcliffe, Stephen, Leslie Scalapino, eds. *Talking in Tranquility Interviews with Ted Berrigan*. Avenue B/O Books. 1991.

Schuyler, James. *Freely Espousing*. Doubleday/Paris Review Editions. 1969.

-----. *The Crystal Lithium*. Random House. 1972.

-----. *Hymn to Life*. Random House. 1974.

-----. *The Home Book*. Z Press. 1977.

-----. *What's for Dinner?* Black Sparrow. 1978.

-----. *The Morning of the Poem*. Random House. 1980.

-----. *Early in '71*. The Figures. 1981.

-----. *A Few Days*. Random House. 1985.

-----. *Selected Poems*. Farrar, Straus & Giroux. 1988.

Stern, Gerald. *Lucky Life*. Houghton Mifflin. 1977.

-----. *The Red Coal*. Houghton Mifflin. 1981.

-----. *Paradise Poems*. Vintage Books. 1984.

-----. *Lovesick*. HarperCollins. 1987.

-----. *Leaving Another Kingdom: Selected Poems*. HarperCollins. 1990.

-----. *Bread Without Sugar*. Norton. 1992.

-----. *Everything Is Burning*. Norton. 2005.

-----. *Save the Last Dance*. Norton. 2008.

-----. *In Beauty Bright*. Norton. 2012.

-----. *Divine Nothingness*. Norton. 2015.

-----. *Perish the Day*. Miramar Editions. 2015.

-----. *Galaxy Love*. Norton. 2017.

Towle, Tony. *North*. Columbia UP. 1970.

-----. *Autobiography and Other Poems*. SUN Press. 1977.

-----. *Works on Paper*. The Swollen Magpie Press. 1978.

-----. *Gemini* (with Charles North). The Swollen Magpie Press. 1981.

Violi, Paul. *In Baltic Circles*. Kulchur Foundation. 1973.

-----. *Harmatan*. SUN. 1977.

-----. *Splurge*. SUN. 1982.

-----. *Likewise*. Hanging Loose Press. 1988.

-----. *The Curious Builder*. Hanging Loose Press. 1993.

-----. *Fracas*. Hanging Loose Press. 1999.

-----. *Overnight*. Hanging Loose Press. 2007.

Waldman, Anne. *Baby Breakdown*. Bobbs-Merrill. 1970.

-----. *Cabin*. Z Press. 1981.

-----. *Nice to See You Homage to Ted Berrigan*. (Anne Waldman, ed.). Coffee House Press. 1991.

Wheelwright, John. *Collected Poems*. New Directions. 1971.

www.ingramcontent.com/pod-product-compliance
Lightning Source LLC
Chambersburg PA
CBHW070125080526
44586CB00015B/1560